PUFFIN BY DESIGN

PUFFIN BY DESIGN

70 Years of Imagination 1940–2010

Phil Baines

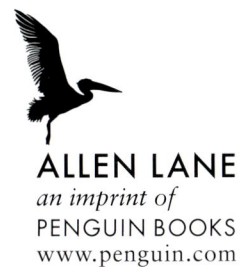

ALLEN LANE
an imprint of
PENGUIN BOOKS
www.penguin.com

To Hane and Bulldoc, with love

ALLEN LANE

Published by the Penguin Group
Penguin Books Ltd, 80 Strand, London WC2R 0RL, England
Penguin Group (USA) Inc., 375 Hudson Street, New York, New York 10014, USA
Penguin Group (Canada), 90 Eglinton Avenue East, Suite 700, Toronto, Ontario, Canada M4P 2Y3
(a division of Pearson Penguin Canada Inc.)
Penguin Ireland, 25 St Stephen's Green, Dublin 2, Ireland (a division of Penguin Books Ltd)
Penguin Group (Australia), 250 Camberwell Road, Camberwell, Victoria 3124, Australia
(a division of Pearson Australia Group Pty Ltd)
Penguin Books India Pvt Ltd, 11 Community Centre, Panchsheel Park, New Delhi – 110 017, India
Penguin Group (NZ), 67 Apollo Drive, Rosedale, North Shore 0632, New Zealand
(a division of Pearson New Zealand Ltd)
Penguin Books (South Africa) (Pty) Ltd, 24 Sturdee Avenue, Rosebank, Johannesburg 2196, South Africa

Penguin Books Ltd, Registered Offices: 80 Strand, London WC2R 0RL, England

www.penguin.com

First published 2010
1

Copyright © Phil Baines, 2010

The moral right of the author has been asserted

All rights reserved
Except in the United States of America, this book is sold subject to the condition that it shall not, by way of trade or otherwise, be lent, re-sold, hired out, or otherwise circulated without the publisher's prior consent in any form of binding or cover other than that in which it is published and without a similar condition including this condition being imposed on the subsequent purchaser

Set in Adobe Sabon and Gill Sans
Designed by Tom Sanderson
Based on *Penguin by Design*, designed by David Pearson
Colour reproduction by MDP Ltd
Printed in Singapore

A CIP catalogue record for this book is available from the British Library

ISBN: 978-0-141-32614-6

PREVIOUS SPREAD:
A Puffin promotion for British Rail, 1992.

Contents

Introduction	7
I. Pictures	10
II. Stories	62
III. Expansion	94
IV. Consolidation	144
V. Reinvention	188
Logo Development	247
Bibliography and Sources	250
Index	252
Acknowledgments	256

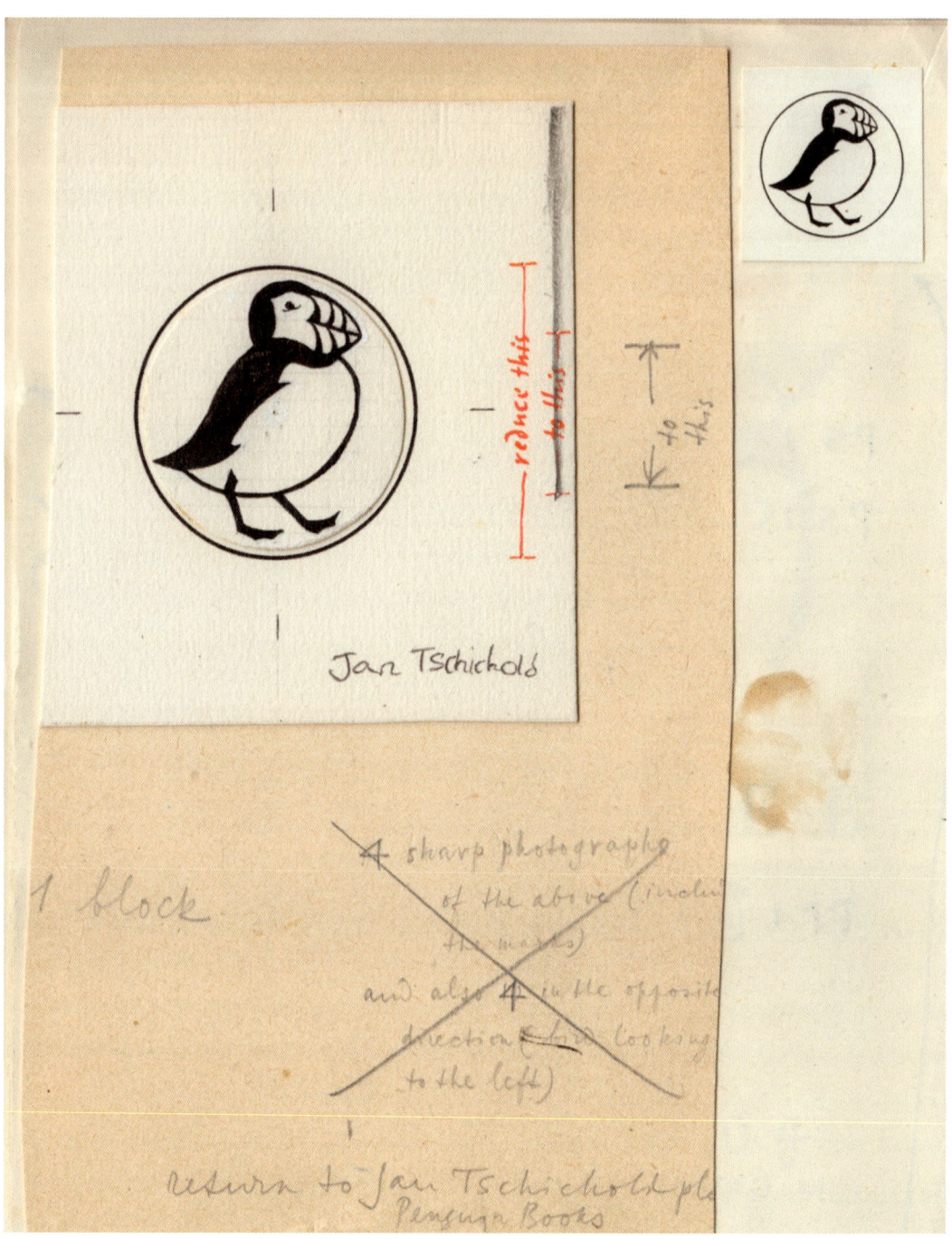

Introduction

Penguin before Puffin

In 1940 Penguin was still a young company, having been founded five years earlier by Allen Lane, (1902–70), and his brothers Richard and John as an imprint of The Bodley Head where the three were directors. Their initial idea had been to make books affordable to a mass market by printing long runs of each title in a small, convenient format and with a simple but memorable paperback binding. The venture was successful enough for the brothers to make Penguin Books a separate company the following year, albeit working from rented premises, with offices above a car showroom in Great Portland Street and a warehouse in the crypt of Holy Trinity, Marylebone. But by 1937 business was secure enough for a three-and-a-half-acre site to be developed on the Bath Road in Harmondsworth opposite what is now Heathrow Airport. The company's ambition and growth can be illustrated by the way it began to diversify that year: a Shakespeare series (April); non-fiction under the Pelican imprint (May); a periodical, *Penguin Parade* (November); and, in the same month, the first Penguin Special, one of a series of books specially commissioned on topical issues.

The success of the Specials – the political titles had sales of 100,000 copies in a few weeks, compared to 40,000 in a few months for standard titles – was crucial when paper rationing was introduced in 1940. Rationing was based on paper consumption in the twelve months before hostilities began, which left Penguin in a much better position than many other publishers. Nevertheless, the practicalities of creating books in wartime were considerable, and it is astounding to realize that although the total number of books produced by Penguin during the war inevitably fell, the number of different series, reaching out to the broadest possible cross section of the population, actually grew dramatically. Puffin books for children were part of that expansion, the name following naturally after Penguin and Pelican.

Puffin and design

The story of cover design at Puffin is markedly different from the other Penguin series. While they were generally clothed in a version of the company's striped uniform, Puffins appeared as colourful outsiders – picture books dressed as suited each title. A brief regimentation was imposed for the first eight story books, and then vibrant disorder resumed. And that is generally how it has been ever since, with the imprint's visual brand taking second place to the individual title or author.

As noted in my previous book, *Penguin by Design*, a survey of seventy years of Penguin cover design, few paperback books have the same relationship with their contents as pop-record sleeves, which never change, have with theirs. While this is true of adult books, it is far less true of children's books where illustration is such an intrinsic part, and where the cover has a more fundamental link to the book itself.

Like Penguin books generally, Puffin covers spanning the period 1940–2010 reflect the emergence of British graphic design and illustration, but in a slightly different way. With the Puffin titles, the illustrator is central, and particularly dominant for the first twenty years. During that time illustrators would have been taught lettering as a matter of course, and on the majority of covers in the 1940s and 1950s the title lettering was drawn or painted by the illustrator as part of the whole. While that in itself was no guarantee of quality, in good hands it gave the covers a wonderful unity. However, at the beginning of the 1960s that visual unity started to give way as hand-lettering was superseded by typography. Later, illustration was joined by photography, further changing the look of covers. Throughout the 1960s and 1970s there were periodic attempts to assert Puffin's brand more strongly, and a greater visual differentiation between the age ranges of books developed through the creation of sub-series. Today, individual titles still take precedence over the Puffin brand, and many authors have become, or are encouraged to become, brands in their own right. Long-term successful titles are grouped into the Classics or Modern Classics sub-brands and, as such, their individuality is muted in favour of the series and publisher.

This book – part history, part critique and part celebration – charts those changes through nearly 500 book covers, together with illustrated pages and a selection of material from the Puffin Club's magazine *Puffin Post* (see Chapter III). It is necessarily subjective, and only scratches the surface of the vast number of books published by Puffin during the last seventy years. As with *Penguin by Design* I have attempted to show the significant design changes and describe them against the broader history of the imprint and the parent company.

Like *Penguin by Design*, to make comparisons easier, reproductions have been restricted as far as possible to three sizes (100%, 46% and 30%). The date given in the caption refers to the when the scanned copy was printed rather than its original publication date. A date given in square brackets indicates that the year is not given in the original and has come from other sources.

Illustrators, designers or photographers are as credited on the book's cover or inside pages. If the illustrator is known because they have signed their artwork, or if the information has come from another source, it is given in square brackets.

I. Pictures

COWELL LTD
...GRAPHIC PRINTERS
329. HIGH HOLBORN...

PUFFIN PROGRESS SHEET.   June 30th., 1946.

Book.	Author-Artist.	Printer.	State of Production
Animals of Countryside.	Arnrid Johnston.	Lowe and Brydone. OWN PLATES.	Ready to machine.
Animals of N. America.	Arnrid Johnston.	Van Leer. OWN PLATES.	Artist at work on
Animals of India.	Arnrid Johnston.	Van Leer. OWN PLATES.	Artist at work on
Building of London.	M. and A. Potter.	Cowells. OWN PLATES.	Artists' revision
Brer Rabbit.	Walter Trier.	DeLittle Fenwick. OWN PLATES.	All material at F
Butterflies.	Richard Chopping.	Cowells. OWN PLATES.	Colour proofs of passed- ready to Cowells.
...ina.	Tsui Chi and C. Jackson.	Jesse Broad. OWN PLATES.	All material at proofs.
...al.	Peggy Hart.	Van Leer. OWN PLATES.	Artist at work o
...ntry ...liday.	Dr. Scott-James and Lee Dowd.	Cowells. NOT OWN PLATES.	Final stages of Waiting proofs
...tory of ...ntryside.	M. and A. Potter.	Cowells. OWN PLATES.	
...ses.	Lionel Edwards.		New photolitho printer to be fo Reprint not yet decided.
...sh.	J. Cannan and Anne Bullen.		
...ss ...cts.	James Holland.		Reprint decided against.

The coloured illustrations in this book are from drawings made by the artist directly on to lithographic zinc plates. They are therefore originals and not reproductions of drawings made on paper. (Noel Carrington in *Life in an English Village*, King Penguin, 1949, p. 32)

Noel Carrington and the first series of Puffin Picture Books, 1940–65

In the first years of Penguin's existence Allen Lane had exhibited an ability to sense a good idea when it was presented to him, and the courage to take a calculated risk. The appearance of the first Puffin Picture Books in December 1940 were an example of both.

By 1939 Noel Carrington (1894–1989) had been involved in book publishing for some fifteen years and was then editing and producing books for Country Life. He had for some time nurtured the idea of a series of simply written, well-illustrated books, which would explain things to children: books about the natural and man-made environments, about history, geography, recreational pursuits, and some stories. Books that were immediate and inexpensive.

Books that combined all those features did not exist but he was encouraged in his convictions by the example of educational Russian titles shown to him by the artist Pearl Binder, and also by the French Père Castor books, illustrated by Rojan (Feodor Rojankovsky 1891–1970). The latter books had been translated into English and published by Allen & Unwin from 1938, but were expensive at two shillings and sixpence (12.5p), five times the price of a standard Penguin paperback.

Carrington was also familiar with the posters commissioned by companies such as London Transport and Shell-Mex, and the work of artists such as Barnett Freedman (1901–58), Charles Mozley (1914–91), Kathleen Hale (1898–2000) and Eric Ravilious (1903–42), who were using the technique of autolithography. Although the number of artists working in this way was limited, its potential as a purer expression of their intentions was clear:

Noel Carrington

PREVIOUS PAGE:
Correspondence concerning
Puffin Picture Books, 1940

Autolithography is a term I use to describe the several techniques through which the artist creates his own lithograph. Often he does not reproduce. There is really no need for him to make a finished sketch – he can create his lithograph step by step and colour by colour. This seems to me to be the keynote to the success of autolithography. He knows the results he wants, knows the limitations of the process, and, continually learning as he goes along, often achieves the result he requires – or rather the feeling he wants to convey – without having to compromise. (Smith, 1949, p. 71)

Geoffrey Smith (of Ipswich printer W. S. Cowell), who wrote the above, was a friend of Carrington's and had printed Hale's *Orlando the Marmalade Cat*, while Curwen Press in London had printed Ravilious's *High Street* and Sacheverell Sitwell and John Farleigh's *Old Fashioned Flowers* – all published by Country Life. Smith made Carrington realize that if the number of colours was carefully considered, autolithography offered both reduced costs and a more faithful rendition of an artist's intent.

With his ideas about subject matter, printing technique and possible artists established, Carrington now needed a publisher and approached his employers, Country Life, but when they turned it down, he naturally thought of Allen Lane.

They first met after a Double Crown Club dinner on 28 February 1938, at which cheap reprints were discussed, a subject Lane naturally defended. Lane took little persuasion in agreeing to Carrington's idea for children's books, which had already been at the back of his mind – his only stipulation was that the selling price must be sixpence. Shortly after, however, Lane left London on business and by the time he returned war had been declared. Carrington assumed that the project would be shelved but Lane was soon in touch.

The worst has happened . . . but evacuated children are going to need books more than ever, especially your kind on farming and natural history. Let us plan to get out half a dozen as soon as we can. (Lane, in Rogerson, 1992, p. xii)

Working with Cowell's, Carrington established the most economical way of producing the titles. Each book was to be the same height as, but twice the width of, a standard Penguin paperback (which made packing economical), and was to be printed on a large single sheet with sixteen pages on each side. One side was to be printed in colour and the other black only. In order to maintain the desired cost, print runs needed to be at least 20,000 per title.

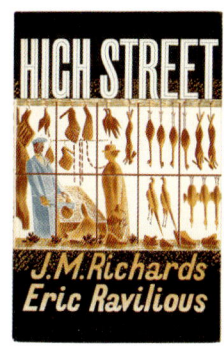

High Street by Eric Ravilious

War on Land, 1940.
The reproduction of this in
Penguin by Design (pp. 34–5)
inadvertently shows the back cover.

The first four titles appeared in December 1940 – *War on Land* and *War at Sea* by James Holland, and *War in the Air* and *On the Farm* by James Gardner – with a further nine published the following year. Like all Penguin series these too bore a series code, in this case PP, and were numbered in order of publication. Lane's intention had been to produce twelve titles a year, but, with shortages of paper and skilled labour, publishing thirteen in the first two years was a remarkable achievement.

After the war, the practice of autolithography was simplified somewhat by the introduction by Cowell's of plastic plates, which were marketed as 'Plastocowell'. These replaced zinc plates, were lighter, more portable, and being semi-transparent, made the accurate register of coloured work much easier.

Despite this, autolithography did not suit all artists, and from 1945 photolithography – where artwork was photographed through coloured filters to separate it into the required 'process' colours for printing – began to be used for some titles, and a few used a combination of both techniques. From 1950 photogravure was used for a handful of titles, but one title – *Printing* by Harold Curwen and Jack Brough – used letterpress because of its subject matter.

With the exceptions of the first three titles and PP8, *Great Deeds of the War* by Roland Davies, and PP21, *The Battle of Britain* by David Garnett and illustrated by James Gardner, (both 1941), the range of published titles progressed very much to Carrington's original brief. And despite the appearance in 1941 of the first Puffin Story Books (see Chapter II), illustrated fiction titles were also published in the series' first five years, with titles by Kathleen Hale and Chiang Yee among the earliest.

All factual titles were based on careful research and as the series developed their use spread from the home to schools – which necessitated more expensive board covers – and even, in the case of S. R. Badmin's *Trees in Britain*, to agricultural colleges. The titles, accompanied by (generally) stunning illustrations by many of the leading artists of the day, captured children's imaginations, were widely praised by the printing trade, and – very importantly – were for many years a commercial success.

A number of Puffin Picture Books were published in other languages, including fourteen in French translation, published by Nathan, and five in Portuguese. The main series are supplemented by three associated series – Baby Puffins (see pp. 56–7), Puffin Cut-out Books (see pp. 40–1) and Porpoise Books (see pp. 58–9). In the late 1940s Allen Lane decided to confine Puffin Picture Books to educational titles. With his agreement a number of the illustrated story books were reprinted – some even using the same plates – under the

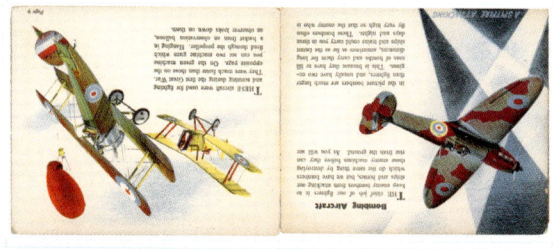

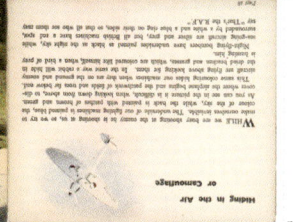

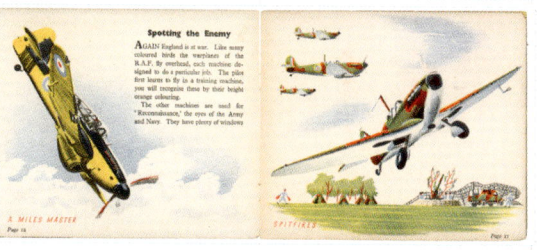

The artists of the Puffin Picture Books drew their artwork, imposed (arranged) for printing sixteen pages to view on plates measuring 38 x 33 inches. Each book was printed on a single sheet: one side in colour as shown here, the other black only as shown overleaf. When printed, the sheet was folded five times, then wire-stitched and trimmed to make the final book. The reverse is shown overleaf.

I. Pictures

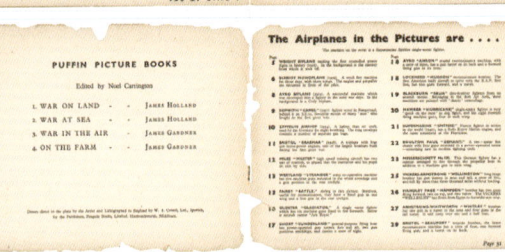
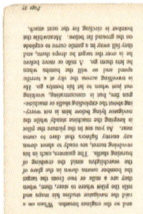

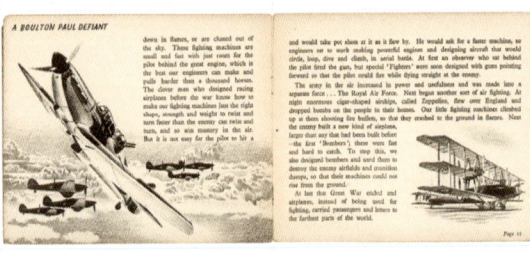
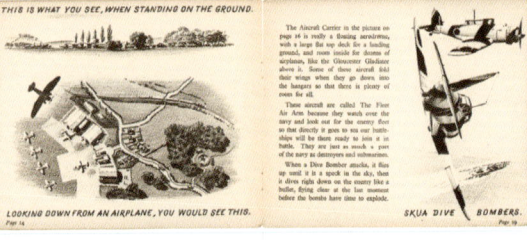

The imposed black-only side of the printed sheet looked like this.

Harlequin imprint, overseen by Carrington and distributed by Transatlantic Arts. Carrington and Transatlantic Arts were also involved in publishing similar titles, such as Bantam Picture Books.

Of the 120 Puffin titles there are around 260 variants: some are minor details, such as occur when reprinting, but many titles were successful over a long period and were revised or updated with new illustrations. Some titles were re-illustrated by another artist, and at least one was revisited by another author *and* illustrator. Number 116, Paxton Chadwick's *Life Histories*, did not appear until 1996 (see pp. 60–1). It was revised by Lee Chadwick and Sheila Dorrell and published by the Penguin Collectors Society, together with an extra twelve-page monograph by Steve Hare.

The series began to wane after Carrington's retirement in the early 1960s. Within Puffin, Kaye Webb had become Senior Editor and was about to change the scale and ambition of children's publishing. She was one of a number of new, younger editors whose presence was being felt within the company. For years it had been noted that the many things which made the Puffin Picture Books attractive – their size and simplicity – also prevented their easy display in bookshops. Where they were understood and given space to be shown full cover they sold well, but without that, and lacking a spine, they failed.

Nevertheless, many of the ideas that Carrington had started would be continued in some form by Webb. More generally, they had raised the standard of children's illustrated books – and expectations of them – immeasurably. They were at the heart of significant changes in the reproduction of artwork and gave a tremendous boost to the popularity and uses of illustration.

THIS PAGE: *War at Sea*, [1940].
Illustrated by James Holland

Great Deeds of the War, [1941].
Illustrated by Roland Davies

OPPOSITE: *Animals of the Countryside*, [1941].
Illustrated by Arnrid Johnston

A Book of Insects, [1941].
Illustrated by James Holland

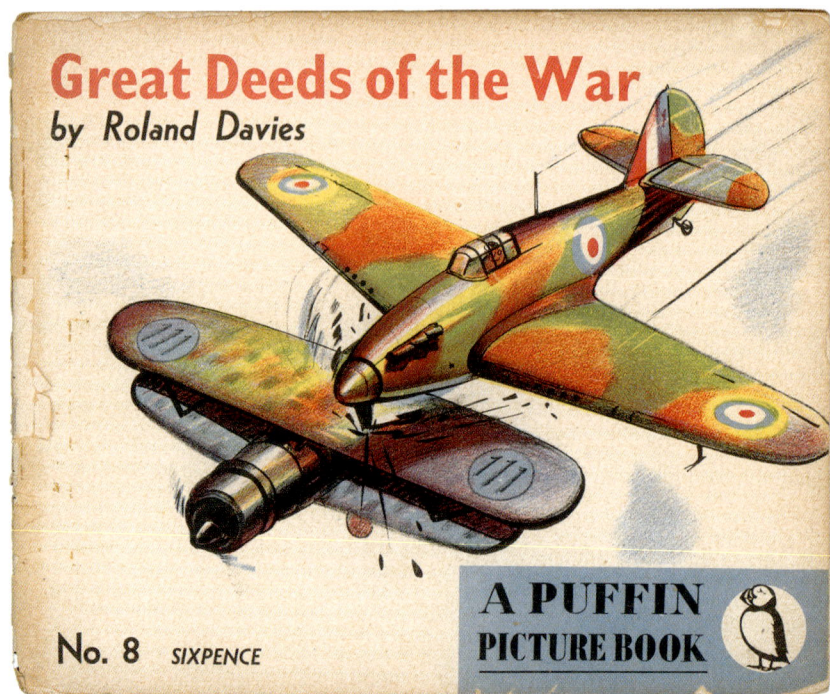

The first Puffin Picture Books

Carrington's original idea for the series was as a set of informative books for children about both the natural and man-made environments. Given the changed circumstances in 1940 the first three titles were devoted to explaining aspects of war (PP1, *War on Land*, p. 14; PP3, *War in the Air*, pp. 15–6), and wartime subject matter was returned to with PP8, *Great Deeds of the War* and PP21, *The Battle of Britain*.

Allen Lane reasoned that with so many evacuated city children, who had never encountered the countryside before, titles about the natural world would be both necessary and popular, and they dominate the early list, forming a significant part of the 120 published titles.

All the books shown on this spread are from 1940–1 and the quality of the artists' drawing can be clearly be seen: working directly to plate necessitated slightly simpler mark-making than preparing finished artwork to be photographically separated for colour, as happened with later titles. The difference in 'feel' that this technique brought can be seen in the selection of covers on the following pages.

As the series progressed it diversified considerably. Aside from the war, recent and current historical events became the subject of a number of titles (see p. 23) while medieval history featured in others (see p. 22).

Pond and River Life, [1941].
Illustrated by Brynhild Parker

Animals of India, [1942].
Illustrated by Arnrid Johnston

Birds of the Village, [1944].
Illustrated by P. F. Millard

Fish and Fishing, [1948].
Illustrated by Bernard Venables

Our Cattle, 1948.
Illustrated by Lionel Edwards

Mountain and Moorland Birds, [1947].
Illustrated by R. B. Talbot Kelly

Insect Life, 1950.
Illustrated by Arthur Smith

Wild Flowers, [1949].
Illustrated by Paxton Chadwick

Birds of the Estuary, 1952.
Illustrated by C. F. Tunnicliffe

Pond Life, 1964.
Illustrated by Paxton Chadwick

Wild Animals, 1957.
Illustrated by Paxton Chadwick

Seashore Life, 1965.
Illustrated by Peter Parks

Signs and Symbols, 1953.
Illustrated by G. E. Pallant Sidaway

A Book of Armour, 1954.
Illustrated by Patrick Nicolle

Everest is Climbed, 1954.
[Illustrated by Richard Taylor]

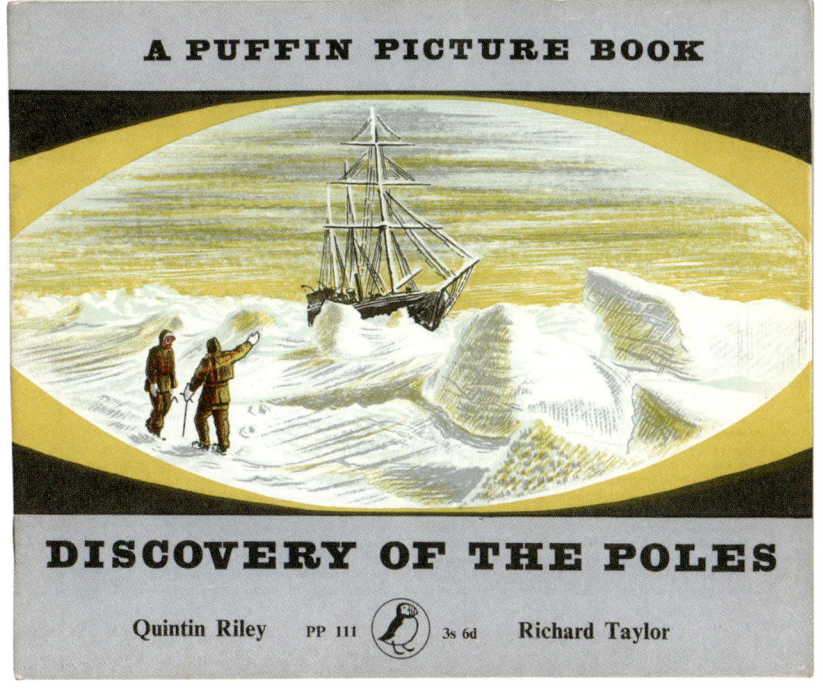

Discovery of the Poles, 1957.
[Illustrated by Richard Taylor]

1. Pictures

Picture stories for children

Carrington had always intended the series to include fiction alongside non-fiction, and the work of Kathleen Hale (see pp. 26–7) was an important catalyst in establishing the series' viability. The fiction published as part of the series is diverse in theme and in artistic expression, which reflects the backgrounds of the author/illustrators.

Walter Trier (1890–1951) was Jewish, and was born in Prague and emigrated to Britain from Berlin in 1936. Pearl Binder (1904–90) had spent much time in the USSR in the 1930s, and *Misha Learns English* can be seen as pro-Anglo-Soviet propaganda at a critical period of the war (1942). José Sancha is from Spain and Chiang Yee (1903–77) left China in 1933 due to unhappiness with the regime there. Yee, the self-styled 'Silent Traveller', spent twenty-two years in England, and wrote and illustrated books about different parts of the country, beginning with *The Silent Traveller: A Chinese Artist in Lakeland* for Country Life in 1937.

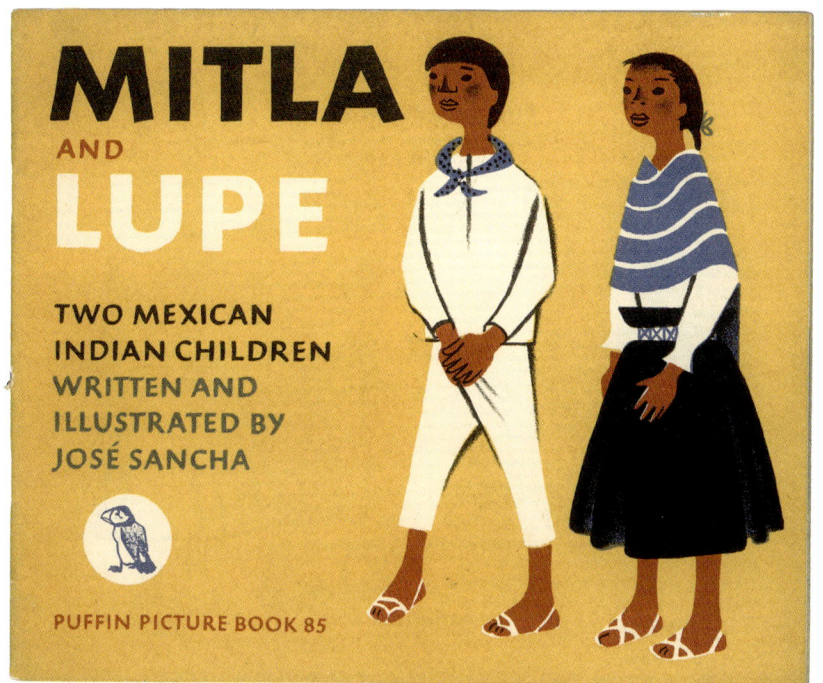

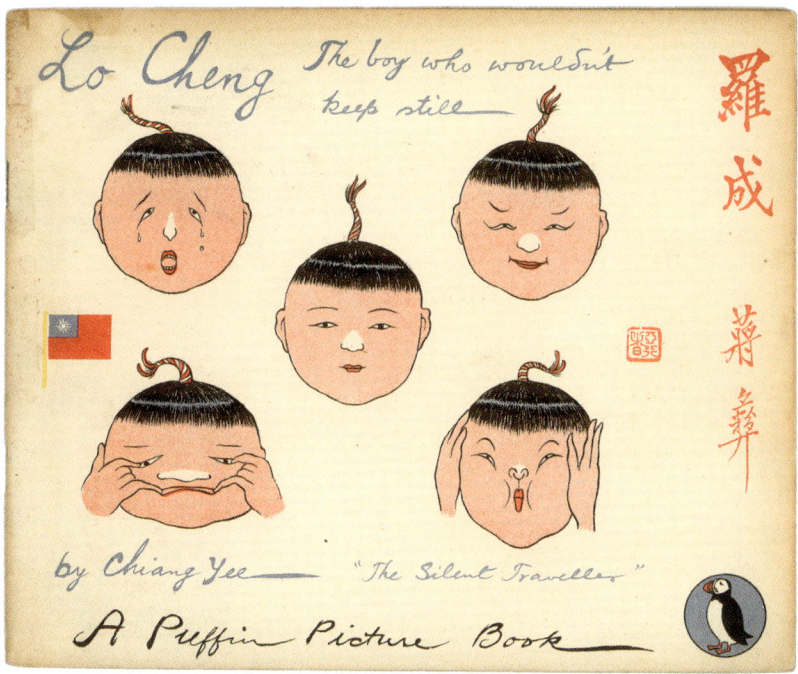

OPPOSITE: *Brer Rabbit*, [1945]. [Illustrated by Walter Trier]

Misha Learns English, [1942]. Illustrated by Pearl Binder

THIS PAGE: *Mitla and Lupe: Two Mexican Indian Children*, 1948. Illustrated by José Sancha

Lo Cheng: The Boy Who Wouldn't Keep Still, [1942]. Illustrated by Chiang Yee

1. Pictures

OPPOSITE: *Orlando's Evening Out*, [1941]. Illustrated by Katherine Hale

Kathleen Hale (1898–2000)

Kathleen Hale's work at Cowell's, the Ipswich printers, when preparing her book *Orlando the Marmalade Cat* for Country Life, was an important factor in Carrington's decision to use auto-lithography for the Puffin Picture Books when he pitched the idea to Allen Lane in 1938.

Hale had moved to London in 1917 with the intention of becoming an artist and she found a home in the artistic circle centred on Fitzrovia. After marrying in 1926, she moved to South Mimms in Hertfordshire to raise a family, and the first Orlando book grew out of her bedtime stories for her sons.

Two Orlando stories were published as Puffin Picture Books: PP14 *Orlando's Evening Out* (1941) and PP26 *Orlando's Home Life* (1942). Orlando was very popular and featured on the BBC's *Children's Hour*, and went on to become a ballet and a mural at the 1951 Festival of Britain. Eventually the Orlando books extended to eighteen titles, with the last in 1972.

BELOW: *Orlando's Home Life*, [1942]. Illustrated by Katherine Hale

THIS PAGE: *Pantomime Stories*, [1943]. Illustrated by Hilary Stebbing (front and back cover shown)

OPPOSITE: *Mary Had a Little Lamb and Other Nursery Songs*, 1951. Illustrated by H. A. Rey

Punch and Judy, [1942]. Illustrated by Clarke Hutton

A Book of Rigmaroles or Jingle Rhymes, [1945]. Illustrated by Enid Marx

Puffin by Design

Victoriana

An important undercurrent gaining momentum in British art in the 1940s was a return to favour for Victoriana. Reflecting this were a number of Puffin Picture Books, some of which are shown here.

Pantomime Stories is one of many examples of Puffin titles that make significant play with the back and front of a cover. Whereas Hilary Stebbing's other books (including PP55 *Extinct Animals*) were unrelated to this theme, Enid Marx (1902–98) had previously had an established interest in the subject matter. She had written *When Victoria Began to Reign* with Margaret Lambert for Faber in 1937. Clarke Hutton (1898–1984) would later illustrate Noel Carrington's King Penguin *Popular English Art* in 1945 (see *Penguin by Design*: p. 27), and other Puffin Picture Books (see pp. 50–1).

H. A. Rey's *Mary Had a Little Lamb* had originally been commissioned as a Porpoise, a short-lived imprint of hard-cover books (see pp. 58–9).

ABOVE: *Woodworking for Children*, [1945]. Illustrated by John Dumayne

OPPOSITE: *Sailing*, 1953. Illustrated by Laurence Sandy

Postage Stamps, 1950. Illustrated by Sydney R. Turner

Pottery and Its Making, 1950. [Illustrated by Mary Sikes]

A Book of Swimming, [1945]. [Illustrated by Lunt Roberts]

Riding for Children, 1949. [Illustrated by Michael Lyne]

How to Play Cricket, 1957. Illustrated by Leonard Hagerty

Hobbies and pastimes

Titles relating to hobbies and pastimes feature heavily in the series and the range shown here – like those on pp. 20–1 – also serves to illustrate how cover designs changed over time.

With the earliest versions the title, lettering was usually drawn by the artist as part of their artwork but for later versions it was often set as type and added by the production department. There is a stylistic unity, therefore, to the earlier covers even if some of the combinations of lettering and image are somewhat awkward. The later covers with added type don't have the same direct appeal at all, and feel far less like books for children.

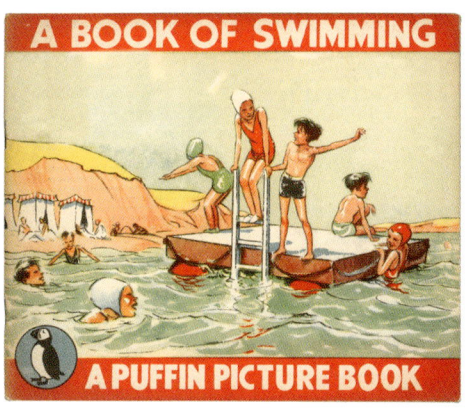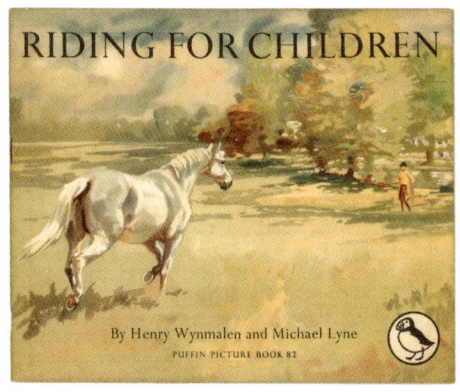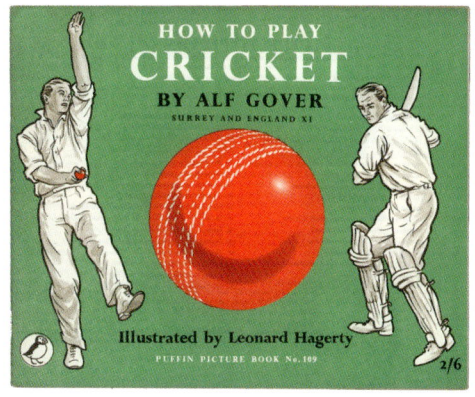

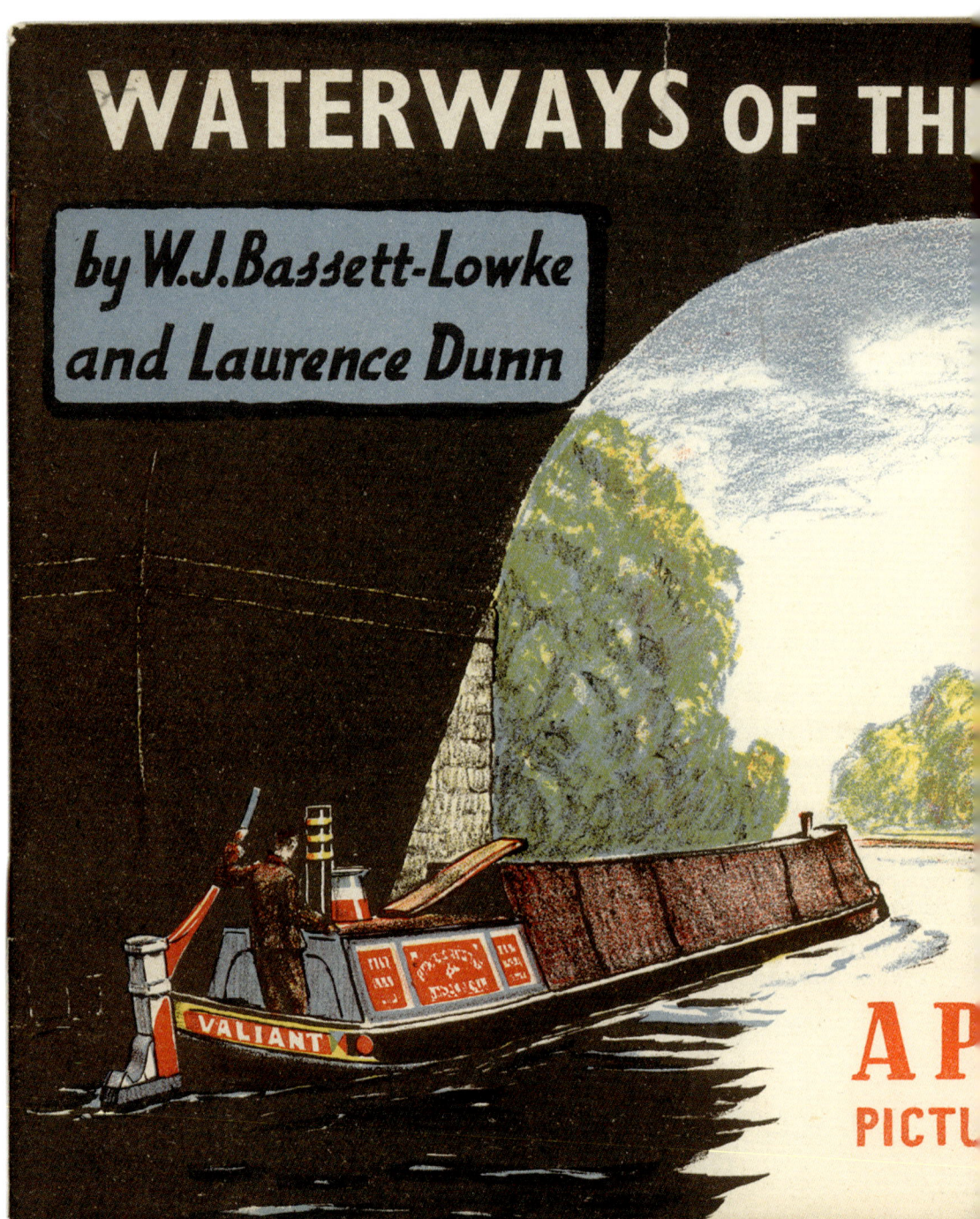

Transport – on the water . . .

From the late 1930s to the early 1960s there was a strong interest in the subjects of engineering and transport, and this was reflected in Puffin's picture books. Carrington's policy of using artists sympathetic to both subject matter and medium was matched by the commissioning of appropriate authors.

W. J. Bassett-Lowke was the founder and owner of Bassett-Lowke, a Northampton-based model-making firm established in 1899, which had started with model boats and ships but quickly moved into railways. He was the ideal author to write for the series and, in addition to *Waterways of the World*, he wrote about his primary interest, trains (see pp. 52–3).

Laurence Dunn, the illustrator, specialized in maritime subjects and also illustrated the original PP11 *Book of Ships*. On *Waterways of the World*, which creates drama by using a carefully chosen viewpoint, the relative crudity of the early direct-to-plate technique can clearly be appreciated, especially in the build-up of blue and yellow for the trees.

Waterways of the World, [1944]. Illustrated by Laurence Dunn.

OPPOSITE: *Airliners*, 1949. Illustrated by John Stroud

. . . and in the air

John Stroud joined Imperial Airways aged fourteen in 1933 and spent his working life writing and editing books and articles about all aspects of air travel. For *Airliners* he was both author and illustrator, and to my mind this is one of the best Puffin Picture Book covers: a combination of a classic three-quarter view of a wonderful mechanical object (the Saunders-Roe 45 Princess flying boat), a distant view of the mode of travel it was designed to replace, simple use of colour and well-balanced typography that supports the composition.

The book charts planes now almost forgotten and ends with a foretaste of what was about to come: 'One of Britain's great hopes for the future in air transport is the de Havilland 106 Comet now being built for long-range airline operation.' The ill-fated Comet features on the far less satisfactory cover (with the type fighting the image) of PP94 *How Planes Fly*.

BELOW: *How Planes Fly*, 1953. Illustrated by E. A. Wren

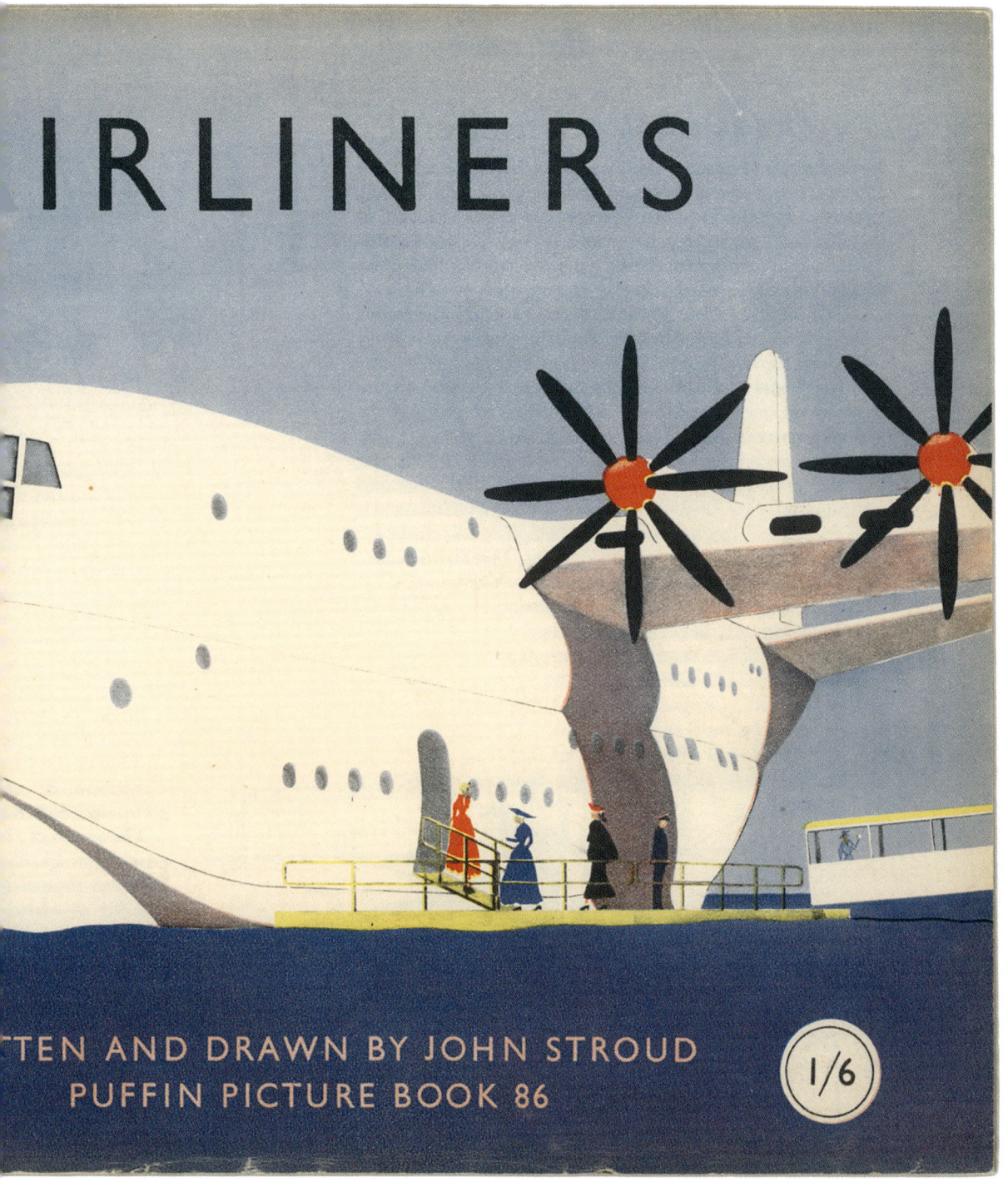

1. Pictures

Fashion old and new

Here are two contrasting styles for a pair of books related to fashion. For a historical survey, *English Fashions*, Victor Ross (a German emigré) chose a style not dissimilar to those used for the Victoriana titles shown on pages 28–9. While Jack Townsend's *The Clothes We Wear*, which is about manufacturing, is much more contemporary – modern, even – in feel with its italic, almost sans-serif letters and go-faster stripes.

OPPOSITE:
The Clothes We Wear, [1947].
[Illustrated by Jack Townsend]

BELOW: *English Fashions*, [1947].
[Illustrated by Victor Ross]

I. Pictures

OPPOSITE: *The Story of China*, [1940s]. Illustrated by Carolin Jackson

The Building of Ancient Egypt, [1954]. Illustrated by Richard Leacroft

Other lands

The breadth of the list is here reflected in a number of titles that bring far-off lands and times to life during a period when long-distance travel was the preserve of the rich. Perhaps the most noteworthy of these is *The Arabs* by R. B. Serjeant, an established authority, with illustrations by Edward Bawden (1903–89). Bawden had been introduced to autolithography before the war by Harold Curwen of the Curwen Press and had spent the last two years of the war – when he was an official war artist – in Iraq and Saudi Arabia. In this book he brings a lightness and verve to the illustrations, which seem very sophisticated compared to the other titles.

The Building of Ancient Egypt by Helen and Richard Leacroft has one of the daftest Puffin logos to have graced a book's cover. The Leacrofts were also responsible for a number of other building-related titles in the series, including *Building a House* (see pp. 44–5).

RIGHT AND OPPOSITE: *The Arabs*, [1947]. Illustrated by Edward Bawden (front cover and inside spread shown)

Puffin by Design

1. Pictures

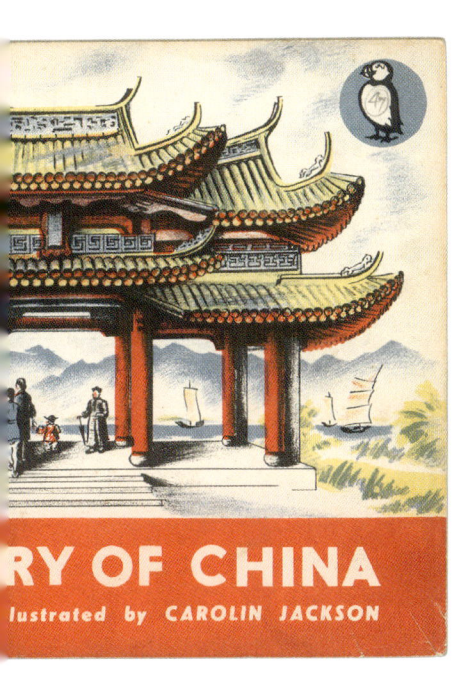

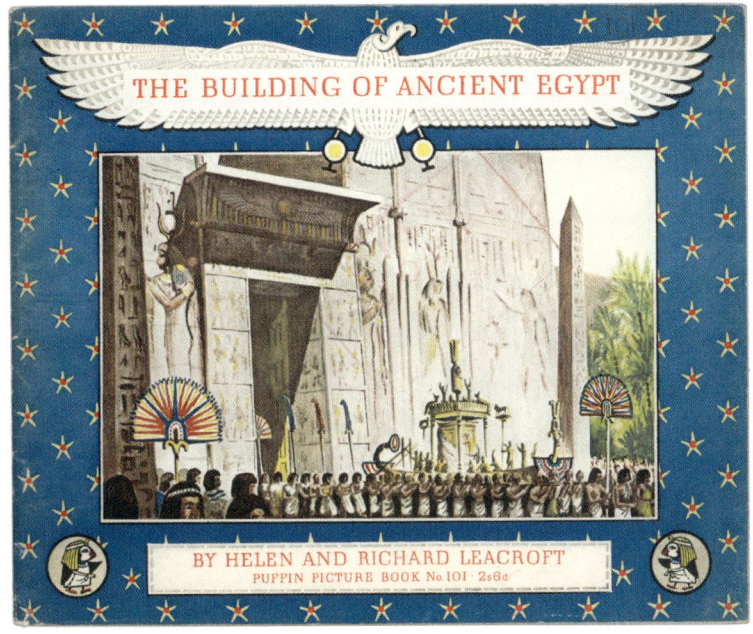

THIS PAGE: *The Emett Festival Railway*, [1951]. Illustrated by Rowland Emett

Paper Birds, [1947]. Illustrated by R. B. Talbot Kelly

OPPOSITE: *Make Your Own Zoo*, [1945]. Illustrated by Trix

Noah's Ark, 1960. Illustrated by John Miles

Puppets, 1958. Illustrated by Tony Hart

Paper, scissors, glue: Puffin cut-outs

In 1947 Puffin published a series of cut-out books. Some, although in Picture Book format, were actually a separate series (prefix PC) and ran to six published titles, including the large-format three-part *Cotswold Village* and *Half-Timbered Village*, as well as the standard-sized *The Emett Festival Railway*. This book recreated the attraction Rowland Emett designed for the Battersea Pleasure Gardens at the 1951 Festival of Britain. This was the most complex of the cut-out titles; making this model is reputed to take an experienced model-maker 200 hours.

Other cut-out books appeared as Picture Books, the earliest of which was described in *Penguin's Progress* (no. 5, 1947) '. . . the latest to appear is *Paper Birds*, anatomized by R. B. Talbot Kelly. On successive pages he provides silhouettes of such birds, common and uncommon, as the Song Thrush, the House Sparrow, Kestrel, Plover, Teal and Golden Eye. His instructions for assembling the parts are clear to the last detail, including his guidance on painting these toy birds in their natural colours, and inventing backgrounds for them to stand on.'

Of interest among the others shown here is *Noah's Ark* by John Miles who was working with Hans Schmoller in the Penguin design department. This idea was pitched to Puffin just before he left to set up the design company Banks & Miles with Colin Banks. *Puppets* was by Tony Hart, who at the time was a resident artist on the children's TV show *Saturday Special*. He later became a presenter, most famously on *Vision On* (1964–77) and *Take Hart* (1977–83).

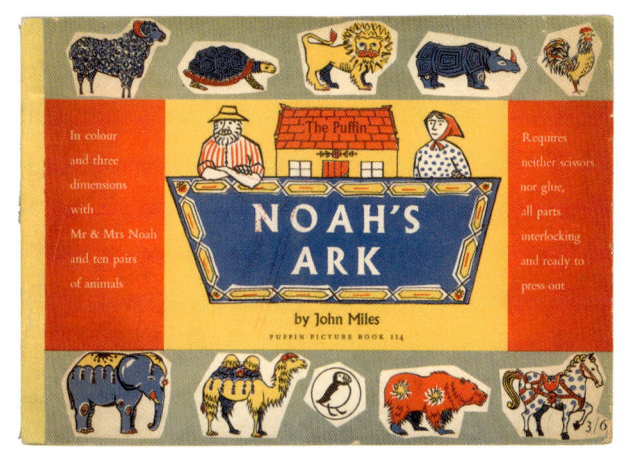

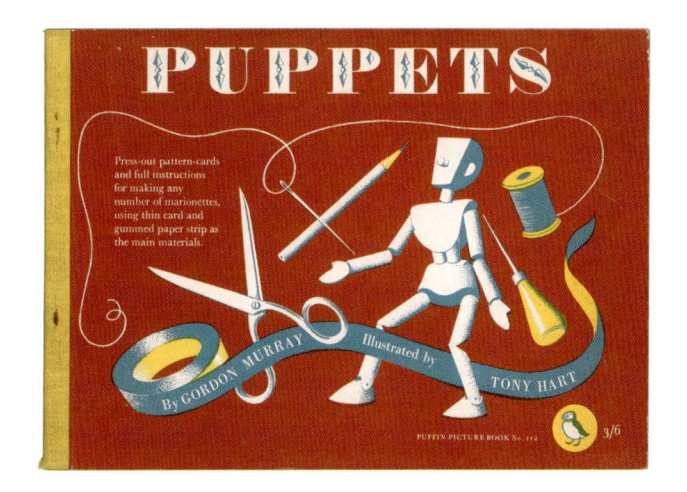

THIS PAGE: *Better Handwriting*, 1954. [Illustrated by George L. Thomson]

The Puffin Book of Lettering, 1961. [Illustrated by Tom Gourdie]

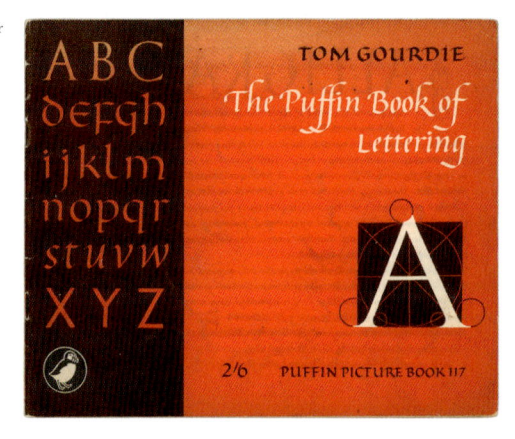

Printing, 1948. Illustrated by Jack Brough

OPPOSITE: *A Child's Alphabet*, [1945]. Illustrated by Grace Gabler

Spelling Book, 1948. Illustrated by Grace Gabler

A Counting Book, 1957. Illustrated by Grace Gabler (front and back cover shown)

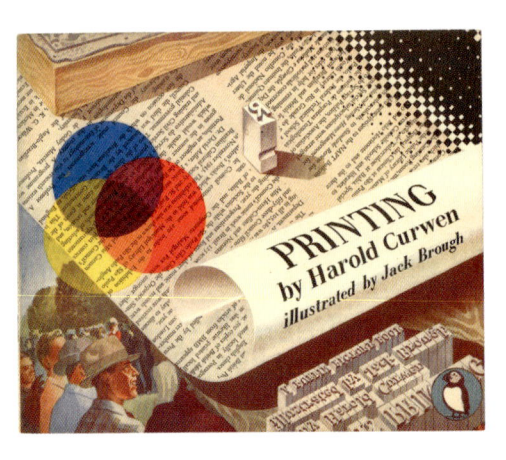

Arts of mankind

A great many of the Puffin Picture Book titles could be termed 'instructive', and those shown here concentrate on the fundamentals of communication and the dissemination of information. They are also indicative of the wide range of ages that the books catered for.

Grace Gabler's three titles are clearly aimed at pre-schoolers and early learners and are the only books in the series in portrait format. Gabler was another Puffin Picture Book author who was an illustrator of covers for the Story Books (see p. 71). *Better Handwriting* and *The Puffin Book of Lettering* are for a wider spread of ages and would be as useful to art students as school children.

Printing, with its technical descriptions of process, is clearly aimed at a teenage market and was unusual in being the only title to be printed letterpress. Harold Curwen was Director of the Curwen Press in Plaistow and had been a champion of autolithography before the Second World War, helping many of the artists associated with the series.

Puffin by Design

I. Pictures

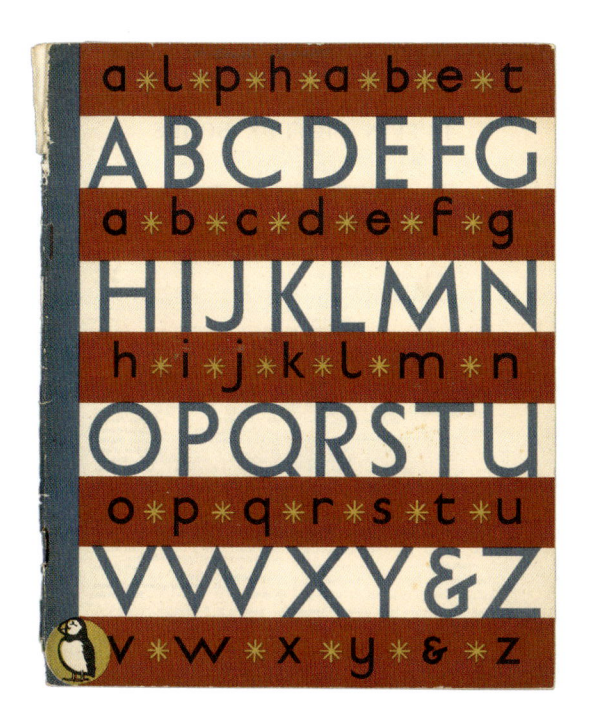

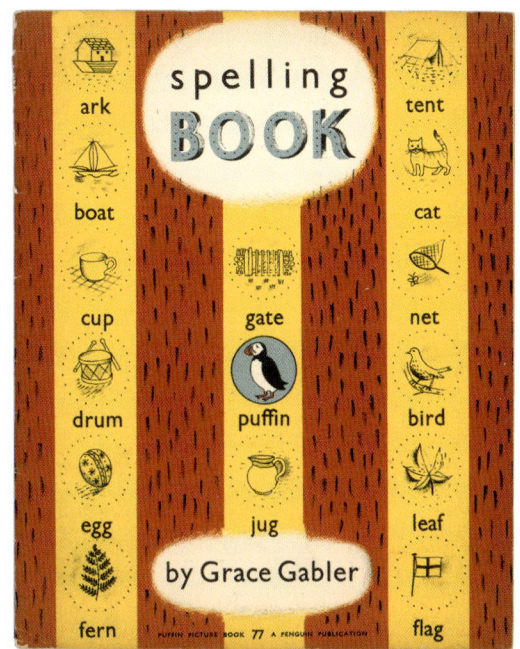

43

Building a House, 1949. Illustrated by Richard Leacroft (front cover and inside spread shown)

Factual description

An aspect of the Picture Books already commented on is their breadth of subject matter. The concept of simplifying the material for children does not appear to have been a primary concern, as it was for books produced by the Isotype Institute working at the same time. *Building a House* by Richard Leacroft is a case in point. In other hands this spread showing water and waste disposal could have been rendered as a simplified diagram illustrating principles. But not here at Puffin. When you look at the detail and the terminologically exact captions it feels as though it is addressed to a class of trainee building-control officers or engineers. And yet it is an absolutely clear, unambiguous cross-section – the terms used are those you need to know, and if you want to know how a house is really built then actually you will love this kind of detail. The implication is clear: if you want to know, you have to step up.

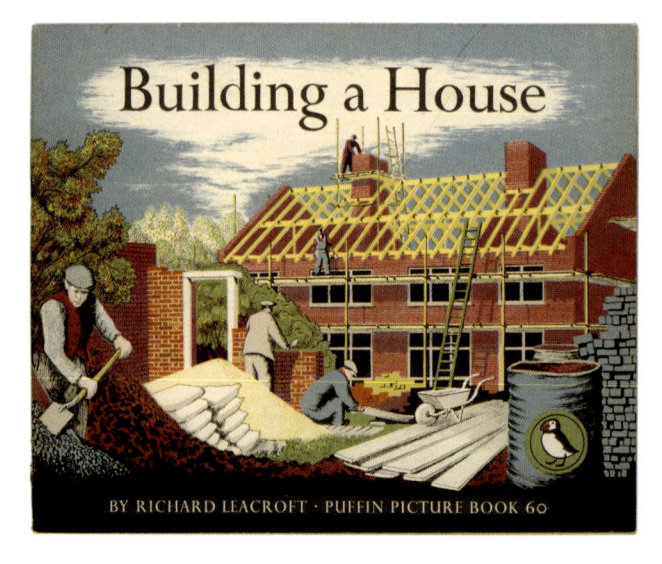

Galvanized iron or copper cage

Cast iron rain water gutter

Cast iron soil pipe carried up 3' 0" ab nearest window to act as vent pipe to drainage system

Cast iron rain water down pipe

Copper or lead vent pipe

Copper or lead waste pipe from lavat basin and bath

S-trap with water seal

Overflow pipe from bath with windfla

W.C. connection to soil pipe

Overflow pipe from W.C. cistern

Flush pipe

Kitchen sink

S-trap to sink with water seal

Washing machine

W.C. connected direct to stoneware o earthenware pipes

Gulley trap with two back inlets

Gulley trap with one back inlet and w waste from washing machine dischar over grating

Earthenware pipes jointed with yarn a cement mortar and laid to a fall of 1: to 1: 60

Brick manhole on concrete base

24

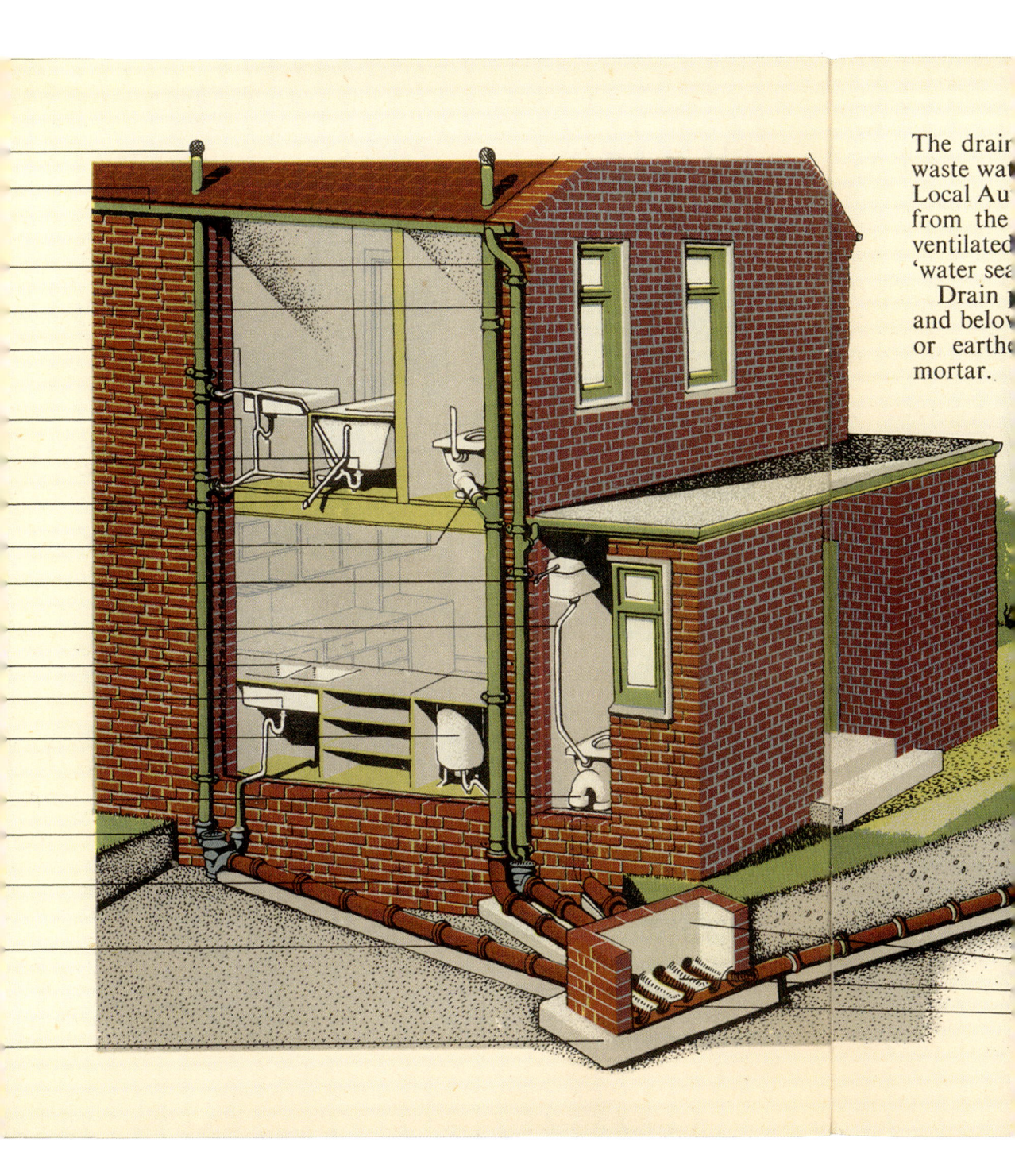

The drain
waste wa
Local Au
from the
ventilated
'water sea
Drain
and below
or earthe
mortar.

1. Pictures

BELOW: *Farm Crops in Britain*, 1955. Illustrated by S. R. Badmin

OPPOSITE: *Village and Town*, [1947]. Illustrated by S. R. Badmin (front cover and inside spread shown)

Trees in Britain, [1943]. Illustrated by S. R. Badmin

S. R. Badmin (1906–89)

Badmin studied at Camberwell School of Art and the Royal College of Art, and later combined teaching with his work as an illustrator. He worked mainly in watercolour, but also in pen and ink, and his favoured subject was the British natural landscape. Compared to virtually all the other autolithographed books in the series, Badmin's are meticulously crisp and detailed. *Trees in Britain* was described by David Thomas in the 1962 *Penrose Annual* as 'one of the most beautiful illustrated books of this century'.

In line with many other books in the series, *Village and Town* has a quiet agenda underpinning its text. At a time when the country was starting to dream about a post-war world, it urges restraint and respect rather than wholesale redevelopment. Badmin also illustrated *The Ladybird Book of Trees* in 1963.

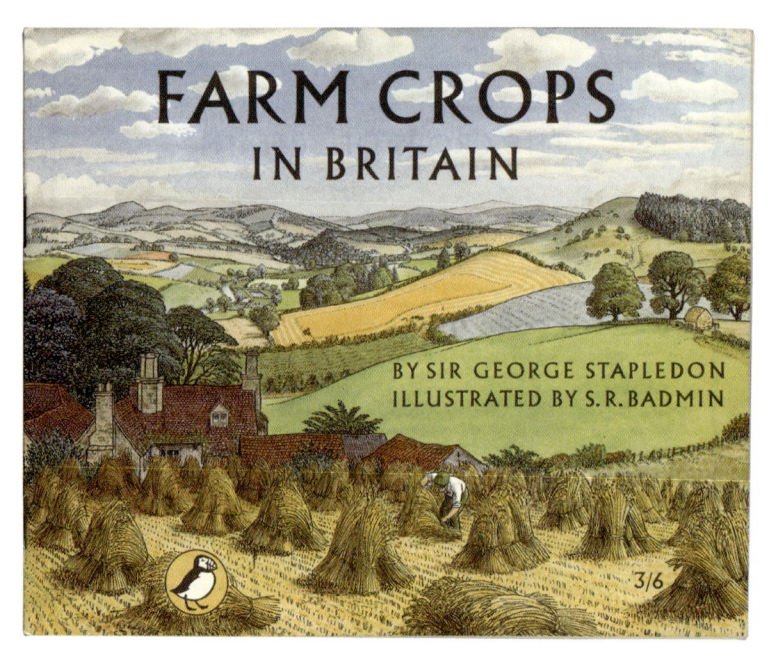

46

Puffin by Design

had been used by the Roman builders, but
idea. This reinforced concrete is extremely
le. Buildings can be very tall. Big windows
el girders. Homes can be balanced on two
into the light and air, and allowing
neath. In building in this new material
need the help of a third person, the
carefully the use to which the building
is to be put; whether it is to house
imals or machines,
kind of building **suitable for penguins**
o. The curious shapes representing ice
s could only be constructed in reinforced
concrete. How comfortably the grown-up
leans on the top
parapet while the child
easily looks over the
lower wall.

CONCRETE HOUSES

This new way of building has given us a way of preventing the towns spreading and creeping over the countryside. Tall blocks of flats have been built that house hundreds of people. The best ones have been built to look beautiful and to be convenient to live in. These buildings take up so little ground space that there is plenty of room for gardens and trees. The service lifts, central heating, communal restaurant, nursery, club-rooms, and sports facilities in them make daily life pleasanter and easier.

Concrete is being used to build new, clean-looking, individual houses too. They have long sliding windows so that you can push the whole of one side of the room away if you wish, and wide balconies and flat roofs on which to grow things or sunbathe. Proper use of reinforced concrete has made these buildings look very different from the old buildings, but they rely for their beauty on simple shapes and simple patterns made by the windows just as do the buildings on pages 8 and 23 and 30.

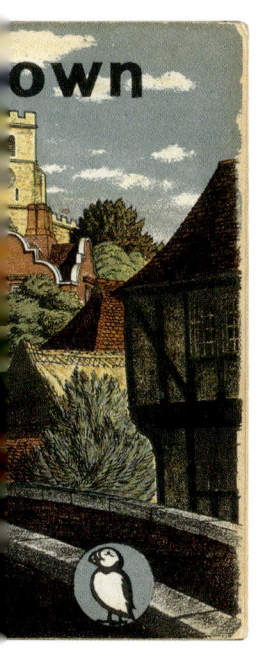

TREES IN BRITAIN
by S. R. Badmin

SWAMPS AND HILLTO[PS]

FROM GORSE BRACKEN THISTLES

Crops have been grown on many hundreds of square miles of unused land from 1939 to 1943. Formerly this ground was swamp and bog. Mountain tops, moors, bare downs, commons also were made to grow crops, some of which had never been productive before. In this way men are now adapting the landscape, which was wild. New machines made this possible, such as big caterpillar tractors, which are able to work on slopes, and wet ground, where horses or wheel tractors would be useless. Such crops as potatoes, oats and rape grow in place of gorse, bracken and thistles.

ABOVE AND OPPOSITE: *A History of the Countryside*, [1944]. [Illustrated by Margaret Potter] (inside spread and front cover shown)

Margaret and Alexander Potter

Margaret (1916–1997), an illustrator, married Alexander 'Alick' Potter (1912–2000), an architect and conscientious objector, in 1939. They ran a hostel for Irish agricultural workers in mid-Wales during the war and produced their first Puffin Picture Book there in 1944. *A History of the Countryside* typifies their style: her lively illustrations as counterfoil to the more serious text, which finishes with an indictment of 1930s ribbon development.

On this spread the tractor sweeps all before it, its heroic depiction softened by the quality of the line work around it. As with many books in the series, however, there is not quite enough room allowed

MADE INTO FIELDS

TO POTATOES OATS & RAPE

These pictures are of some stages in reclamation of land. First the ground is cleared, and may have to be drained. The first picture shows Gorse Burning. Afterwards the ground is ready for ploughing. Disc Harrows follow to make the soil fine, with their sharp metal discs. A plough and harrow are shown working in the second picture. The third shows a Spike Harrow, and workers filling a Drill with seed and fertiliser which it sows together. Later the Spike Harrow is drawn over the ground to cover the seed. Four shows a Combined Harvester cutting and threshing corn at the same time.

for the text and the justification of the narrow columns is unavoidably poor.

They wrote another Picture Book, PP42 *The Building of London* in 1945 and illustrated L. A. Dovey's *Half-Timbered Village* and *Cotswold Village* in the related Puffin Cut-out series (see pp. 40–1).

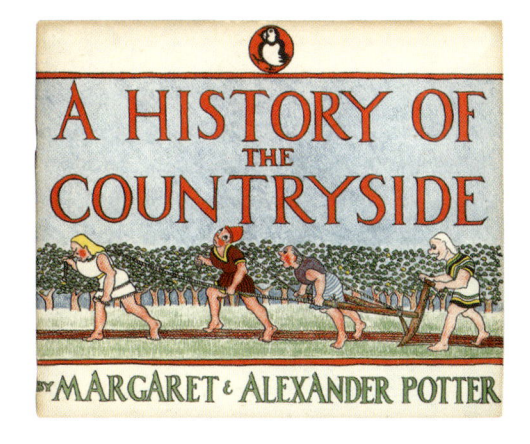

A HISTORY OF THE COUNTRYSIDE
by MARGARET & ALEXANDER POTTER

I. Pictures

BELOW AND OPPOSITE:
The Tale of Noah and the Flood,
[1946]. Illustrated by
Clarke Hutton (front cover and
inside spread shown)

Clarke Hutton (1898–1984)

Clarke Hutton had worked as a set designer before turning to art and studying lithography under A. S. Hartrick at the Central School. Upon Hartrick's retirement in 1930 he then took over the class from him, continuing until 1968.

The two titles shown here exhibit different characteristics of his work. *A Tea-Time Story* is controlled and economical in composition, colour and line, whereas *The Tale of Noah and the Flood* is an altogether more tempestuous affair. A strong use of line underpins dark, brooding images with their surreal colour and dramatic use of white.

Hutton illustrated two other books in the series, PP17 *Nursery Rhymes* and PP27 *Punch & Judy* (see p. 29). He went on to write and illustrate the very popular Pictorial History of . . . series for Oxford University Press and produced lithographs for their Wall Picture series for schools.

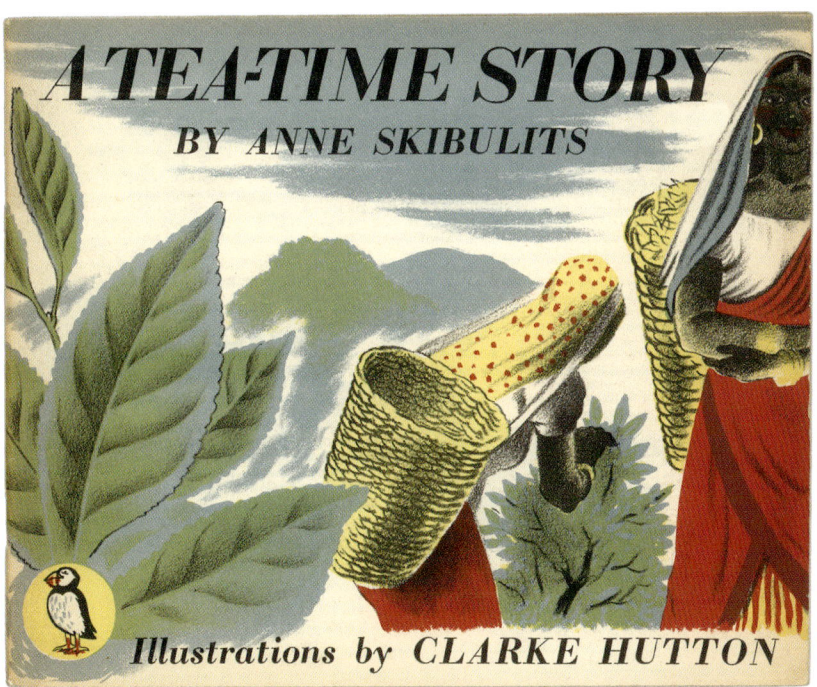

A Tea-Time Story, published as *The Story of Tea*, [1948]. Illustrated by Clarke Hutton. This shows a proof copy; although the illustration is the same in the published version, the typography differs, crediting Anne Skibulits and Clarke Hutton jointly below the title, while the lower panel states 'A Puffin Picture Book Number 72 A Penguin Publication'.

I. Pictures

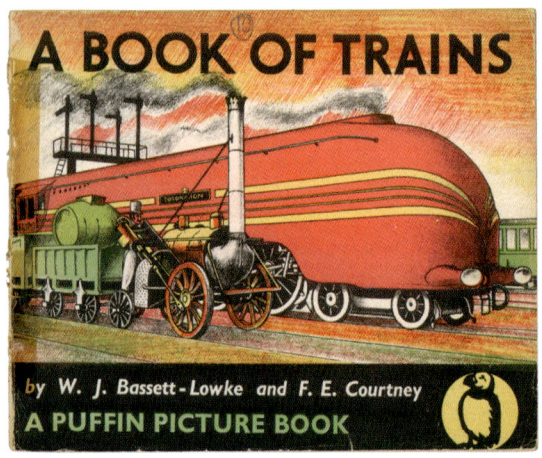

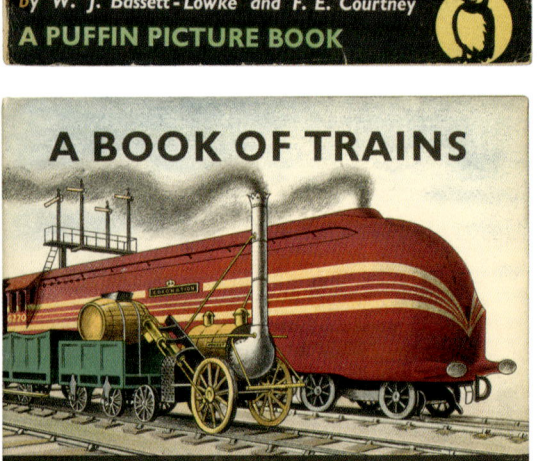

Changing covers, techniques and authors

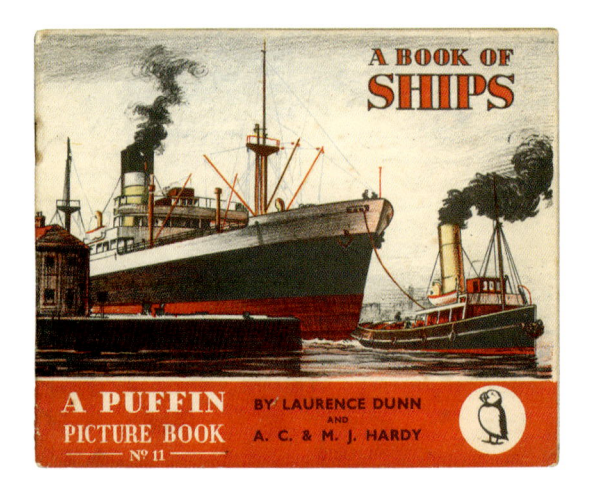

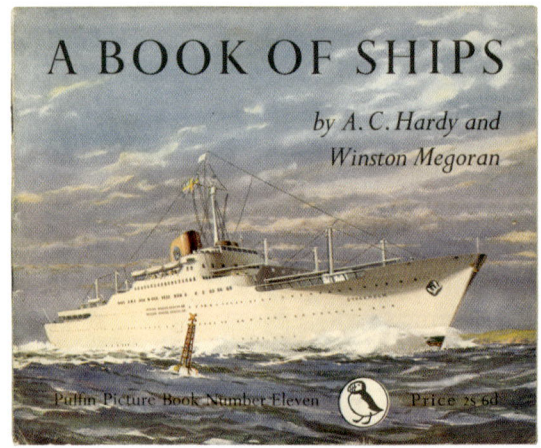

A Book of Trains, [1941].
[Illustrated by F. E. Courtney]

A Book of Ships, [1942].
[Illustrated by Laurence Dunn]

A Book of Trains, 1951.
[Illustrated by F. E. Courtney]

A Book of Ships, 1952.
[Illustrated by Winston Megoran]

Although the series was started – for both financial and philosophical reasons – on the premise of using autolithography, photolithography came to be used from 1945 onwards. Many titles ran to several printings and editions and reflect this in subtle, and not so subtle, ways.

A Book of Trains had two later revised editions containing changes to reflect the nationalization of the railways on 1 January 1947. For the revisions the printing technique changed from auto- to photolithography, which has quite a different 'feel' in this example. The typography is also tidied up, reflecting the arrival of Jan Tschichold at Penguin.

The second edition of *A Book of Ships* appeared ten years after the first and is aimed at an older age group. Printed by photogravure it is quite dull looking, with the same polite typography that also lets down *How Planes Fly* (see p. 34) and many other titles.

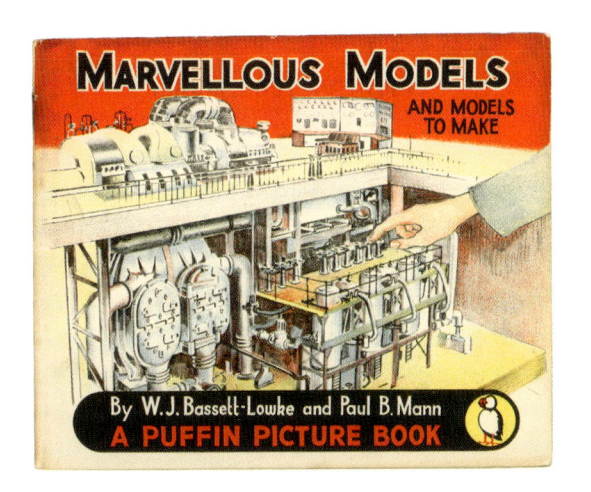

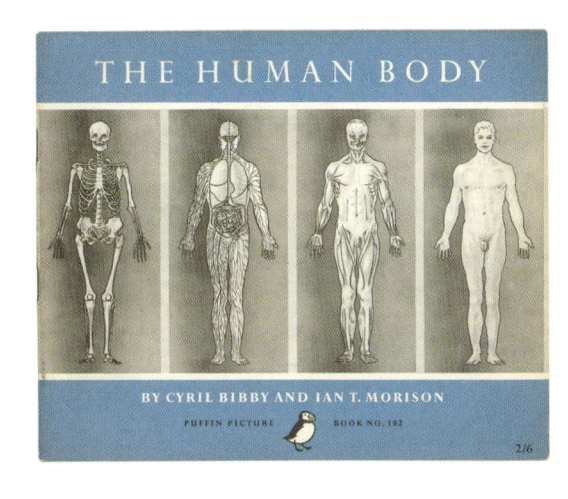

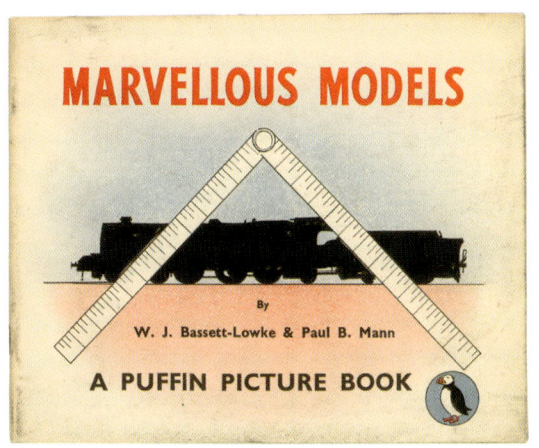

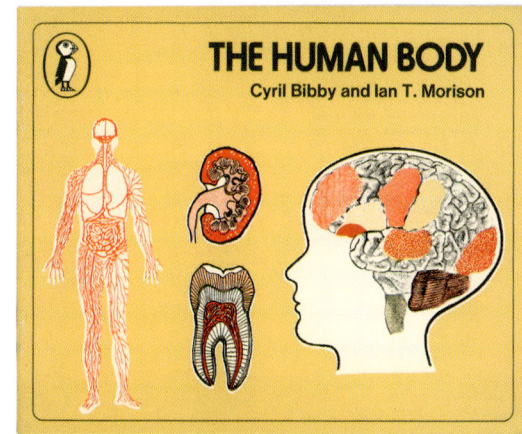

With *Marvellous Models and Models to Make* the reprint was a substantial revision to the text and illustrations inside, a simplified title and a new cover outside, and again tighter typography.

The Human Body was one of the longest running titles in the series with a final reprint in 1983, long after the series officially ended. The covers shown are the first and last of the variants.

Marvellous Models and Models to Make, [1945]. [Illustrated by Paul B. Mann]

The Human Body, 1955. [Illustrated by Ian T. Morison]

Marvellous Models, 1947. [Illustrated by Paul B. Mann]

The Human Body, 1976. [Illustrated by Ian T. Morison]

1. Pictures 53

THIS PAGE: *About a Motor Car*, [1946]. [Illustrated by Phyllis Ladyman]

Changing times, 1943–8

About a Motor Car, like *The Human Body*, was another long-lasting title, with its final reprint in 1975. While the absolute essentials of a car's mechanics changed little throughout the book's history, there was a considerable sophistication of many parts as well as general appearance. The two covers and spreads here show some of this clearly, as well as the visually different feel of auto- and photolithography.

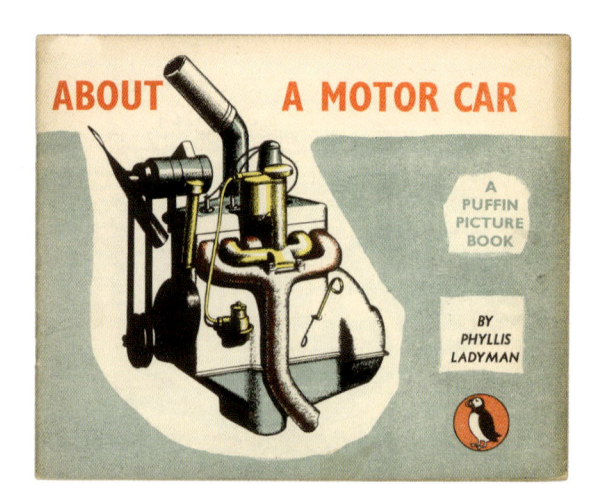

About a Motor Car, 1965. [Illustrated by Phyllis Ladyman]

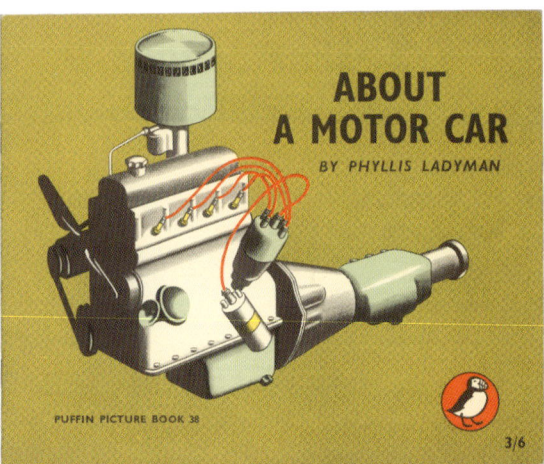

OPPOSITE: Inside spreads from the 1946 (top) and 1965 (bottom) editions of *About a Motor Car*.

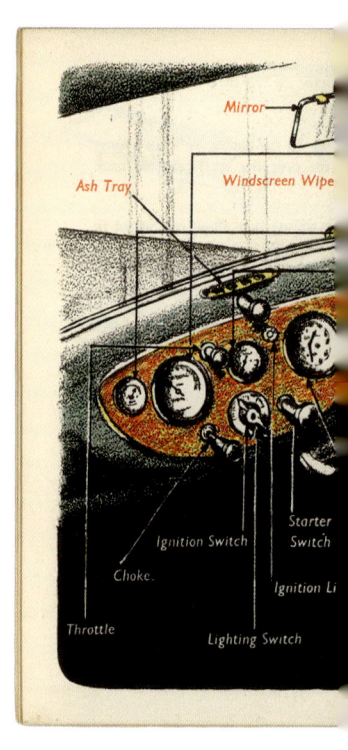

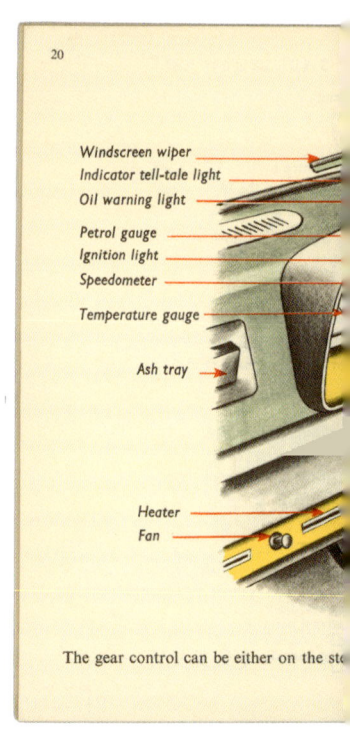

54

Puffin by Design

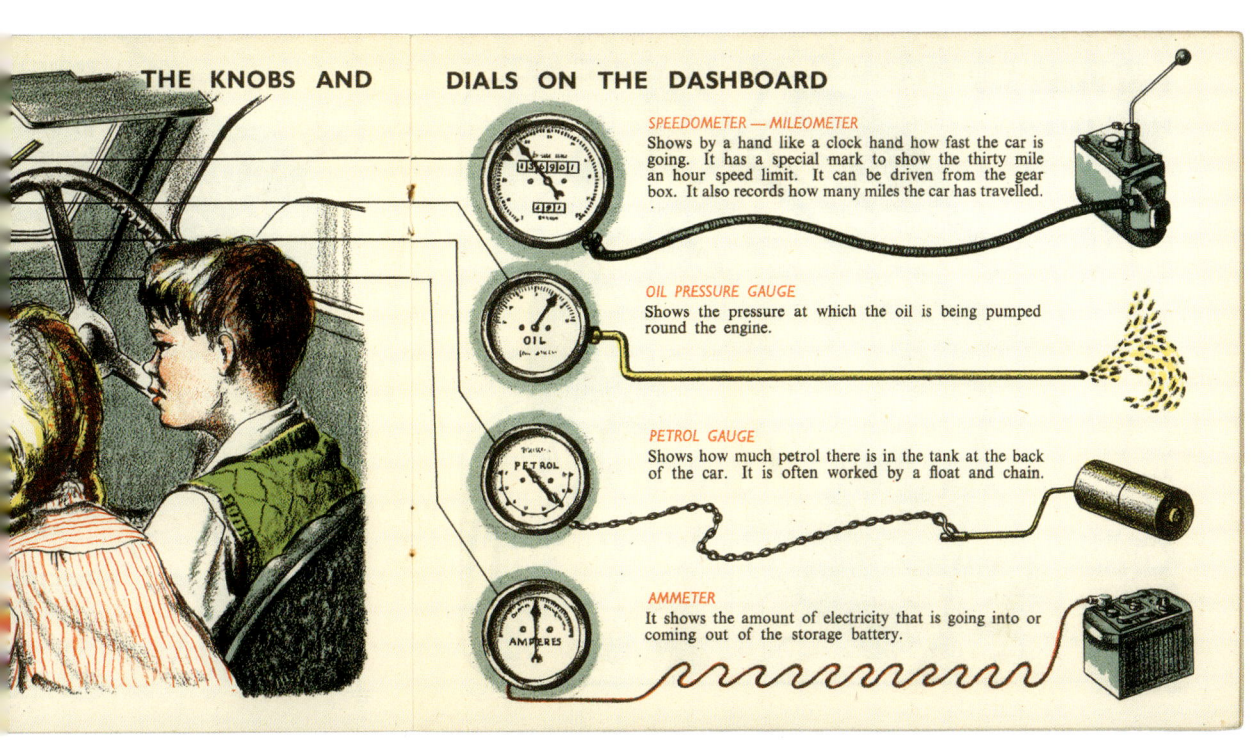

THE KNOBS AND DIALS ON THE DASHBOARD

SPEEDOMETER — MILEOMETER
Shows by a hand like a clock hand how fast the car is going. It has a special mark to show the thirty mile an hour speed limit. It can be driven from the gear box. It also records how many miles the car has travelled.

OIL PRESSURE GAUGE
Shows the pressure at which the oil is being pumped round the engine.

PETROL GAUGE
Shows how much petrol there is in the tank at the back of the car. It is often worked by a float and chain.

AMMETER
It shows the amount of electricity that is going into or coming out of the storage battery.

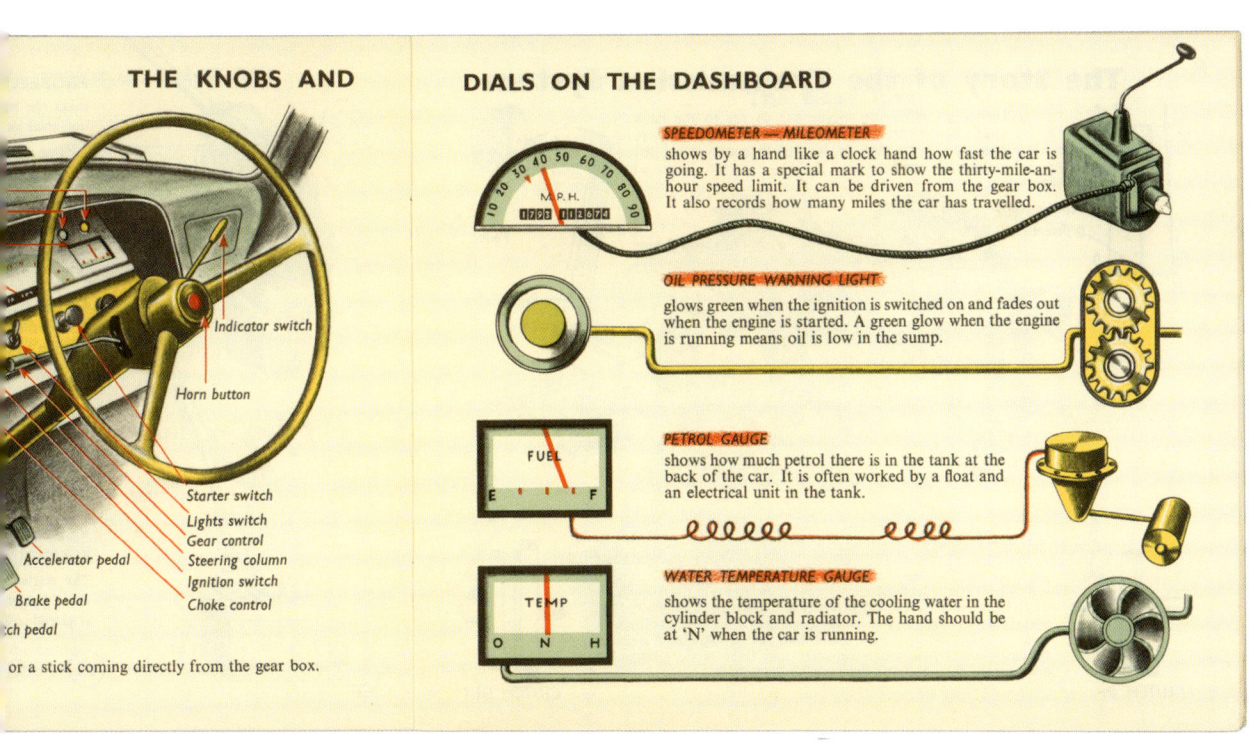

THE KNOBS AND DIALS ON THE DASHBOARD

- Indicator switch
- Horn button
- Starter switch
- Lights switch
- Gear control
- Steering column
- Ignition switch
- Choke control
- Accelerator pedal
- Brake pedal
- ch pedal

or a stick coming directly from the gear box.

SPEEDOMETER — MILEOMETER
shows by a hand like a clock hand how fast the car is going. It has a special mark to show the thirty-mile-an-hour speed limit. It can be driven from the gear box. It also records how many miles the car has travelled.

OIL PRESSURE WARNING LIGHT
glows green when the ignition is switched on and fades out when the engine is started. A green glow when the engine is running means oil is low in the sump.

PETROL GAUGE
shows how much petrol there is in the tank at the back of the car. It is often worked by a float and an electrical unit in the tank.

WATER TEMPERATURE GAUGE
shows the temperature of the cooling water in the cylinder block and radiator. The hand should be at 'N' when the car is running.

1. Pictures

55

The Holiday Train, 1944.
Illustrated by Peter Heaton

The Holiday Train Goes to the Moon, 1946.
Illustrated by Peter Heaton

Baby Puffins

Following on from the success of the Picture Books and the Puffin Story Books described in the following chapter, Baby Puffins were an attempt to address the needs of the very young. They were produced by autolithography in exactly the same manner as the Picture Books but were only half the size, i.e. virtually the same A format of standard Penguin books. Although this made them easier to handle, their slim extent – thirty-two pages – gave them the same problems of shelf display as the larger books.

Only nine titles were published in the series, which lasted just five years. *The Old Woman and Her Pig* was by John Harwood, who was also illustrating covers for the Story Book series, including the Worzel Gummidge titles shown on pages 72–3 at around the same time.

ABC, 1943. Illustrated by Dorothy Chapman (front cover and inside spread shown)

123, 1943. Illustrated by Dorothy Chapman

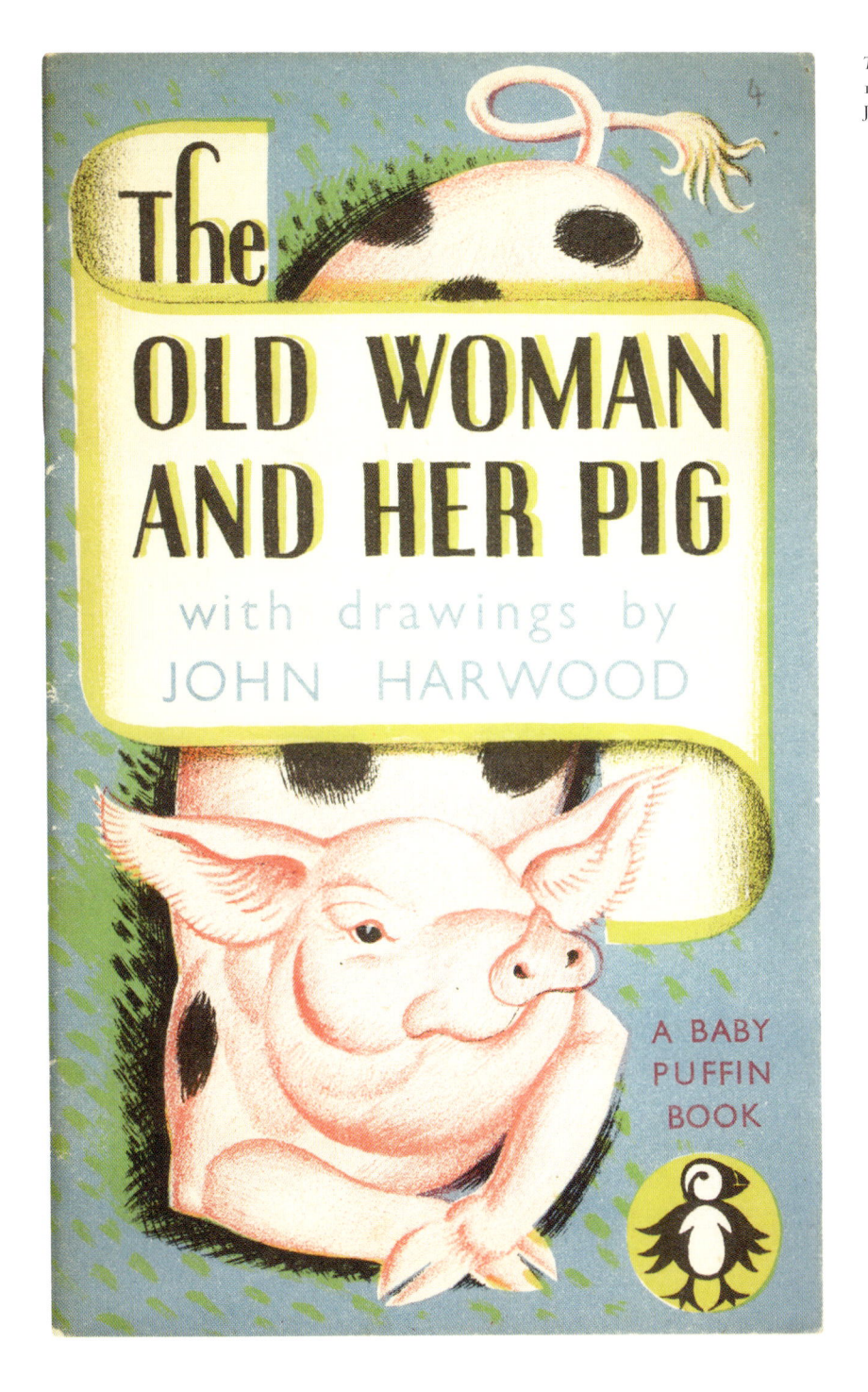

The Old Woman and Her Pig, 1944. Illustrations by John Harwood

1. Pictures

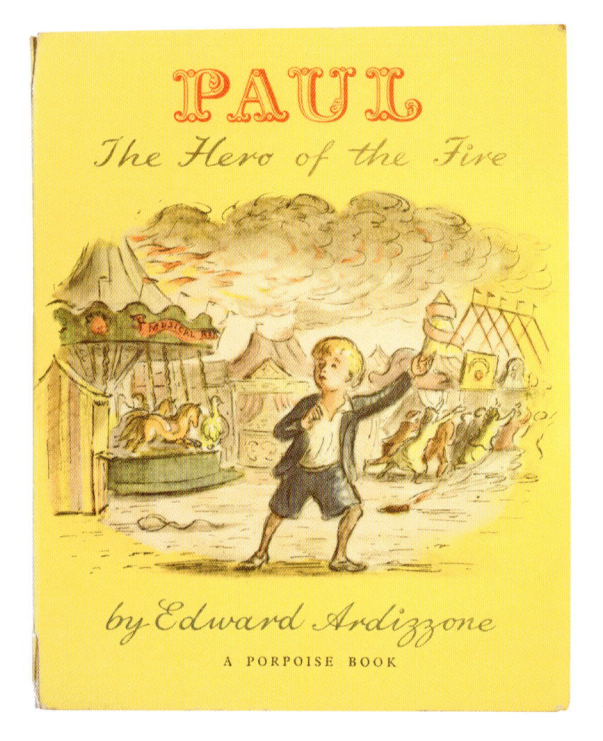

Paul the Hero of the Fire, 1948. Illustrated by Edward Ardizzone

The Ugly Duckling, 1948. Illustrated by Will Nickless

Porpoises

These four titles were a short-lived experiment in hardback children's illustrated fiction. Noel Carrington had initially proposed a series of large-format hardback books with cloth spines selling for a shilling (5p) – twice the price of the Picture Puffins. The management of the series was given to the American-born Grace Hogarth (1905–95). The US publisher Houghton Mifflin was a named co-publisher but seems to have been no more than a sleeping partner. Hogarth had experience of producing similar titles for OUP, including the first of Edward Ardizzone's Little Tim books. Late in 1945 she approached Ardizzone and Violet Drummond who had ideas for new stories (*Paul the Hero of the Fire* and *The Flying Postman* respectively), while Will Nickless and John Harwood were asked to interpret classic stories (*The Ugly Duckling* and *Aladdin*). Eventually these became the four published titles, but over a two-year period a dozen other artists were also approached about the series.

During the following two years various printers – but strangely not Cowell's – were trialled, proofs were made, and eventually around 100,000 copies of each title were printed.

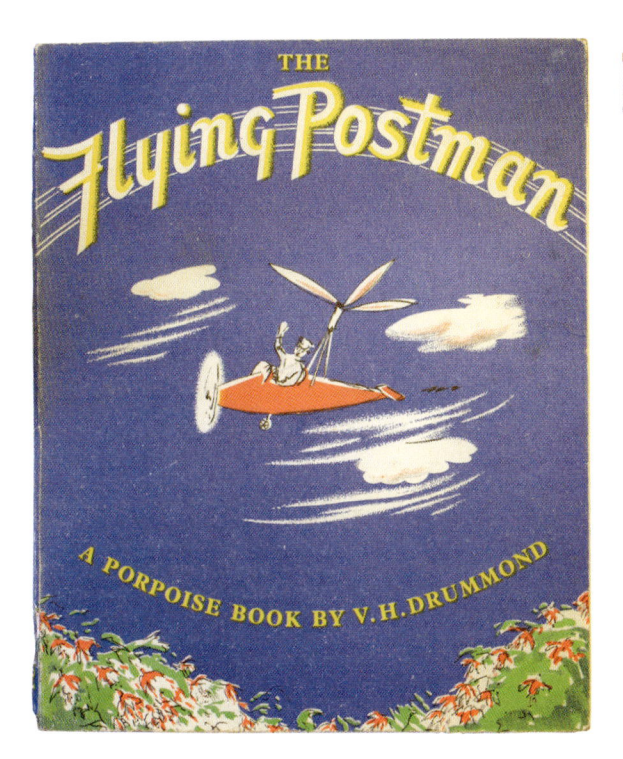

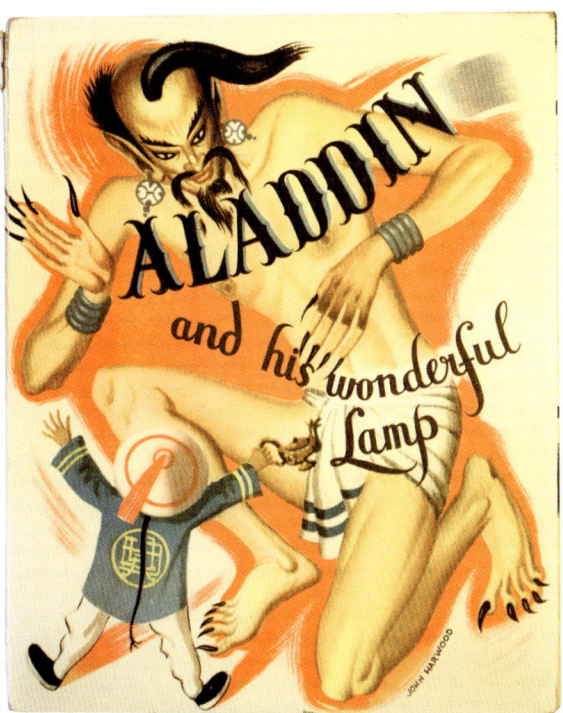

Compared to the Picture Books, no expense seems to have been spared, with six colours being used for all except *The Ugly Duckling*, which required nine. Nevertheless, Ardizzone and Drummond were very unhappy at the mismatch between proofs and the final published result.

More problematic than the quality of colour reproduction was the selling price: 3/6d (17.5p). This made it a very expensive children's book in post-war Britain, and they never sold in anything like sufficient quantities. After the first four titles the series was dropped and by the early 1950s rumours that the bulk of the print run had been pulped began to emerge. Their fate still remains unclear.

Of other titles that had been in production, *The Emperor's New Clothes*, illustrated by Virginia Lee Burton, was published by Houghton Mifflin in 1949: Dudley Jarrett's *The Pink Pony* was published as an Odhams Little Colour Book in 1951; and H. A. Rey's *Mary Had a Little Lamb* appeared as PP91 in 1951 (see p. 29).

The Flying Postman, 1948. Illustrated by V. H. Drummond

Aladdin and His Wonderful Lamp, 1948. Illustrated by John Harwood

Life Histories, 1995.
Illustrated by Paxton Chadwick

Late for the party

Artist (and communist) Paxton Chadwick (1903–61) had produced three books for the series – PP81 *Wild Flowers*; PP93 *Pond Life*; and PP105 *Wild Animals in Britain* – and had an agreement for a fourth, PP116 *Life Histories*. Unfortunately, he died before fully completing his work on it and, with Noel Carrington's retirement not long after, the book never appeared, and the series number was not allocated to another title. Throughout the 1960s Kaye Webb considered publishing it, but eventually the series disappeared before any final agreements had been made.

In 1995 with the consent of both Puffin and Chadwick's estate the Penguin Collectors Society published the book using Chadwick's plates, which still existed, with a text layout by John Miles, who had begun his career at Penguin in 1954. It was printed in three colours by Battley Brothers, under the supervision of the London College of Printing.

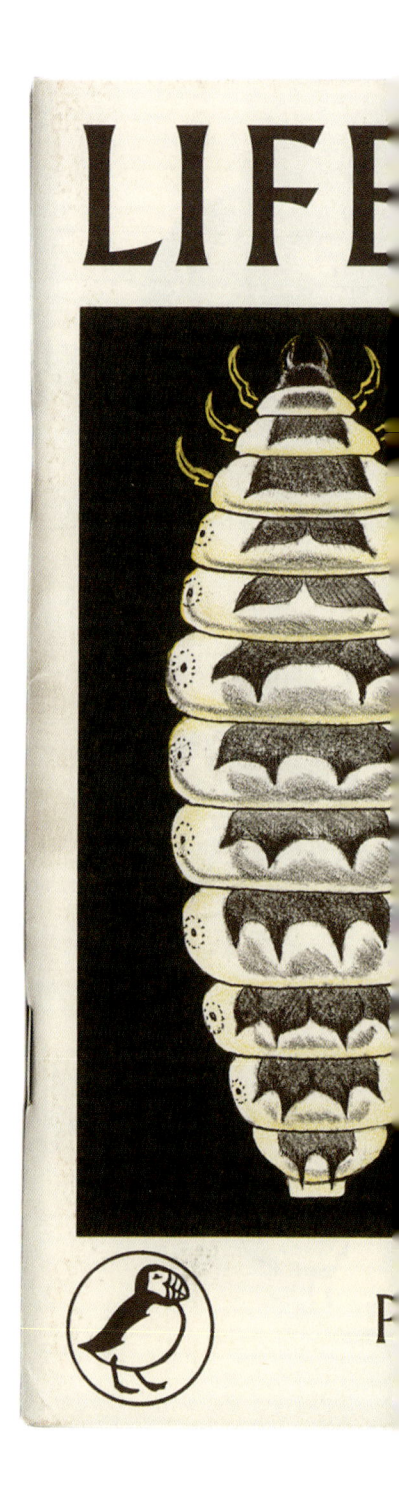

HISTORIES

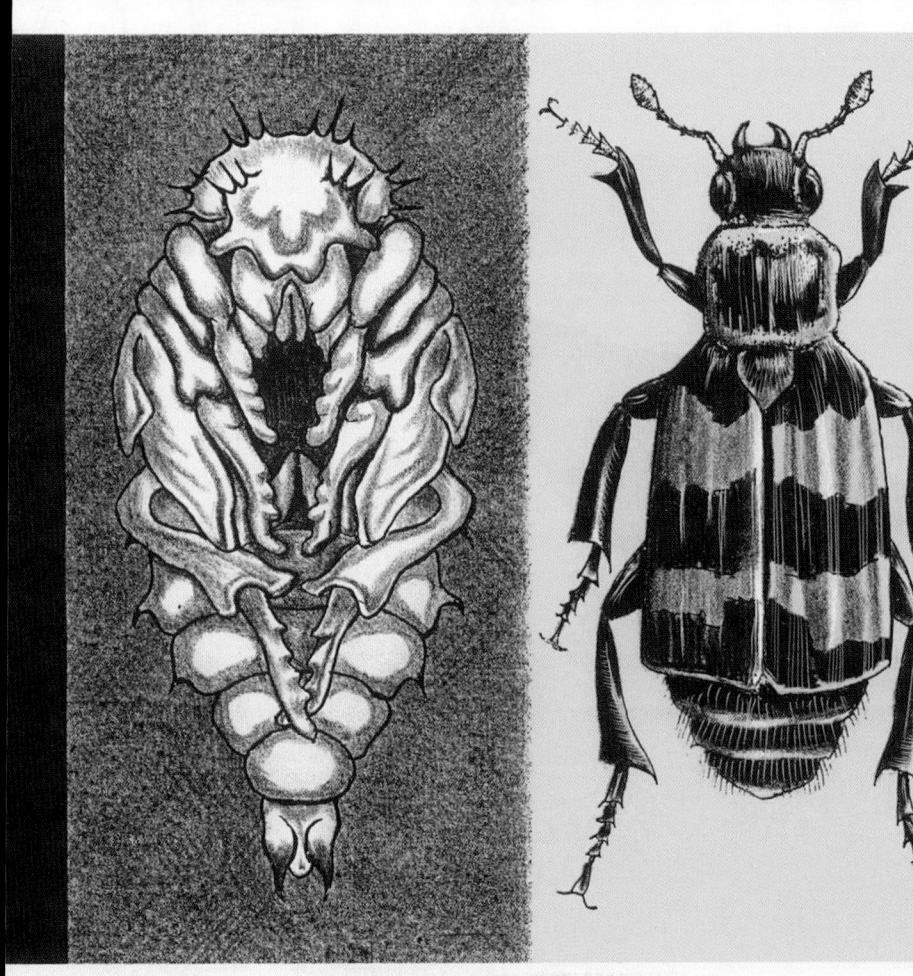

BY PAXTON CHADWICK

FFIN PICTURE BOOK 116

I. Pictures

II. Stories

FELL FARM HOLIDAY

Marjorie Lloyd

When I saw the finished copies my heart sank, for I could see the booksellers' dilemma. You couldn't make a show of five thin books, however good. But so we got off – to a not very rosy start. (Eleanor Graham in Gritten, 1991 p. 14)

Eleanor Graham and the start of the Story Books, 1941–61

After the Picture Books it was a natural step for Penguin to consider publishing children's stories. In many ways, the launch of these Story Books, as they became known, echoed the situation six years earlier when inexpensive books did not exist and Allen Lane wanted to supply them to the market. There was the small problem of a war and an acute shortage of paper, but, on the other hand, Penguin was becoming increasingly established and had a reputation for innovation and quality.

Eleanor Graham (1896–1984) had been a medical student before joining the children's department of London's Bumpus bookshop in 1927. With a childhood predisposition for books, but no previous experience, she learnt quickly by observation, questioning and by testing what kinds of books appealed to children. Further experience was gained through working subsequently in a private library, writing reviews for the *Sunday Times* and by being secretary and selector for the Junior Book Club. She had known Allen Lane for some years before he contacted her in 1940 to discuss his ideas for children's story books. Graham was by this time working for the Board of Trade when Lane offered her the job of Editor, but once she heard the seriousness of his plans she accepted.

As with the Picture Books, there were difficulties due to shortages of paper and skilled labour, but the main challenge that Graham faced was the lack of titles to publish. Neither she nor Lane wanted to publish out-of-copyright books – they wanted the best of new titles. However, despite the success of Penguin's main series, the children's book trade and librarians were even more resistant to releasing paperback rights than their adult equivalents. Gaining

Eleanor Graham

PREVIOUS PAGE: '. . . and when the artist came to design the jacket he followed directions in the book [. . .] So the cover is a true (and I think very lovely) picture of High Arnside Farm.' (Marjorie Lloyd to Kaye Webb, 10 August 1962) (see p. 88)

those rights was a drawn-out, tactful business for Graham, so Puffin evolved slowly by balancing ambition with practicality. Permissions were obtained where possible, and without sacrificing quality. Because of this, a number of books on her 'wanted list', such as the Doctor Doolittle books and *Swallows and Amazons*, became Puffins only after she had retired.

The first five titles, bearing the series identifier PS – Barbara Euphan Todd's *Worzel Gummidge*, Derek McCulloch's *Cornish Adventure*, Mrs Molesworth's *The Cuckoo Clock*, Herbert Best's *Garram the Hunter* and Will James's *Smoky* – appeared in December 1941. Like the original launch of Penguin itself, these appeared in the three-horizontal-stripes design but with the colour of red a little darker in shade than the Specials (see pp. 67–8), and because it was now wartime – there was no dust jacket. A line illustration was incorporated rather uncomfortably in the central panel. As Graham herself recalled after her retirement, it was not a visually exciting start.

The Puffin Story Books' covers did not last long in this initial design. After PS9 covers started to appear with full-bleed colour illustrations – many with integrated front and back – and reprints of earlier titles were re-covered to match (see pp. 72–3). In 1945 this was very unusual for a Penguin book; only the Puffin Picture Books and the more expensive, collectible King Penguins had coloured covers at this date. In Penguin's main fiction series the few covers sporting images were only printed in black and are now regarded as curiosities. Illustrations didn't feature on Penguin fiction until the vertical-stripes design of *c.*1948 (see *Penguin by Design*: pp. 78–84), and full colour was not properly trialled until 1957 (see *Penguin by Design*: pp. 85–9). Another feature of the Puffin Story Books was the inclusion of integrated illustrations. These were simple black line drawings secondary to the text, often by the illustrator who worked on the cover.

While Graham was editor of the series, she was not a full-time Penguin employee and her contact on a day-to-day basis was with Eunice Frost, who was very much at the heart of everything that was going on at Penguin throughout the 1940s and early 1950s. A talented artist herself, it was she who was responsible for commissioning artists and illustrators for the covers, and to whom they, and many of the authors, wrote.

Like the main Penguin series, Puffin Story Books were initially confined to reprints, and Graham's insistence on quality titles dictated the slow expansion of the list, with no more than twelve titles a year appearing during her editorship. It was some years before the publication of an original manuscript – Marjorie Lloyd's *Fell Farm Holiday* – which was agreed in

1947, but didn't appear until 1951. This was followed by commissioned retellings of popular stories, such as those about Greek heroes, Troy, Robin Hood and others, by Roger Lancelyn Green. These additions gave Puffin a wider range of titles, helped increase readership and reduced their reliance on other publishers, all of which were essential for the development and financial stability of the series.

By 1960 when Penguin turned twenty-five, the Puffin Story Books numbered 148 and Puffin was becoming as established a part of Penguin as the Classics series, which until August that year boasted Penguin Books' bestselling title, *The Odyssey*. The new decade saw many changes within the company. Structurally the most significant, perhaps, followed the publication on 25 August 1960 of D. H. Lawrence's *Lady Chatterley's Lover* and the subsequent obscenity trial. Victory for Penguin cemented its reputation, and ensured that its flotation on the stock market the following year would be oversubscribed 150 times. Penguin, although still dominated by Lane, then became a public company with a board of directors.

Editorially, the close of the 1950s had seen new editors, such as Oliver Caldecott and Dieter Pevsner, starting to make their presence felt, and Tony Godwin's arrival in 1960 re-invigorated the fiction list. He brought with him considerable practical experience in running bookshops, and rapidly rose to become Chief Editor. He insisted that Penguin addressed cover design in the same professional and consistent manner with which they approached their text pages and appointed Germano Facetti as Penguin's first Cover Art Director. This did not affect Puffin greatly, whose Picture Books and Story Books had always had their own identity and more design latitude than other Penguin series, but over the next decade Facetti's reforms transformed the look of every other Penguin series.

Eleanor Graham retired in 1961 and, whatever the reservations about the nature of the list – parts of which look rather middle class and predictable, and parts of which appear overly 'educational' to twenty-first-century eyes – she had established Puffin Story Books as a serious force in children's literature and laid solid foundations for her successors. She also wrote for children, including *The Children Who Lived in a Barn*, as well as non-fiction 'retellings', such as *The Story of Jesus* (see p. 93).

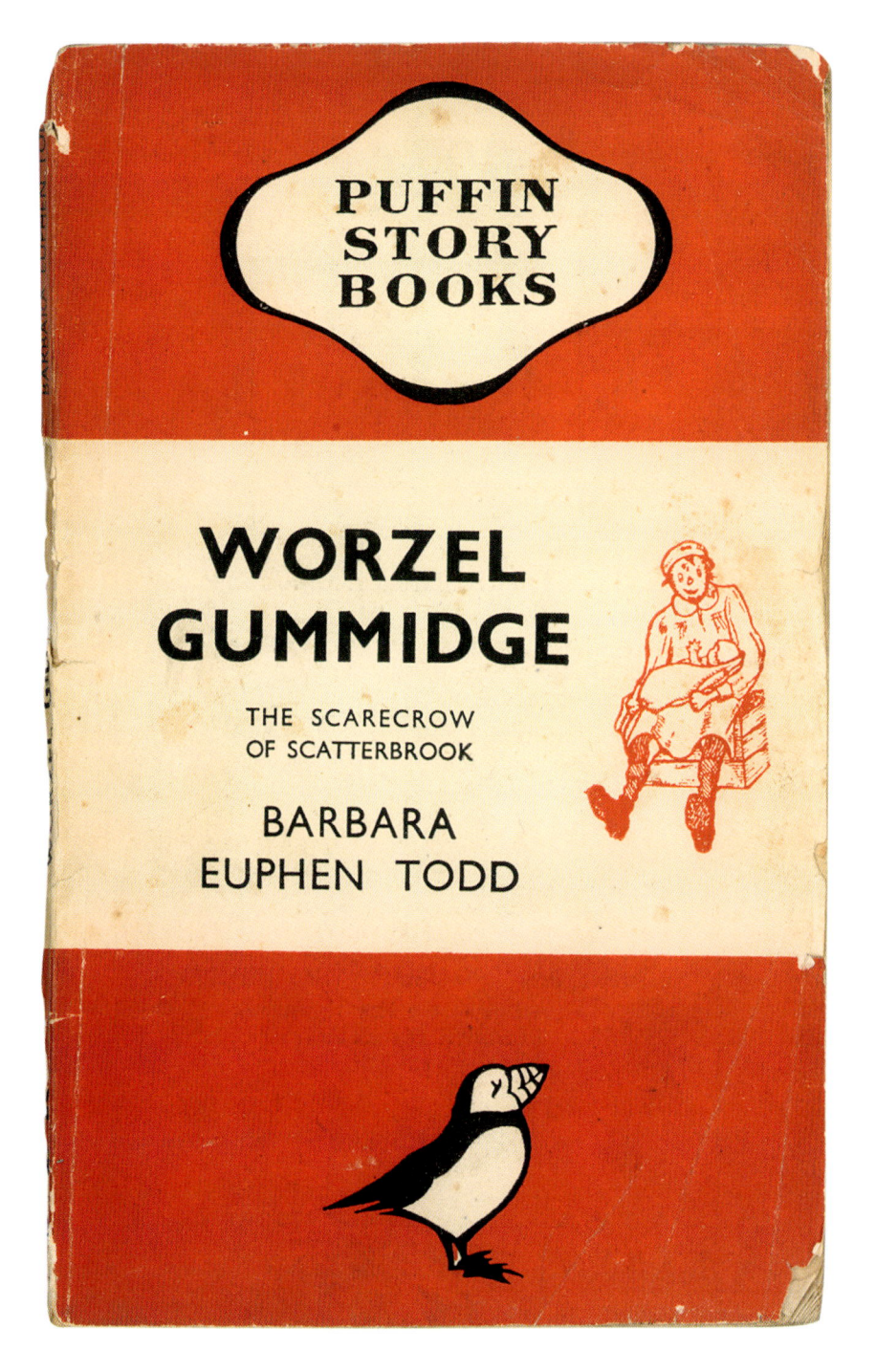

Worzel Gummidge, 1941.
Cover illustration by
Elizabeth Alldridge (note that the
author's name is misspelt on this
first printing)

Garram the Hunter, 1941.
Cover illustration by Erick Berry

Cornish Adventure, 1941.
Cover illustration adapted from photograph by the author

The first titles

The first Puffin Story Books appeared in a version of Penguin's three-horizontal-stripes design with a shade of red darker than that used on the Penguin Specials as the signature colour. Small line illustrations were incorporated into the central panel with the title and author set in Gill Sans and centred awkwardly in the remaining space. The imprint name was set, as with Penguin's main series titles, inside a quartic. The Puffin logo was drawn by Bob Maynard, who had taken over as Penguin's Production Manager after Edward Young joined the RNVR in 1940.

Before these Puffins, this type of cover design had been attempted a few times (see *Penguin by Design:* pp. 20–1), but seldom successfully.

The first eight Puffin titles appeared in this form before full-colour illustrated covers were introduced with the ninth. 'It has recently been decided to make the Puffin Story Books Series much more attractive; we shall use better paper for the text and a four-colour cover design for the cover and your PUZZLE PUFFIN BOOK is the first one to be produced in this way,' wrote Eunice Frost to W. E. Gladstone on 12 November 1943.

This cover set the tone for the majority of Puffin covers until the late 1950s. There is no type: instead, all lettering is drawn by the artist in styles or colours that harmonize with the image, and there is a very relaxed attitude to the logo, i.e. it is often absent. Among illustrators represented on the following pages are established artists, such as Robert Gibbings (*Coconut Island*); Grace Gabler (*Jam Tomorrow*), who would later become an author of several Puffin Picture Books (see pp. 42–3); and the incredibly adaptable William Grimmond (*Jungle John*, see also *Penguin by Design:* pp. 26, 46, 66–7, 76).

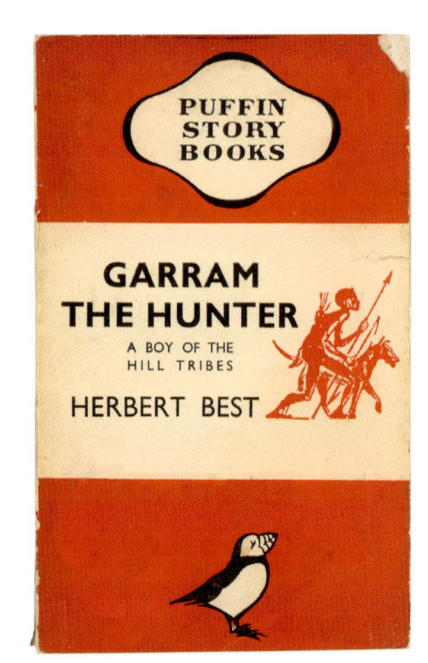

Puffin by Design

The Puffin Puzzle Book, 1944. [Cover illustration by William Grimmond]

II. *Stories*

Jehan of the Ready Fists, 1945.
[Cover illustration by A. H. Hall]

Greentree Downs, 1945.
[Cover illustration by 'S. J.']

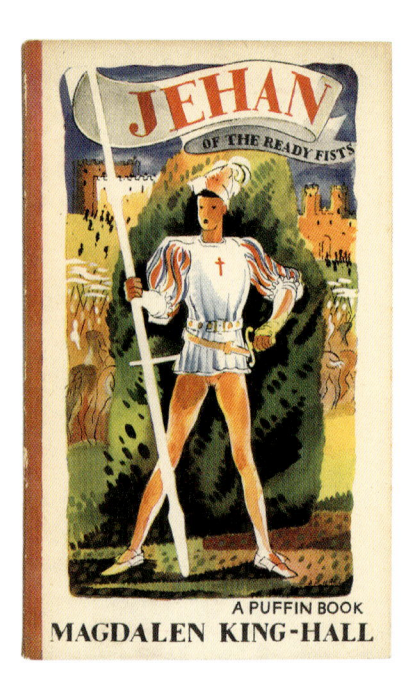

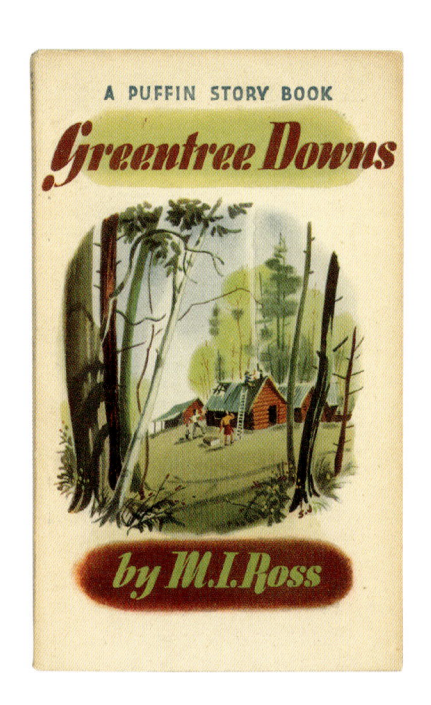

Coconut Island, 1945.
Cover illustration by
Robert Gibbings

My Friend Mr. Leakey, 1944.
[Cover illustration by
John Harwood]

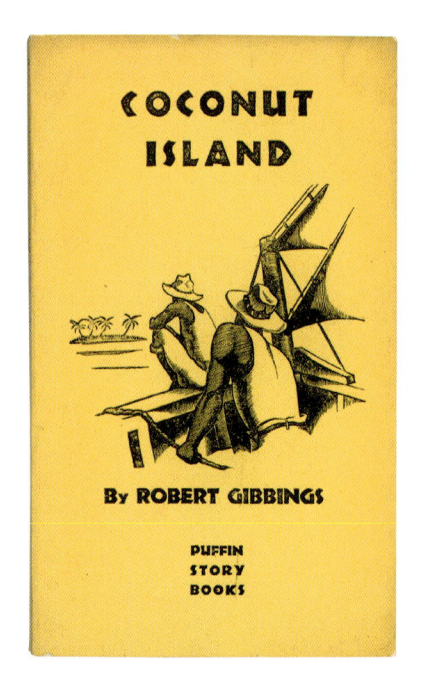

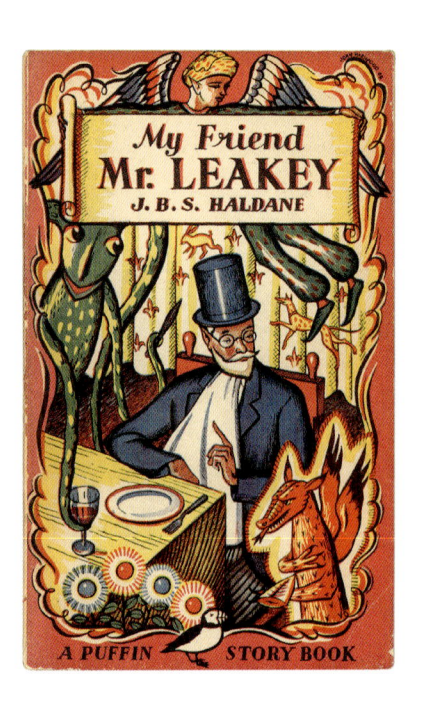

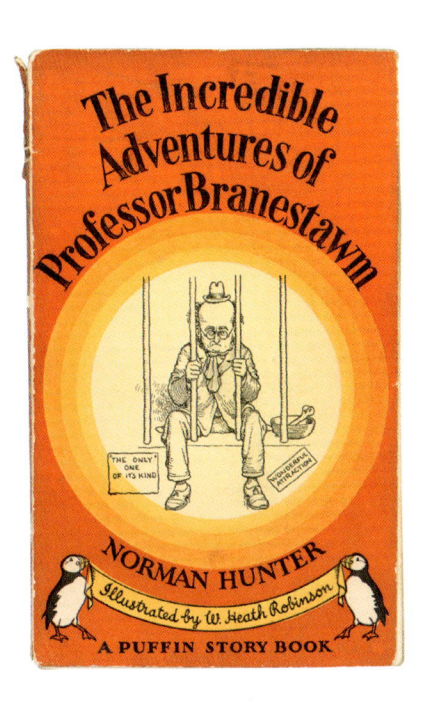

*The Incredible Adventures of
Professor Branestawm*, 1946.
Cover illustration by
W. Heath Robinson

Jam Tomorrow, 1947.
Cover illustration by Grace Gabler

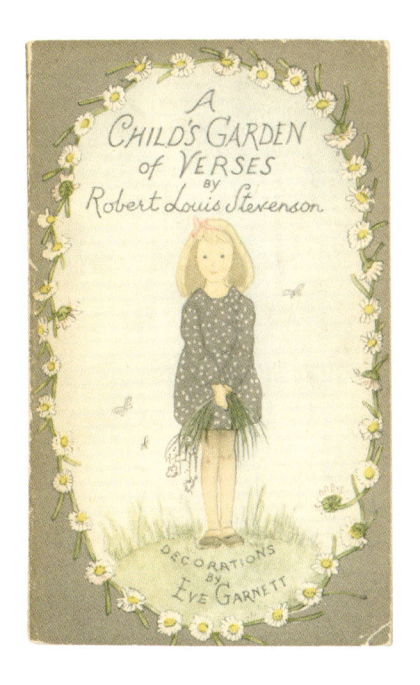

A Child's Garden of Verses, 1947.
Cover illustration by Eve Garnett

Cranes Flying South, 1948.
Cover illustration by Sylvia Dyson

II. Stories

Worzel Gummidge, 1953.
[Cover illustration by John Harwood]

Worzel Gummidge Again, 1949.
[Cover illustration by John Harwood]

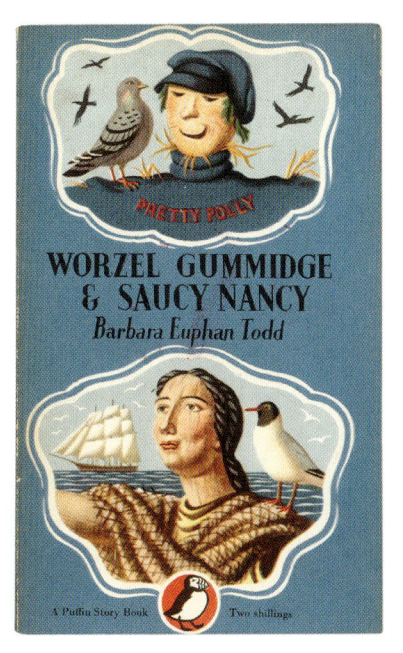

Worzel Gummidge and Saucy Nancy, 1951. [Cover illustration by John Harwood]

Double-sided covers

Seeing the books here and the Puffin Picture Books in Chapter 1 makes it difficult to understand why the immediate post-war period in Britain is so often described as grey; these covers are bright and vibrant, relevant to each book's content and designed to entice and delight.

Throughout the 1940s and 1950s Puffin did not regard back-cover blurb as necessary, meaning that both covers were available for the design. Illustrators responded to the possibilities this offered in a variety of ways, as seen here and on the following pages. On some titles the front and back are part of one larger image (e.g. *Worzel Gummidge* and *David Goes to Zululand*); on others each face shows a different aspect of the book (e.g. *Worzel Gummidge Again* and *No Other White Men*); and others play with the idea of front and back themselves (*Flaxen Braids*). The logo seems to be optional, but is humorously treated on a number of titles – notably *Columbus Sails*.

Because the illustrator was responsible for the lettering there was also a variety of approaches to the relationship between text and image. Although on some titles (e.g. *Flaxen Braids* and *Strangers at the Fair*) the two elements are separated, allowing each element to be 'read' independently, on many others there is an attempt to integrate all the elements. Of the covers shown here, only on *North After Seals* and *No Other White Men* does the lettering look as though it was insufficiently considered.

At this point in Puffin's (and Penguin's) history cover illustrators – unlike text illustrators – were not usually credited in any formal way but many signed their artwork.

II. Stories

Flaxen Braids, 1945.
[Cover illustration by
Grace W. Gabler]

North After Seals, 1946.
[Cover illustration by
Arthur H. Hall]

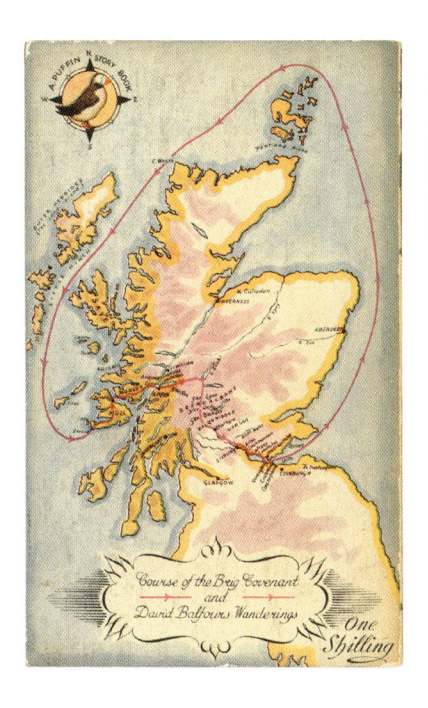

Kidnapped, 1946.
[Cover illustration by Anthony Lake]

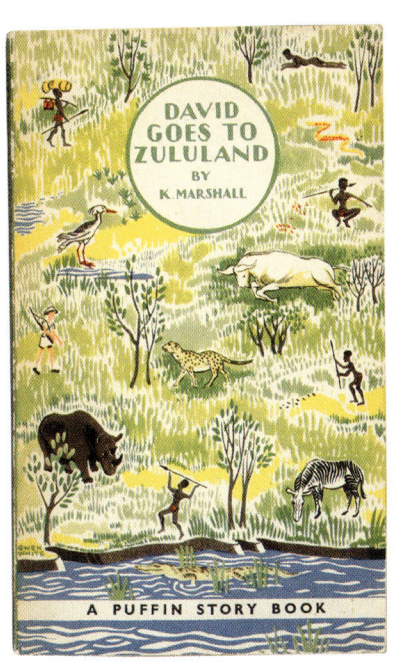

David Goes to Zululand, 1946.
[Cover illustration by Gwen White]

II. Stories

Street Fair, 1949.
[Cover illustration by S. Dyson]

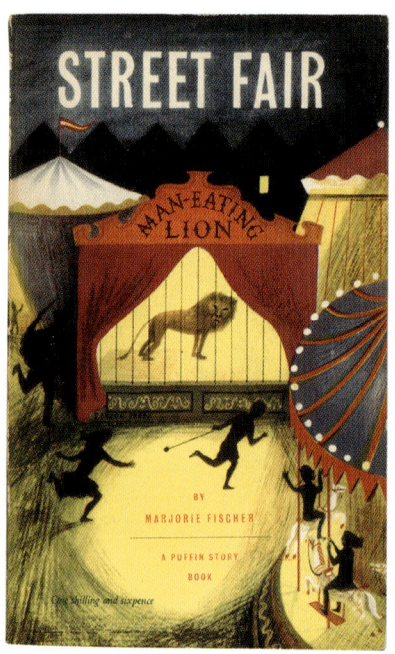

No Other White Men, 1946.
[Cover illustration by John Harwood]

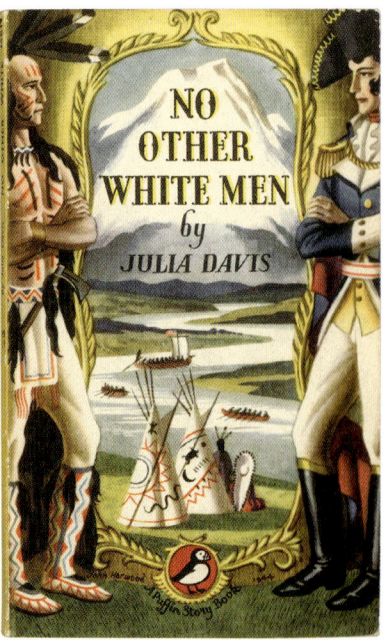

Strangers at the Fair, 1949.
[Cover illustration by
Eileen Coghlan]

Columbus Sails, 1947.
Cover illustration by
C. Walter Hodges

II. Stories

Little Women, 1953.
[Cover illustration by Astrid Walford]

Treasure Island, 1946.
[Cover illustration by Anthony Lake]

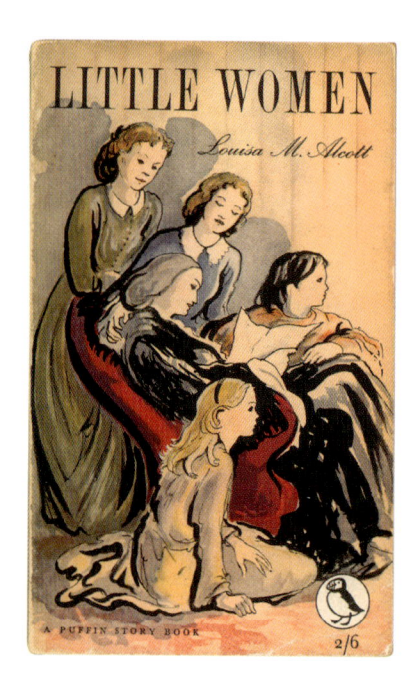

The Adventures of Tom Sawyer, 1950. [Cover illustration by A. H. Hall ('A. H. H.')]

Heidi, 1956.
[Cover illustration by Cecil Leslie]

Puffin by Design

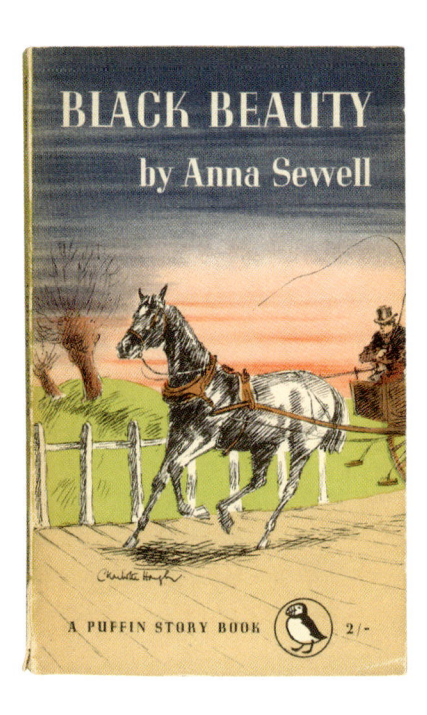

Established titles I

Of the six books shown here, *Little Women*, *Treasure Island* and *Black Beauty* were out of copyright when Puffin first published them. For the others, like the majority of Puffin titles, rights needed to be negotiated with other publishers.

A key factor to the success of Puffin in the first twenty years of its existence was the ability of Eleanor Graham to secure the rights to publish established children's titles in paperback. She would only publish books she regarded as having lasting worth: titles by Enid Blyton and J. R. R. Tolkien were among those she felt less than worthy of publication by Puffin.

Black Beauty, 1954. [Cover illustration by Charlotte Hough]

The Secret Garden, 1958. [Cover illustration by Astrid Walford]

Through the Looking Glass, 1948.
Cover illustration by John Tenniel

Established titles II

An aspect of cover design that applies to children's books far more than adult titles concerns the relationship of illustration to title. With a significant number of children's books this is regarded as fixed, and although titles may, in time, move publisher they keep their existing artwork. An early example of this at Puffin were the Alice titles by Lewis Carroll, which used Sir John Tenniel's illustrations from 1865.

Tenniel's black line illustrations were coloured for this Puffin edition by William Grimmond, one of Penguin's most versatile illustrators, who was also producing covers for *Fell Farm Holiday* (see pp. 62–3, 88), *The Young Detectives* and *The Secret of Dead Man's Cove* at the same time.

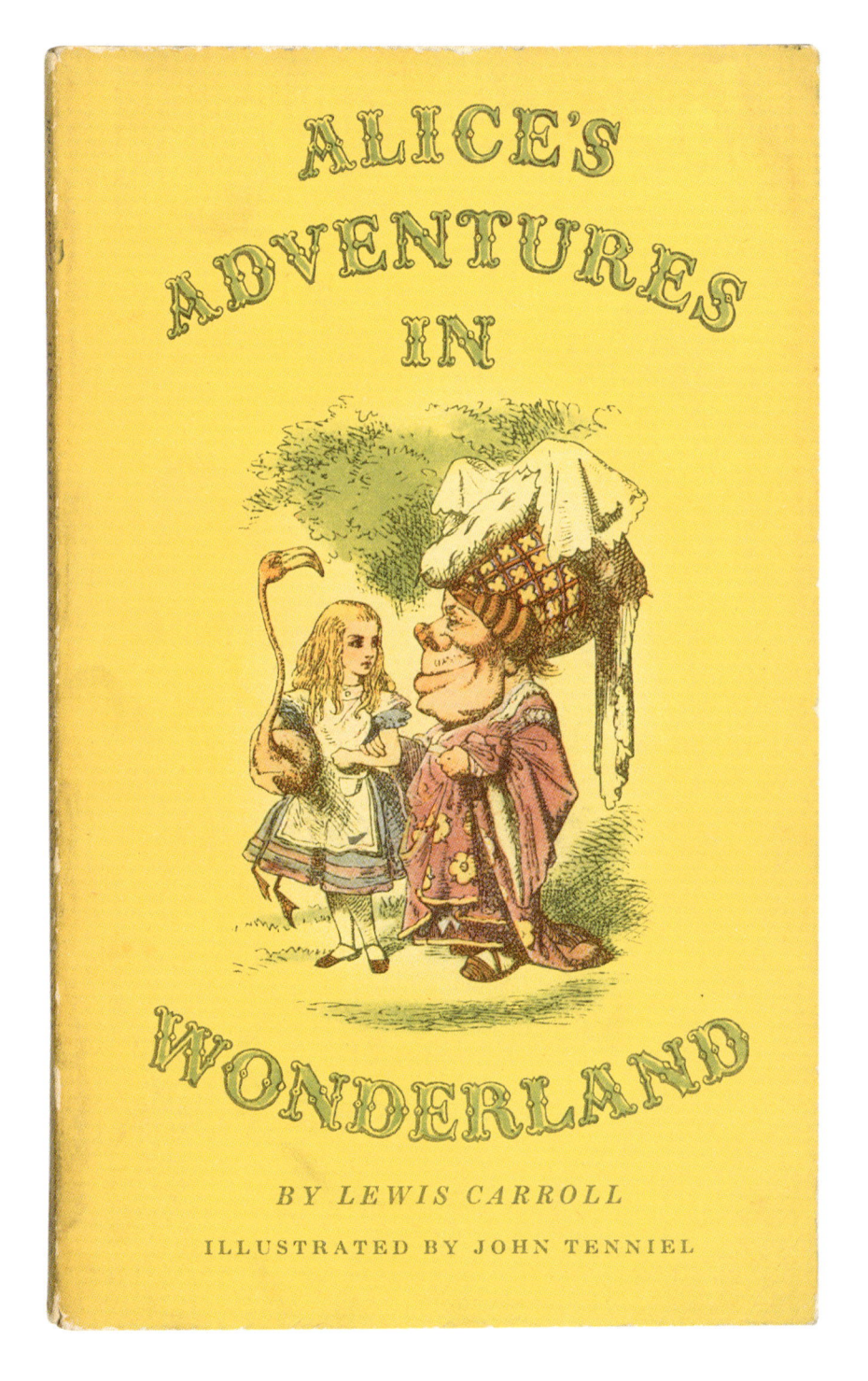

Alice's Adventures in Wonderland, 1949. Cover illustration by John Tenniel

The Puffin Quiz Book, 1956. Cover illustration by John Woodcock

Puzzles and quizzes

The Puffin Puzzle Book was the first in the Story Book series to have a fully illustrated colour cover (see p. 69) and its success led to further titles and books of a similar nature. Related to that idea is *The Puffin Quiz Book*, again the first of many.

While the lettering for *The Second Puffin Puzzle Book* is a playful and spirited interpretation of the subject matter, it is almost overwhelmed by the strength of the red panel below that contains author and publisher name, logo and price. The quiz book appears to be addressed to a slightly older readership. Although arguably less interesting, it is much better considered and works as an integrated whole far better. It was designed by John Woodcock, who also wrote and illustrated a Puffin Picture Book, PP104 *Binding Your Own Books*, before going on to teach at St Martin's School of Art.

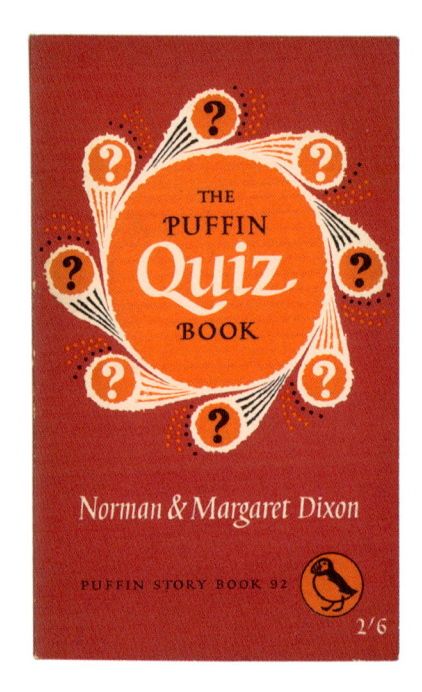

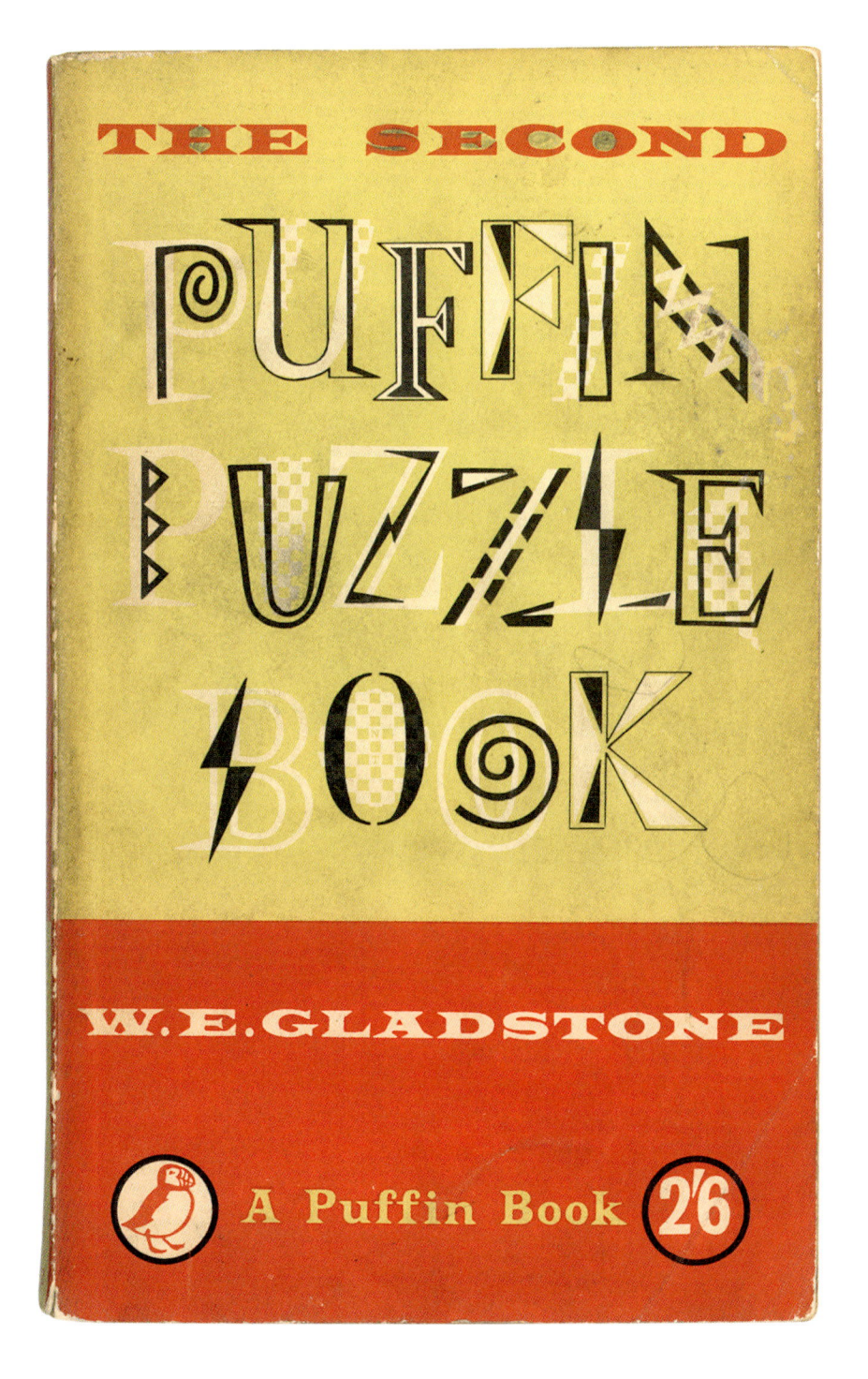

The Second Puffin Puzzle Book, 1958. Cover illustration by Nigel Tuckley

King Arthur and His Knights of the Round Table, 1953. Cover illustration by Lotte Reiniger

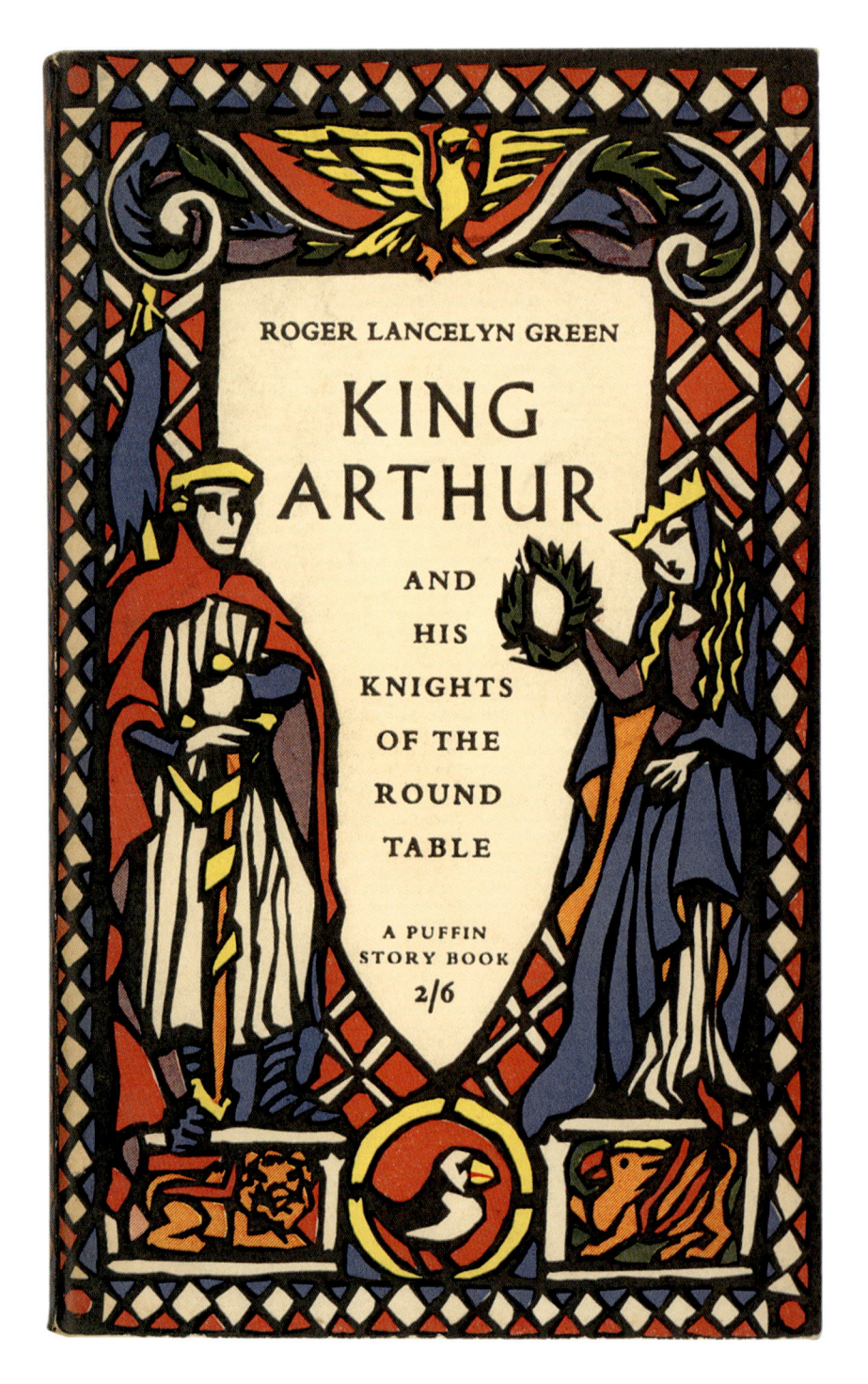

History, myths and legends

A key part of Graham's publishing scheme was balancing fiction and non-fiction titles in the list. Biography was represented early on, with titles about Elizabeth Fry and Marie Curie, and many fictional titles were historically based, e.g. *Columbus Sails* and *A Moor of Spain*.

Roger Lancelyn Green's retelling of ancient legends began with *King Arthur and His Knights of the Round Table* in 1953. The cover was designed by Lotte Reiniger (1899–1981), the German-born film-maker, who specialized in making animated silhouette films. The covers of *Troy* and *Greek Heroes* are quite ungainly by comparison, though nonetheless the books proved enormously popular and have remained so to the present day.

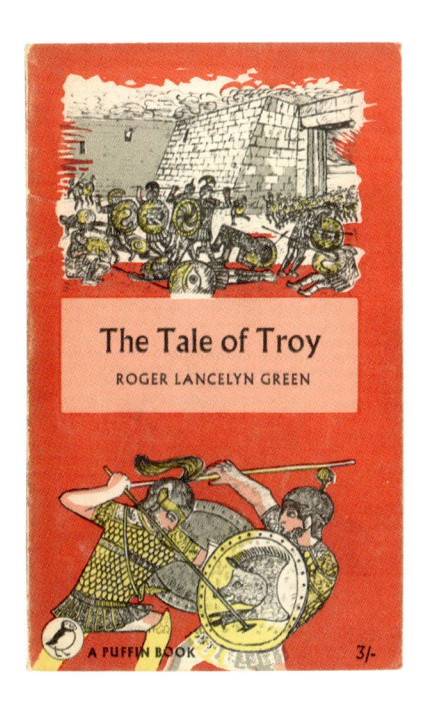

The Tale of Troy, 1958. Cover illustration by Betty Middleton-Sandford

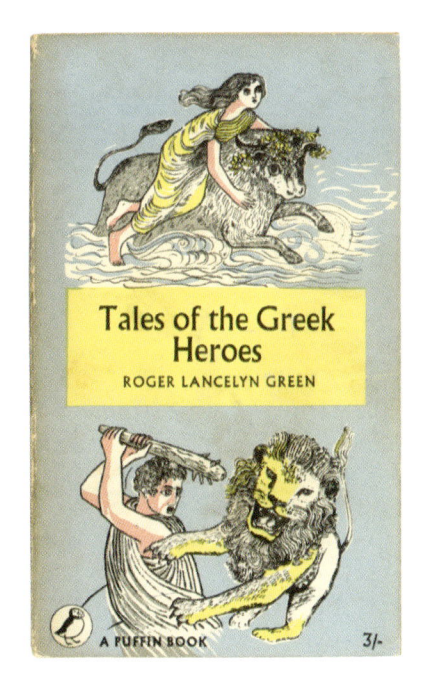

Tales of the Greek Heroes, 1958. Cover illustration by Betty Middleton-Sandford

Bird Watching for Beginners, 1952.
[Cover illustration by James Arnold]

Bird Watching for Beginners, 1959. Cover photograph by Eric Hosking.

Educating the masses

Many Penguin books – from the Specials to the Puffin Picture Books – can be seen to have some sort of educational or instructional quality to them. Getting the tone of such titles right is not always easy. With the Specials the voice was 'this is something you really *need* to know'; with the Picture Books 'this is something we think you'd *like* to know about'. Part of that voice comes from the way the inside of the book is written and illustrated, but as far as a buying public is concerned, the immediate voice comes from the cover. The earliest cover for *Bird Watching for Beginners* here is a simple, evocative, yet realistic watercolour illustration, which speaks like the Picture Books. But something changes with the later covers, which include photography. They look as though they're aimed at adults rather than teenagers and the voice has changed to 'here is something which would be *good* for you'.

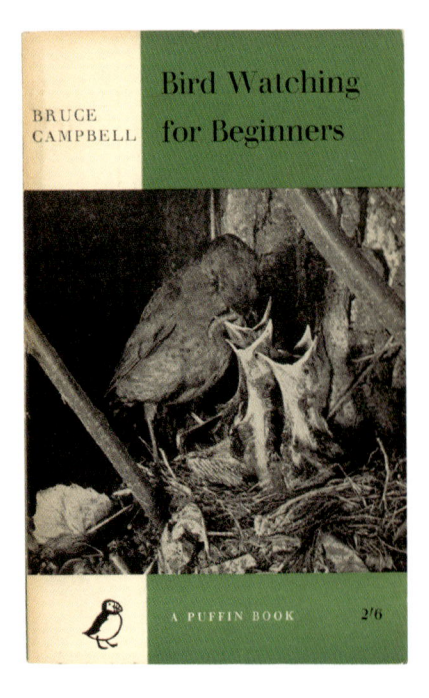

Going to a Concert, 1954.
Cover photograph by permission of the BBC

Going to the Ballet, 1954.
Cover photograph by Baron

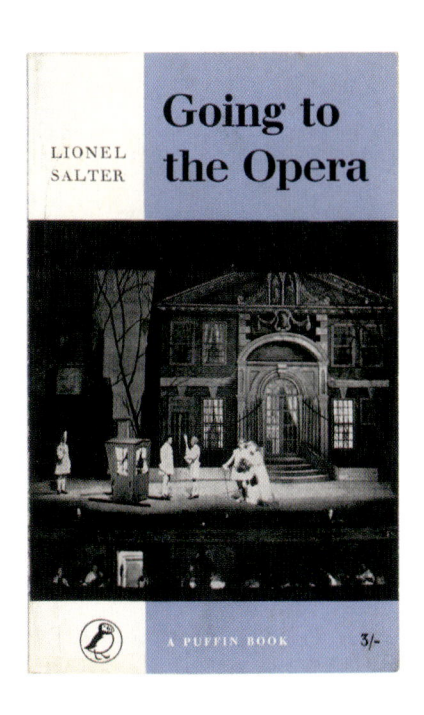

Going to the Opera, 1958.
Cover photograph by Associated Press

Going to the Ballet, 1958.
Cover photograph by Baron

II. Stories

Fell Farm Holiday, 1959.
[Cover illustration by William Grimmond]

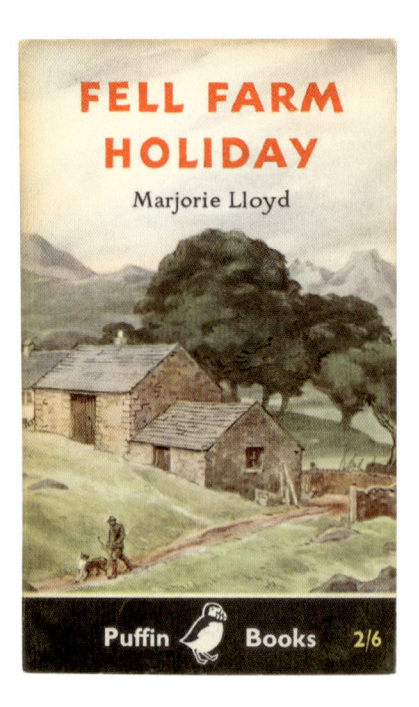

The emergence of Puffin branding

A branding strip appeared on many Penguin series in the late 1950s as cover designs diversified and the company tried to resolve the balance between needing to sell the individual title and preserving a strong brand image. For Puffin, as we have seen, there was little in the way of visual unity and a sense of the brand was upheld by a general awareness of quality and production values. Nevertheless, a black strip was introduced across the foot of covers from 1959 onwards and this contained the publisher's name – usually, but not always, in Gill Sans – the logo and the price. It just seems so heavy-handed, distracting and . . . unnecessary.

Avalanche!, 1959.
[Cover illustration by Alie Evers]

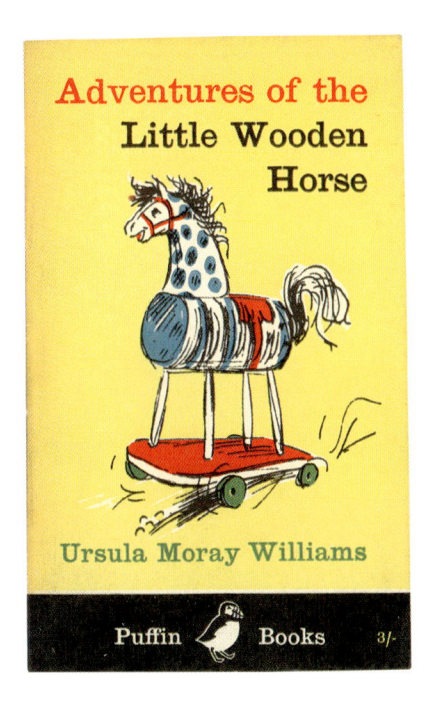

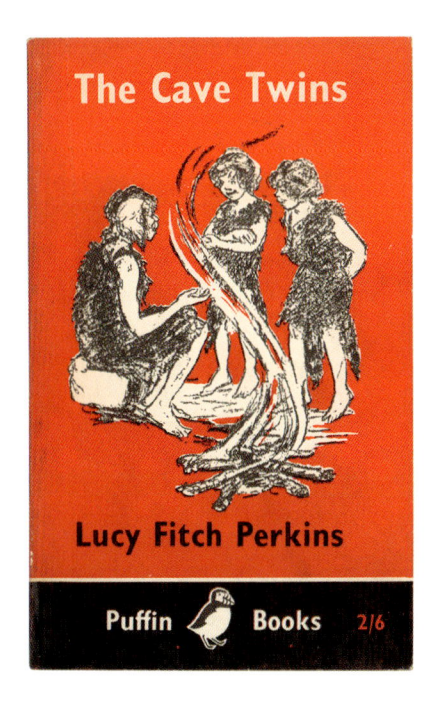

Adventures of the Little Wooden Horse, 1959. Cover illustration by Peggy Fortnum

The Cave Twins, 1959. Cover illustration by Lucy Fitch Perkins

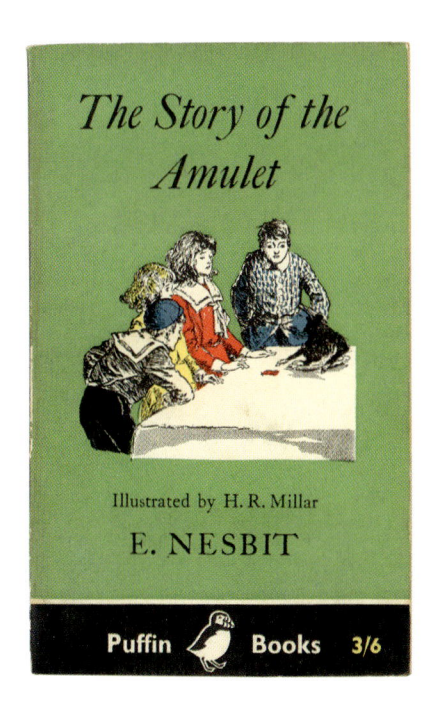

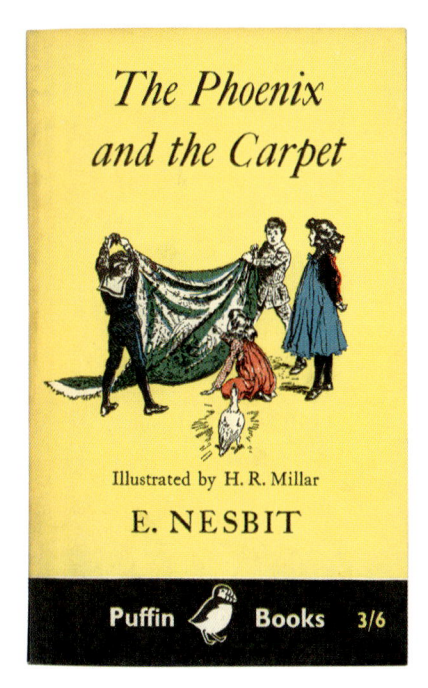

The Story of the Amulet, 1959. Cover illustration by H. R. Millar

The Phoenix and the Carpet, 1959. Cover illustration by H. R. Millar

II. Stories

The Lion, the Witch and the Wardrobe, 1959. Cover illustration by Pauline Baynes

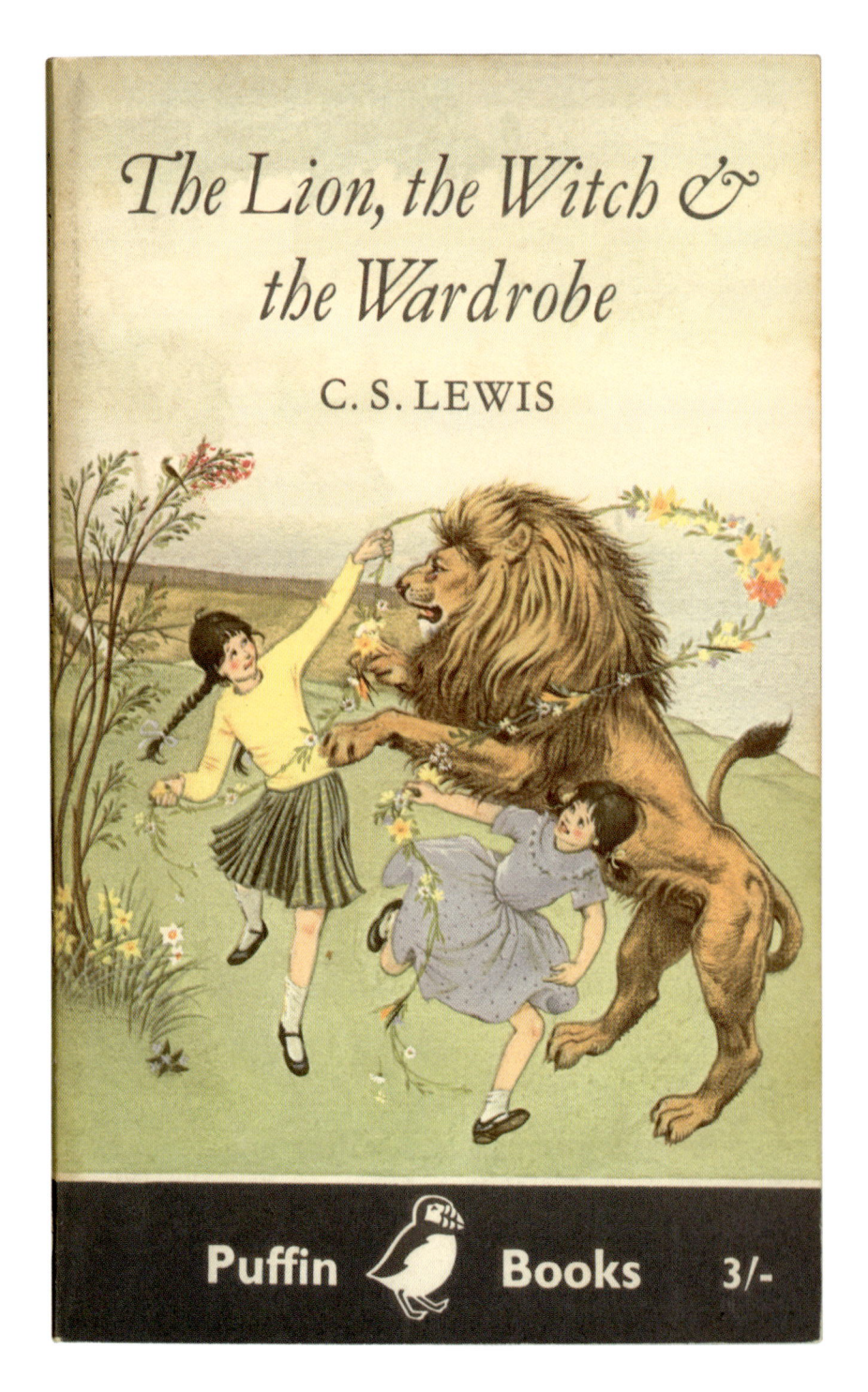

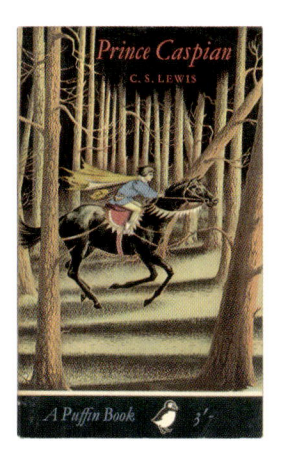

Prince Caspian, 1962.
Cover illustration by
Pauline Baynes

The Voyage of the Dawn Treader,
1965. Cover illustration by
Pauline Baynes

The Silver Chair, 1965.
Cover illustration by
Pauline Baynes

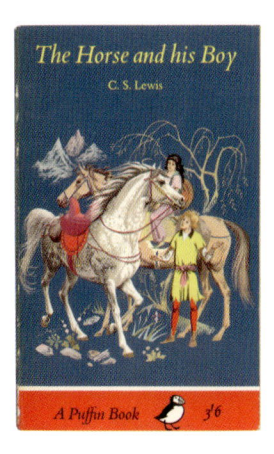

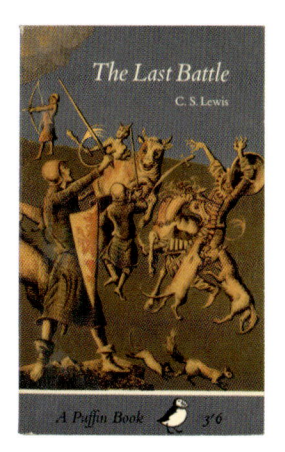

The Horse and His Boy, 1965.
Cover illustration by
Pauline Baynes

The Magician's Nephew, 1963.
Cover illustration by
Pauline Baynes

The Last Battle, 1964.
Cover illustration by
Pauline Baynes

Pauline Baynes, books and their covers

Pauline Baynes (1922–2008) was responsible for the dust-jacket and text illustrations for C. S. Lewis's Chronicles of Narnia when they were published in hardback by Geoffrey Bles in 1952. Baynes had previously illustrated for Tolkien and met Lewis only twice. He was polite about the illustrations to her face, but critical about them to friends, claiming that she couldn't draw a lion. Despite this, in 1959 she was commissioned by Puffin to produce cover illustrations for their paperback editions. The text illustrations are all from the original hardbacks. *The Lion, the Witch and the Wardrobe* appeared first in 1959, and the series was completed in 1965 under Kaye Webb's editorship.

As with a number of children's book covers these illustrations have become synonymous with the titles and, long after Puffin lost the rights, the books retained Baynes's illustrations – and, in fact, one current edition still uses them.

*The Children who Lived in a Barn,
1955. [Cover illustration
by Mary Gernat]*

By, and edited by, Eleanor Graham

In addition to her work as Editor of the series, Graham was also an author in her own right. *The Children who Lived in a Barn* was published in hardback in 1938 by Routledge and appeared as a Puffin in 1955 with a cover illustration by Mary Gernat.

Graham re-told *The Story of Jesus* in 1959. This contains the first illustrations Penguin commissioned from Brian Wildsmith, who went on to do many others. Despite the high quality of his cover illustration for this title it is overpowered by the frame, and the result is unsatisfactory. Graham was also responsible for the compilations *The Puffin Book of Verse* (PS72, 1953) and *A Puffin Quartet of Poets* (PS121, 1958), and in retirement edited further poetry collections for other publishers.

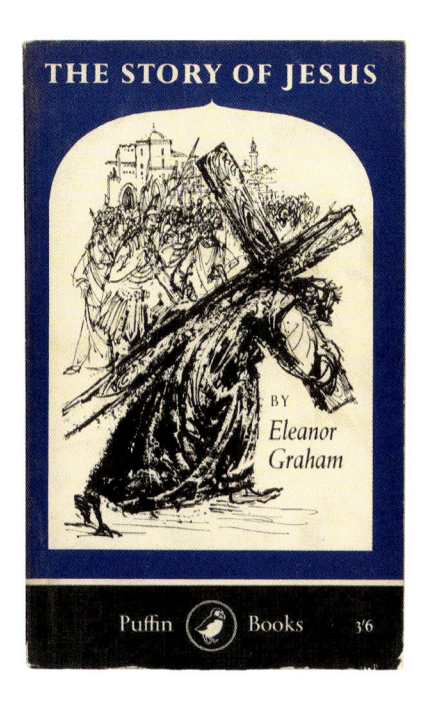

The Story of Jesus, 1959. [Cover illustration by Brian Wildsmith]

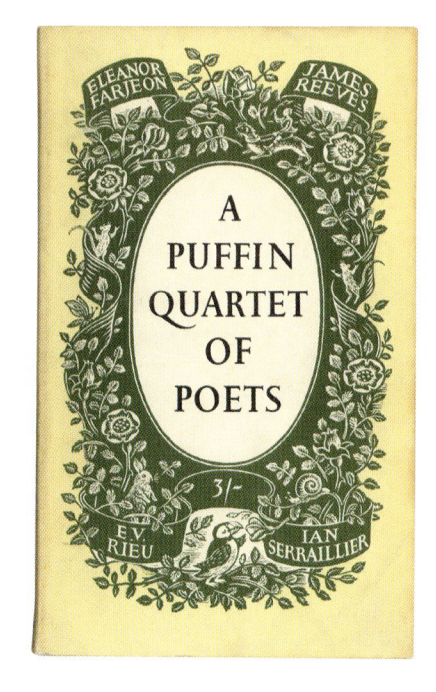

A Puffin Quartet of Poets, 1958. [Cover illustration by Diane Bloomfield]

III. Expansion

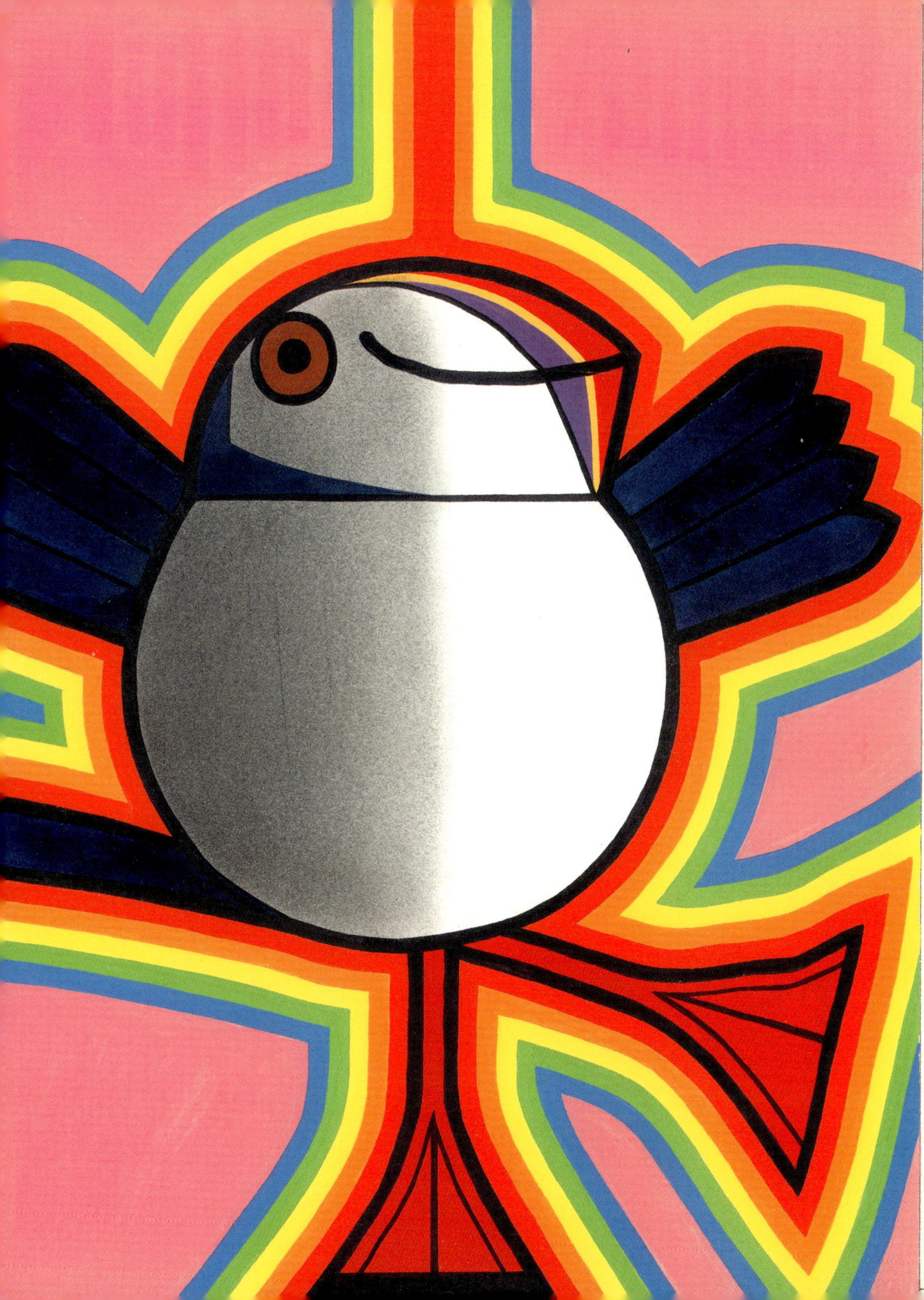

It takes a long time for books to reach children. Books have to go through five lots of adults: the editor who chooses, the traveller who sells, the bookseller who buys, teachers, parents. The whole point of the [Puffin] club was to cut out one or two sets of grown-ups. (Kaye Webb in Gritten, 1991, p. 20)

Kaye Webb: integrated production and marketing, 1961–79

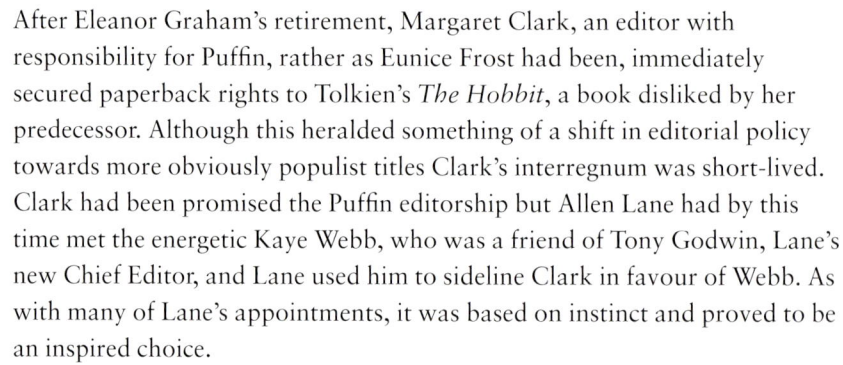

After Eleanor Graham's retirement, Margaret Clark, an editor with responsibility for Puffin, rather as Eunice Frost had been, immediately secured paperback rights to Tolkien's *The Hobbit*, a book disliked by her predecessor. Although this heralded something of a shift in editorial policy towards more obviously populist titles Clark's interregnum was short-lived. Clark had been promised the Puffin editorship but Allen Lane had by this time met the energetic Kaye Webb, who was a friend of Tony Godwin, Lane's new Chief Editor, and Lane used him to sideline Clark in favour of Webb. As with many of Lane's appointments, it was based on instinct and proved to be an inspired choice.

Kaye Webb was born in Chiswick, London, in 1914. Her career path was varied to say the least. Aged fifteen, she wrote replies to children's letters for *Mickey Mouse Weekly* and film reviews for her critic mother. In 1931, she joined *Picturegoer* as 'George the Answerman', moving later on to *Caravan World* and *Sports Car*. In 1938, Webb went to *Picture Post* as a secretary and became Assistant Editor of *Lilliput* magazine in 1941. During the war she was also an ambulance driver, air-raid warden, canteen worker and member of the Fleet Street Women's Rifle Brigade. She left *Lilliput* in 1947 and worked as a freelance theatre correspondent for the *Leader* magazine, wrote weekly features for the *News Chronicle*, and broadcast regularly on *Woman's Hour*. She worked with her then husband, artist Ronald Searle (whom she had first met at *Lilliput*), on a number of titles. They also founded Perpetua Books. In 1955 Webb began to edit the *Young Elizabethan*, a magazine for school children (subsequently renamed *Elizabethan*), and continued to do so until 1961.

Kaye Webb

PREVIOUS PAGE: Jill McDonald's artwork from *Puffin Annual* number 1, 1974

If Eleanor Graham had been somewhat stuffy in outlook, Webb was very different. She was not only able to build on the credibility established by her predecessor, but also to change the spirit of the whole operation. Capitalizing on a renewed interest in children's literature and an increased output in new writing, she changed the Puffin list in as radical a way as Tony Godwin was changing the adult fiction list, but with far less disruption and none of the personality clashes that led to Godwin's departure after seven years.

In the first five years of Webb's leadership the Puffin list trebled in size, with a number of books now regarded as children's classics making their first appearance, such as the newly acquired P. L. Travers's *Mary Poppins* (1962) and Puffin's first publication of Clive King's *Stig of the Dump* (1963).

Difficulties in gaining paperback rights continued, however, and in fact grew worse as hardback publishers began to realize that they could set up their own paperback imprints and keep both aspects under their own control. Webb was proactive in fighting this and even persuaded three publishers – William Collins, Oxford University Press and Faber & Faber – to grant her exclusive rights to their children's fiction list for a number of years on the basis that Puffin could market the titles much more effectively than they could.

Webb was passionately interested in reaching children of all ages and was mindful of the particular demands of a teenage readership. Rather than creating a sub-division of either the Penguin or Puffin lists, she chose instead to create a separate imprint that sat between the two – Peacock – and its covers contained elements introduced by Germano Facetti for other Penguin series and imprints (see pp. 136–7). Peacock grew throughout the 1960s, and there were several variations of cover design, but the number of titles issued annually tailed off in the 1970s. Despite a brief flurry of activity in 1977, Peacock was discontinued as an imprint in 1979 after Tony Lacey took over from Webb as Editor of Puffin.

During Kaye Webb's reign greater links were forged between the marketing and editorial divisions. The strongest example of this was the formation of the Puffin Club in 1967. This grew out of Webb's own enthusiasm for children's books, and aimed to encourage children to read, borrow or buy books. Membership included an enamel badge, a secret code, stickers, diaries, competitions, outings and, not least, the quarterly magazine *Puffin Post*, and its equivalent for younger members *Egg*. Although many Puffin artists and illustrators contributed to the magazine (see p. 122), the dominant visual identity was created by Jill McDonald (1927–82), who was its chief designer from the start. At the height of its popularity the Puffin

Jill McDonald

Club had over 200,000 members and continued to be run by Webb even after her retirement as Editor. In the 1970s the club changed its remit and, in addition to its original role, became a commercial book club based mainly in schools, through which members could buy books.

Not everything was a success, however. After Carrington's retirement in the early 1960s (see Chapter I), Puffin Picture Books continued for only a short time, although a small number remained in print until the 1970s. Despite this, three attempts were made by Webb to revive the idea of picture books in a wider sense. Picture Puffins appeared in 1968, New Puffin Picture Books in 1975 and Practical Puffins in 1978. They covered similar areas to the Carrington series, but only the Picture Puffins proved to possess lasting qualities.

The Picture Puffins (see p. 150) took up the short-lived story-book idea from Carrington's series. They began, inevitably, with reprints of other publishers' titles, the first seven being from The Bodley Head[1] and the eighth – Edward Ardizzone's *Paul the Hero of the Fire* – was originally published as a Porpoise in 1948. The series continues today but is no longer badged as a series.

The New Puffin Picture Books (see pp. 130–3) were an attempt to revive the non-fiction, instructional aspects of Carrington's list. Only fifteen titles were published over a two-year lifespan.

The other attempt at the picture-book format originated from Australia and fared a little better: four years and nineteen titles. Produced as complete books and sold to British and many other Penguin territories, these were hugely successful at a time when Australian profits were supporting the financial stability of the parent company.

Generally speaking, the 1970s proved to be quite a difficult decade for the parent company. Allen Lane, a staunch supporter of Webb, died on 7 July 1970, after having laid the foundation for the company's sale to Pearson Longman. The first three senior executives of Penguin following the takeover – Christopher Dolley, Peter Calvocoressi and Jim Rose – had the unenviable task of steering the firm through a time of great economic difficulty. Parts of the Penguin family felt this more than others. In 1974,

---

1. Flack, Marjorie, & Weiss, Kurt, *The Story about Ping*, (BH 1935), 1968; 2. Fatio, Louise, illustrated by Roger Duvoisin, *The Happy Lion*, (BH 1955), 1968; 3. Zion, Gene, illustrated by Margaret Bloy Graham, *Harry the Dirty Dog*, (BH 1968), 1968; 4. Broomfield, Robert, *The Twelve Days of Christmas*, (BH 1965), 1968; 5. Stobbs, William, *The Story of the Three Little Pigs*, (BH 1965), 1968; 6. Broomfield, Robert, *The Baby Animal ABC*, (BH 1964), 1968; Titus, Eve, illustrated by Paul Galdone, *Anatole*, (BH 1957), 1969.

for instance, Calvocoressi reduced the list of published titles from 800 to 450, and closed the Education division. At Puffin, however, Webb's instincts for a good title continued to reap dividends. Although the rights to some books – e.g. Lewis's The Chronicles of Narnia series – reverted to their original publishers, she always seemed able to secure the rights to others. Titles such as Roald Dahl's *Charlie and the Chocolate Factory* (1973), Richard Adams's *Watership Down* (1973), and authors such as Ursula Le Guin, were acquired against this background of economic gloom and became phenomenal sellers – proof that Webb still possessed a keen sense of what would appeal to her readers.

These successes meant that when Peter Mayer was appointed Managing Director in 1978, charged with revitalizing the company, Puffin needed little of his attention. Webb retired as Puffin Editor the following year but continued to work for the company after her retirement, editing *Puffin Post* until 1981. In addition, she maintained her interests in broadcasting, and in reviewing and editing books.

Her contributions to children's literature were recognized when she won the Eleanor Farjeon Award in 1969, and when she became one of the first female members of the Society of Bookmen in 1972. Further recognition came in 1974 when she was made an MBE. She died on 16 January 1996.

The Hobbit, 1961.
Cover illustration by
Pauline Baynes

Coloured stripes

Tolkien's *The Hobbit* had been rejected by Eleanor Graham but was published by Puffin very soon after her retirement. The cover is by Pauline Baynes (see pp. 90–1) and it carries the black branding stripe introduced in 1959. Very soon into Kaye Webb's editorship, however, this stripe changed to a colour sympathetic with the rest of the cover design.

The illustrations used were, as before, of many styles. *Charlotte's Web* inherits the Garth Williams illustration carried on the original publisher's hardback edition. *A Dog So Small* is by the same illustrator – Antony Maitland – as the Constable hardback of 1962 and is closely related; but most covers carried freshly commissioned artwork.

There now appeared to be a greater allowance made by the illustrator for the inclusion of type, and, because of the stronger, more positive use of colour, there is far less sense that the cover illustration is simply a reused text illustration.

What is also largely missing now is the use of lettering by the illustrator; of the Puffin-originated covers shown on the following spread, only *The Box of Delights* is lettered.

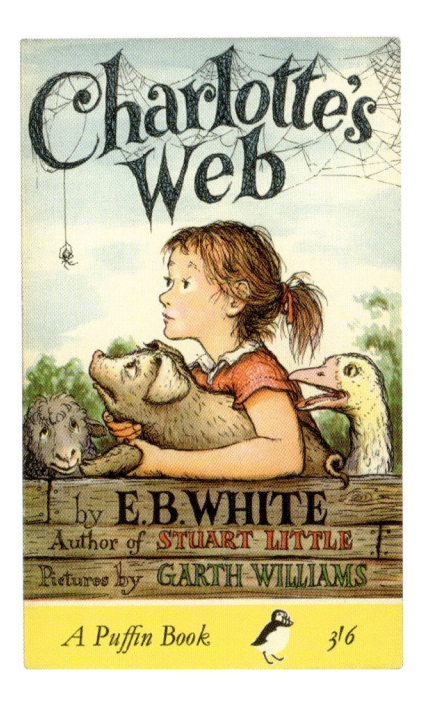

Charlotte's Web, 1963. Cover illustration by Garth Williams

A Dog So Small, 1968. Cover illustration by Antony Maitland

III. Expansion

The Warden's Niece, 1963. [Cover illustration by Dick Hart]

Cue for Treason, 1967. Cover illustration by Zena Flax

Tell Me a Story, 1963. [Cover illustration by Judith Bledsoe]

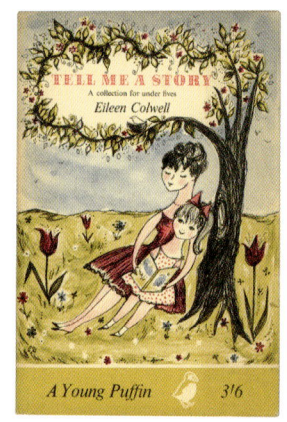

The Hundred and One Dalmations, 1962. [Cover illustration by Janet and Anne Grahame-Johnstone]

Antelope Singer, 1963. [Cover illustration by Peter Barrett]

Landslide!, 1964. [Cover illustration by Brian Wildsmith]

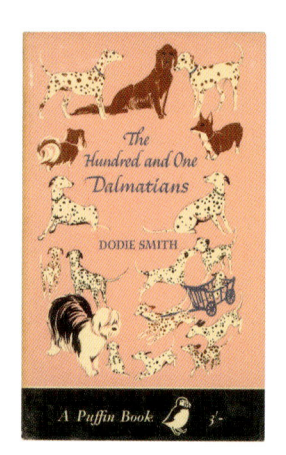

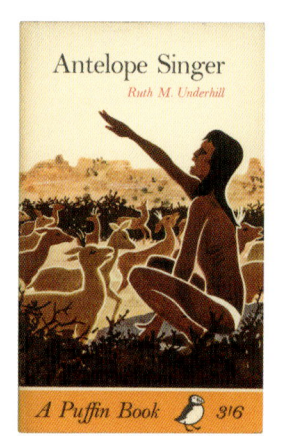

The Day the Ceiling Fell Down, 1966. Cover illustration by Juliet Renny

The Phantom Tollbooth, 1965. Cover illustration by Jules Feiffer

Magnolia Buildings, 1968. Cover illustration by Dick Hart

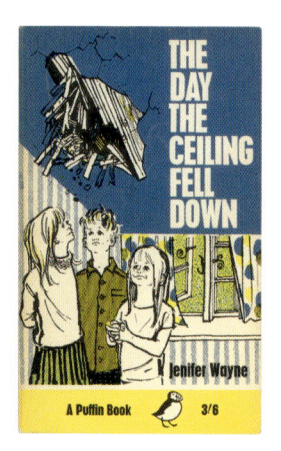

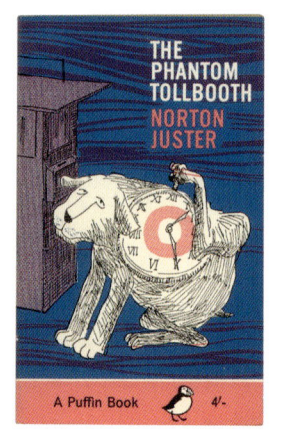

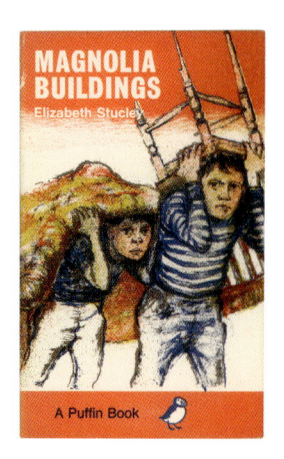

The Box of Delights, 1965.
Cover illustration by
Juliet Renny

PADDINGTON AT LARGE

Michael Bond

A Young Puffin 3/6

Young Puffins

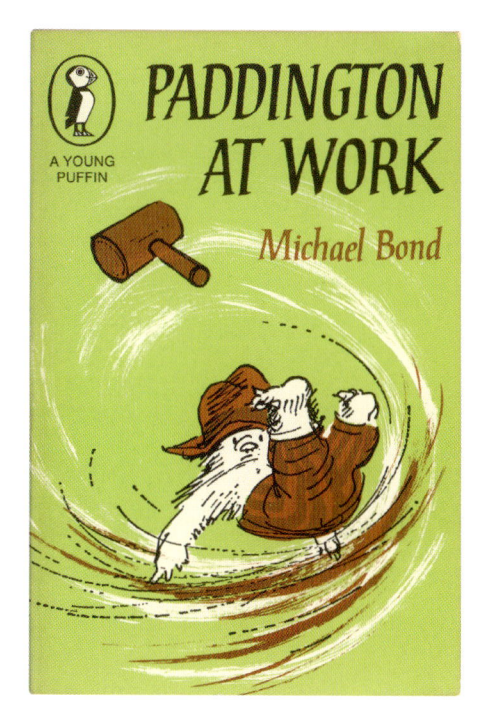

Young Puffins started to appear from 1961 onwards. Initially their identification was handled typographically within the coloured stripe and the titles were still numbered in sequence as Puffin Story Books.

Michael Bond (b. 1926) had his first Paddington Bear book – *A Bear called Paddington* – published in 1958. By 1965 these books were so successful that he left his job as a television cameraman and concentrated on writing full time. Puffin began publishing the books in 1962 and continued to use the illustrations by Peggy Fortnum (b. 1919), who illustrated the stories from the start and continued to do so until 1974. After being invalided out of the Auxiliary Territorial Service, Fortnum was taught by John Farleigh at the Central School of Art and Crafts between 1944 and 1945, and began illustrating children's books soon after. Her distinctive, lively pen drawings were coloured for use on covers by the production department with varying degrees of sensitivity: *Paddington at Large* is particularly clumsy, but *Paddington Helps Out* and *Paddington at Work* both use the natural white of the cover stock to emphasize the central character and the action.

Paddington at Work is in the freer cover design described on the following pages, which first appeared in 1967. The Young Puffin identifier then became a simple sub-heading beneath the Puffin logo.

Paddington Helps Out, 1965. [Cover illustration by Peggy Fortnum]

Paddington at Work, 1969. [Cover illustration by Peggy Fortnum]

OPPOSITE: *Paddington at Large*, 1966. [Cover illustration by Peggy Fortnum]

Little Plum, 1975.
[Cover illustration by Jean Primrose]

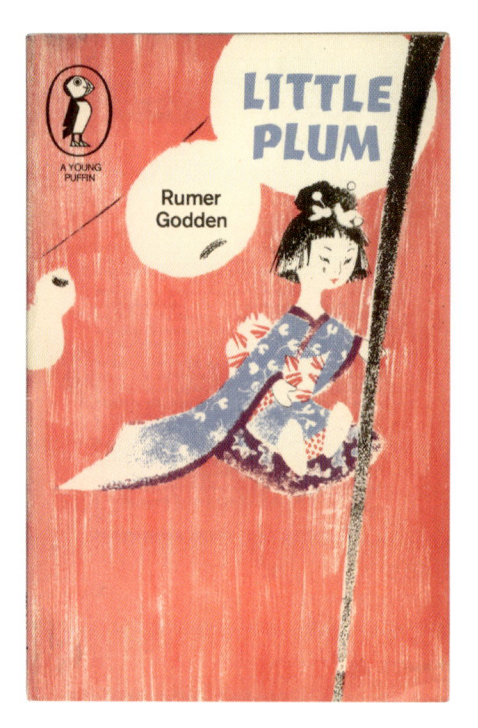

Danny Fox, 1969.
[Cover illustration by Gunvor Edwards]

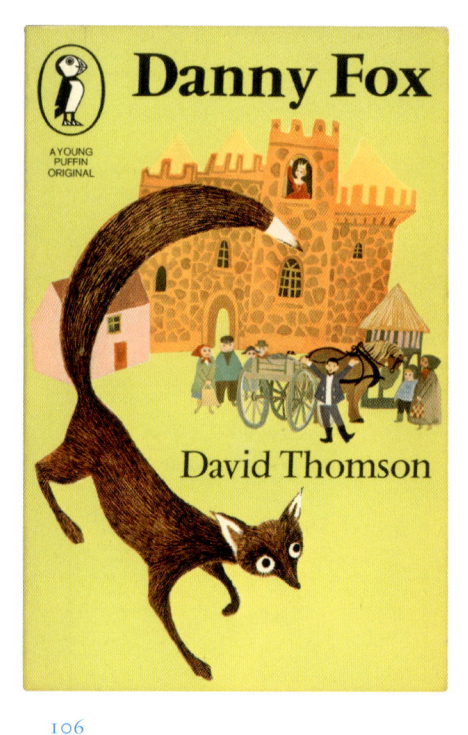

Freedom returns

By 1967 the coloured stripe was abandoned and covers almost reverted to their former freedom. Aside from changing tastes in illustration, there are two other tendencies that distinguish them from the covers of the 1940s and 1950s.

Whereas the Puffin logo could previously be treated humorously, now it became fixed, albeit in the harder-edged 1959 version. Often it appears over-large, similar to the Penguin logo on Fiction titles of the same period.

The most fundamental change, however, was the attitude to composition, simplicity and cropping. Many of the older covers are self-contained as images, using the edge of the book as a frame, while others use the front and back to create two scenes as a mini narrative. The new covers focus more on an instant, and are more tightly cropped, implying action off stage, both left and right. From this time too, photography and photographic collage or effects make a more significant appearance.

Comet in Moominland, 1970.
[Cover illustration by Tove Jansson]

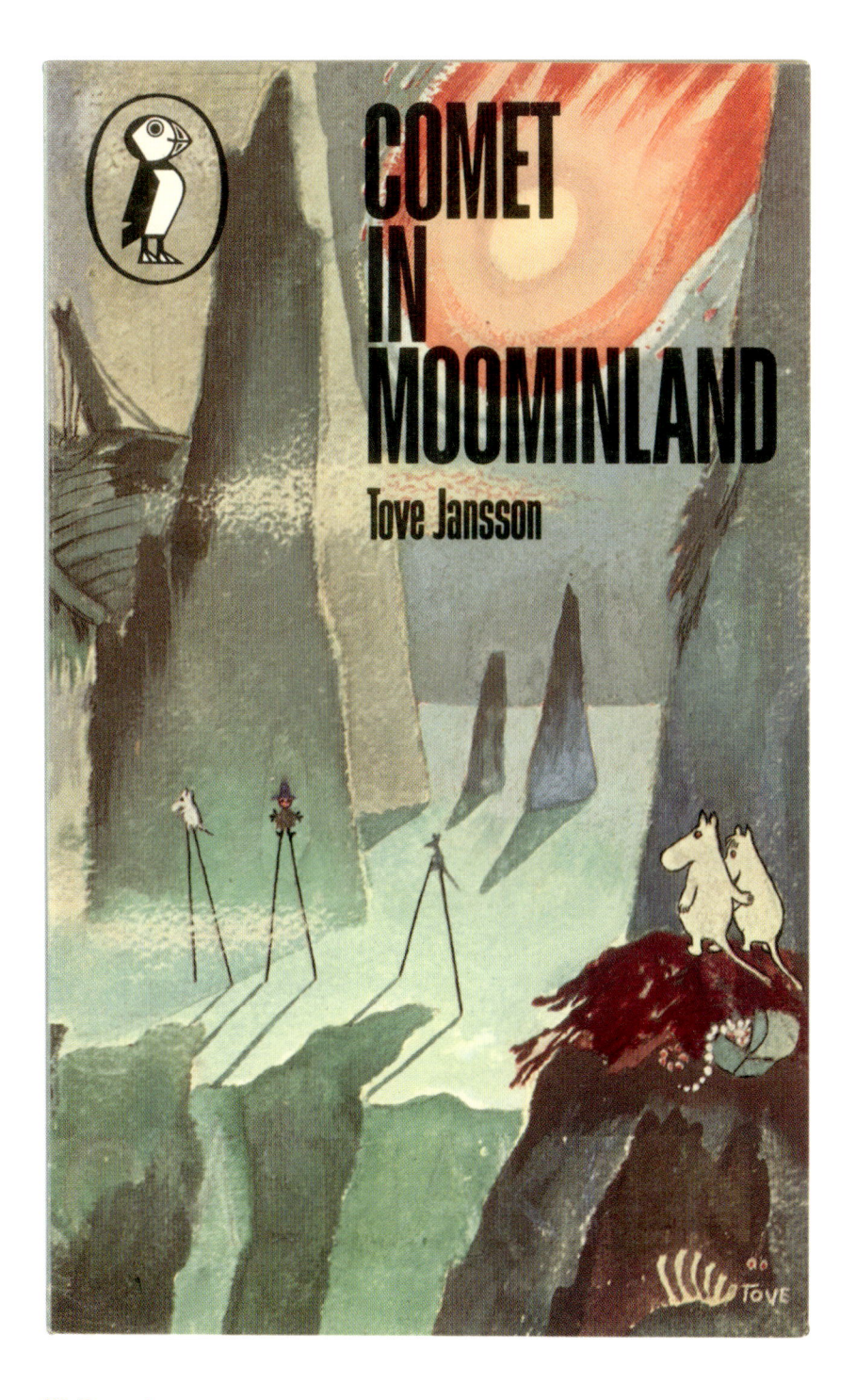

III. Expansion 107

The Wolves of Willoughby Chase, 1971. Cover illustration from drawings by Pat Marriott

Myths of the Norsemen, 1960. [Cover illustration by Brian Wildsmith]

Comet in Moominland, 1967. [Cover illustration by Tove Jansson]

Stuart Little, 1969. Cover illustration by Garth Williams

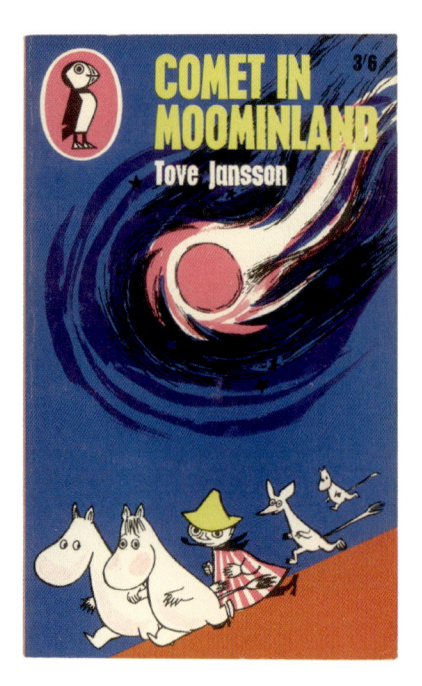

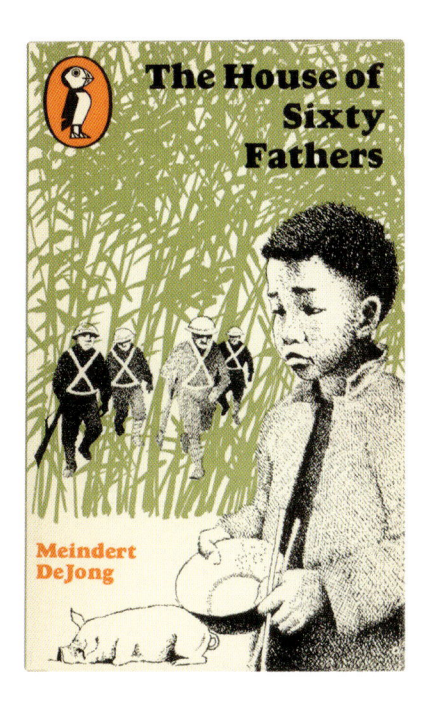

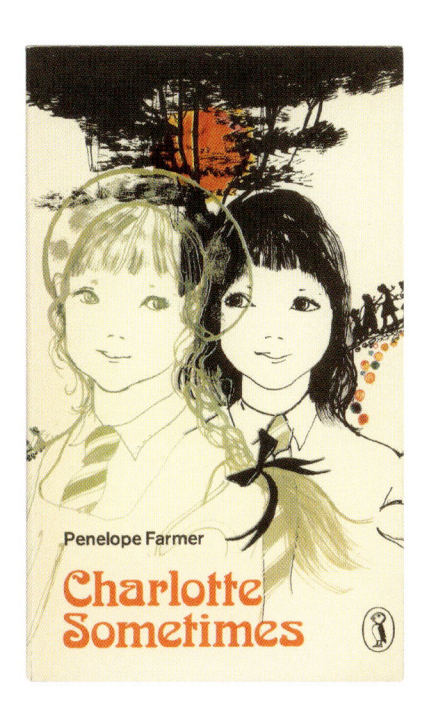

The House of Sixty Fathers, 1971.
Cover illustration by Peter Barrett

Charlotte Sometimes, 1972.
[Cover illustration by Janina Ede]

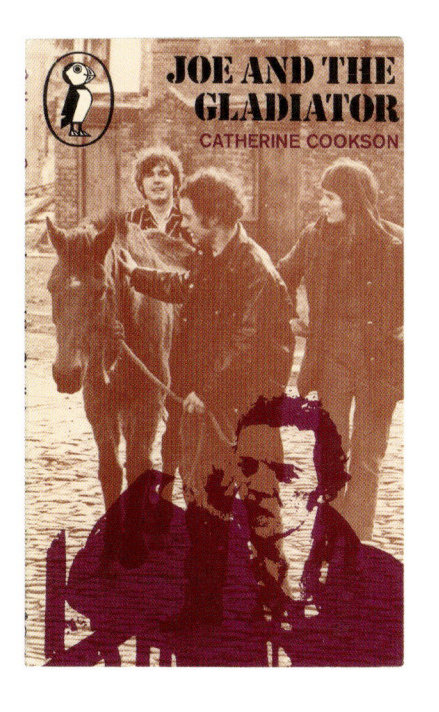

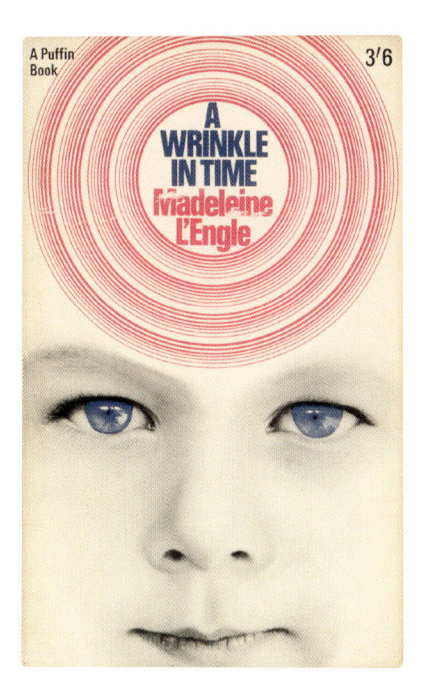

Joe and the Gladiator, 1971.

A Wrinkle in Time, 1967.
Cover illustration by Peter Barrett

III. Expansion 109

Eleanor Farjeon's Book: Stories – Verses – Plays, 1960. Cover illustration by Edward Ardizzone

The Little Grey Men, 1962. Cover illustration by Edward Ardizzone

The Otterbury Incident, 1961. Cover illustration by Edward Ardizzone

Stig of the Dump, 1963. Cover illustration by Edward Ardizzone

The Land of Green Ginger, 1966. Cover illustration by Edward Ardizzone

Edward Ardizzone (1900–79)

Edward Ardizzone is known by many for his Little Tim stories, which first appeared in 1939, but he had been working as an illustrator since 1927, producing work for publishers; magazines such as *Radio Times* and *Strand*; and as a war artist between 1940 and 1945. In 1958 he had produced a cover for Penguin Fiction in the Abram Games cover template (see *Penguin by Design*: p. 88), and his atmospheric pen and wash illustrations were then used for five unrelated Puffins published between 1960 and 1966.

The drawing and lettering style is not confined to the front covers but extends to the spines too, which adds greatly to their distinctiveness. The illustration for *Stig of the Dump* is still used today in the 2003 Puffin Modern Classics version of the title (see pp. 212–3).

III. Expansion

A YOUNG PUFFIN

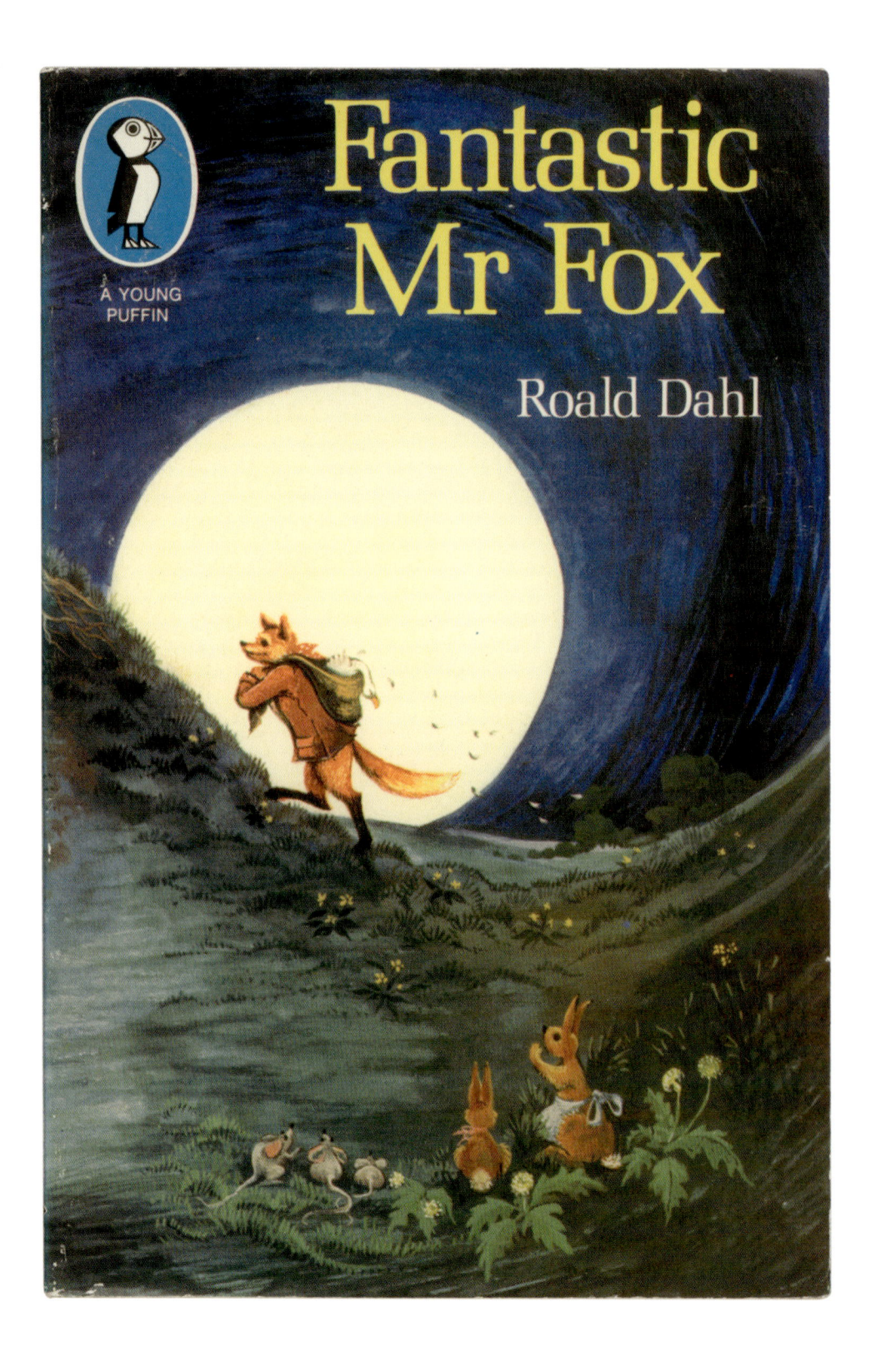

Fantastic Mr Fox

Roald Dahl

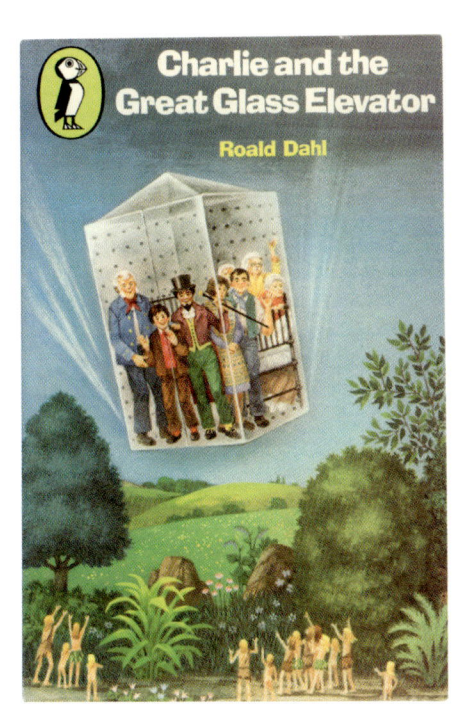

Roald Dahl (1916–90)

After his death in 1990 Roald Dahl was described as the 'most successful children's author in the world', but he didn't set out to be a writer, only doing so in 1942 when asked to write about his war experience having been invalided out of active service. The success of that first piece for the *Saturday Evening Post* via C. S. Forester led to others and, after the war, to short stories for adults. His first children's story was 'Gremlins' in 1943 but this was a one-off and it wasn't until the 1961 publication of *James and the Giant Peach* that he started writing children's stories seriously. *Charlie and the Chocolate Factory* followed, and the worlds of *The BFG*, *The Twits*, *The Witches*, *Fantastic Mr Fox* and more.

In 1976 Quentin Blake began illustrating his books and all the Puffin editions feature these to this day (see pp. 224–7). However, the first Puffin editions were illustrated by several different illustrators and it's interesting to compare these with today's versions.

James and the Giant Peach, 1980. Cover illustration by Nancy Ekholm Burkert

Charlie and the Great Glass Elevator, 1975. Cover illustration by Faith Jaques

OPPOSITE: *Fantastic Mr Fox*, 1974. Cover illustration by Jill Bennett

III. Expansion

A Necklace of Raindrops and Other Stories, 1975. Cover illustration by Jan Pieńkowski

Joan Aiken (1924–2004) and Jan Pieńkowski (b. 1936)

Joan Aiken was born in Sussex and had stories broadcast by the BBC during the Second World War. She pursued writing alongside other work and bringing up a family, until the success of *The Wolves of Willoughby Chase* enabled her to consider writing as an occupation. She worked with a number of illustrators throughout her life, including Quentin Blake and Pat Mariott.

A Necklace of Raindrops and *The Kingdom Under the Sea* were her first two of five collaborations with Jan Pieńkowski. Born in Poland in 1936, Pieńkowski moved to England with his family in 1946. After studying classics and English at Cambridge he began to design posters, set designs, greetings cards and graphics for BBC's *Watch!*, as well as illustrating books. The latter activity soon began to take over and the two books shown are early examples at Puffin of his silhouette style, which is reminiscent of the animated films of Lotte Reiniger. The black images are cut from card and superimposed on coloured backgrounds. It is a technique that he used again for several later Picture Puffin titles (see pp. 208–9).

Pieńkowski is also author of a series of nursery books and worked with Helen Nicoll on the Meg and Mog stories talked about on page 150.

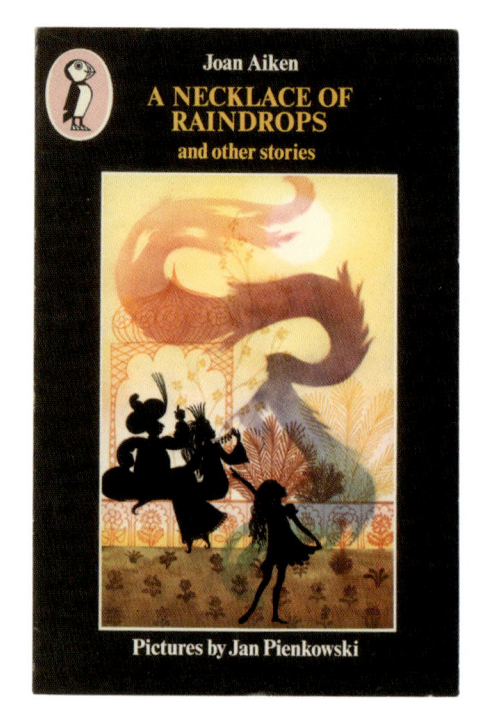

OPPOSITE: *The Kingdon Under the Sea and Other Stories*, 1973. Cover illustration by Jan Pieńkowski

Joan Aiken

THE KINGDOM UNDER THE SEA
and other stories

Pictures by Jan Pienkowski

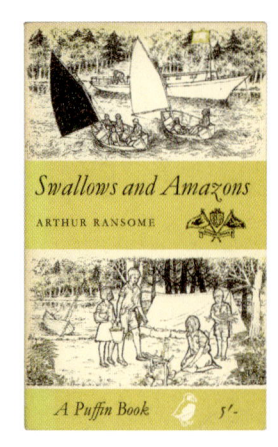

Swallows and Amazons, 1962.
Cover illustration by
Patricia McGrogan

Peter Duck, 1968.
Cover illustration by
Arthur Ransome

Swallowdale, 1968.
Cover illustration by
Arthur Ransome

Arthur Ransome (1884–1967)

Ransome's twelve related stories about the Walker and Blackett children on holiday in the English Lake District, which begin with *Swallows and Amazons*, were first published between 1930 and 1947. Dissatisfied by others' work, Ransome started to illustrate the books himself with rather controlled but accurate line drawings, beginning in 1932 with *Peter Duck*.

The books first appeared as Puffins from 1962, with *Swallows and Amazons* in a cover that is an amalgam of horizontal stripes and the Puffin cover template of that period. By the time the entire twelve books were repackaged between 1968 and 1971, however, the images were more carefully selected and given a strong graphic treatment by the addition of a limited palette of flat colours. In this set Ransome's drawings take on a whole new lease of life and create a very distinctive and collectible series.

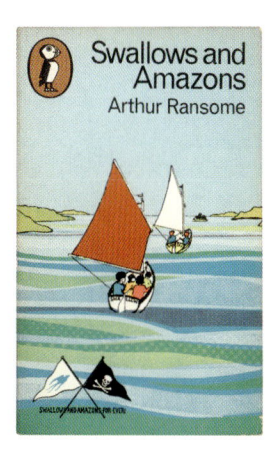

Swallows and Amazons, 1968.
Cover illustration by
Arthur Ransome

The Big Six, 1970.
Cover illustration by
Arthur Ransome

Coot Club, 1969.
Cover illustration by
Arthur Ransome

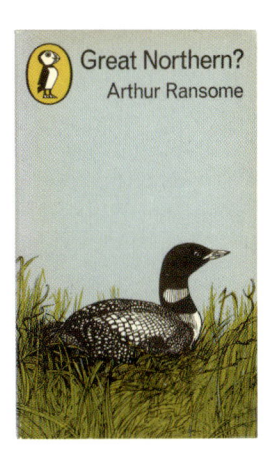

Great Northern?, 1971.
Cover illustration by
Arthur Ransome

Missee Lee, 1971.
Cover illustration by
Arthur Ransome

Winter Holiday, 1968.
Cover illustration by
Arthur Ransome

Pigeon Post, 1969.
Cover illustration by
Arthur Ransome

We Didn't Mean to Go to Sea,
1969. Cover illustration by
Arthur Ransome

Secret Water, 1969.
Cover illustration by
Arthur Ransome

III. Expansion

Watership Down, 1974. Cover illustration by Pauline Baynes (back cover)

Watership Down, a coup

Kaye Webb's policy of publishing or acquiring the best children's books as Puffins continued in the 1970s when *Watership Down* became probably her biggest coup. Published by Rex Collings in 1973 after refusals from thirteen other companies, it appeared as a Puffin the following year and became a huge crossover success as a Penguin with a cover that used a different crop of the same illustration. It quickly became the company's bestseller, replacing *Lady Chatterley's Lover*.

The cover is by Pauline Baynes, who had started illustrating books at the end of the Second World War and in the 1950s produced illustrations for both J. R. R. Tolkien and C. S. Lewis (see pp. 90–1).

Watership Down, 1974. Cover illustration by Pauline Baynes (Penguin edition)

Puffin by Design

Watership Down, 1974.
Cover illustration by
Pauline Baynes

III. Expansion 119

Lorna Doone, 1976. Cover photograph by Douglas Playle, showing Emily Richard as Lorna Doone and John Somerville as John Ridd in the BBC television production of *Lorna Doone* (copyright BBC)

Film and television tie-ins

Publishers have always looked for ways to boost sales of books, and from the late 1950s onwards the success of a film or television show proved an irresistible reason to give a book a new cover, generally with design sensitivity low down on the list of priorities.

As The Television Adventures of Worzel Gummidge shows, by the 1970s this relationship was starting to become circular. Characters were beginning to become commodities in their own right, and TV companies would create new stories for them that could subsequently be published as new additions to the series.

The Television Adventures of Worzel Gummidge, 1979. Cover photograph shows John Pertwee as Worzel Gummidge in Southern Television's networked series

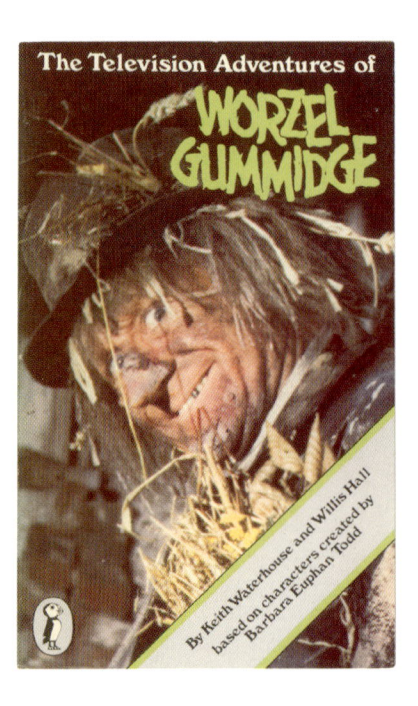

Puffin by Design

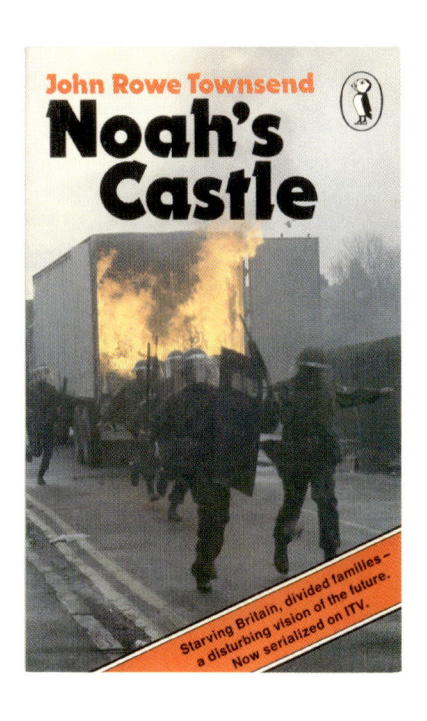

Run For Your Life, 1974. Adapted by Granada Television in the adventure serial *Soldier and Me*: cover photograph shows Richard Willis, who played Soldier, and Gerald Sunquist

Noah's Castle, 1980. Adapted by Southern Television

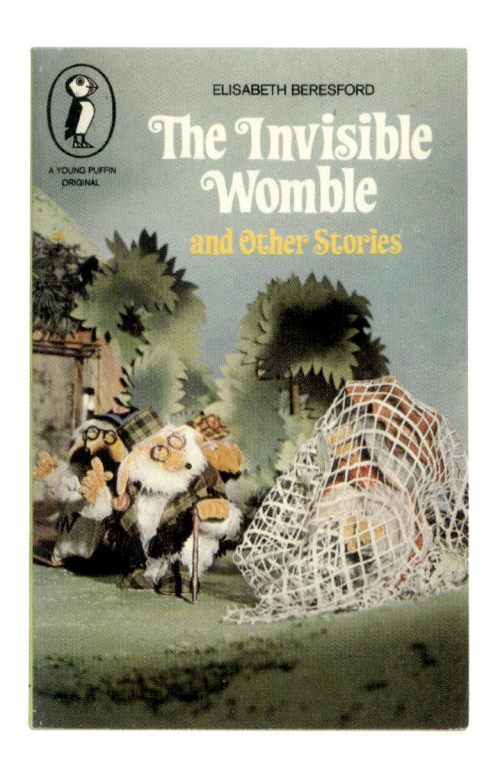

The Invisible Womble and Other Stories, 1973. Cover photograph features the original film puppet designs by Ivor Wood, who also illustrated this book (copyright FilmFair Ltd)

The Growing Summer, 1968. Serialized by London Weekend Television

Puffin Post, volume 1, number 1, 1967. Illustrations by Jill McDonald

'Sniffup Spotera'

The Puffin Club grew out of Webb's own enthusiasm for children's books and aimed to encourage children to read, borrow or buy books. Alongside an enamel badge, a secret code, stickers, diaries, competitions and outings, membership included the quarterly magazine *Puffin Post*.

With articles by Puffin's leading authors, including Norman Hunter, Leon Garfield, Michael Morpurgo, Roald Dahl and Ursula Le Guin, the magazine has been described as 'the first forum that created critics and writers out of children. It took them seriously as consumers and as judges of fiction at a time when words such as "empowerment" were just a twinkle in a facilitator's eye.' (Isabel Berwick, *Financial Times*, 14 October 2008)

Although many Puffin artists and illustrators contributed to the magazine – Quentin Blake, Edward Ardizzone, Jan Pieńkowski, Raymond Briggs – the dominant visual identity was created by Jill McDonald. McDonald grew up in New Zealand and had trained as an architect before illustrating for *The School Journal* in the 1950s. *The School Journal* was founded in 1907 and aimed to provide young readers with stories, plays, articles and poems relevant to their lives. In fulfilling that it gave many New Zealand writers and artists their first break. McDonald became its Art Editor between 1959 and 1965 before coming to Britain and working for Penguin. With the experience of *The School Journal* to draw on, she was the perfect choice for *Puffin Post*'s Chief Designer, and she continued in that role until her untimely death in 1982.

As a subscription magazine liberties could be taken with covers and masthead in a way that would be unthinkable for a magazine selling via a news-stand. And taken they were: the approach is playful, idiosyncratic, sophisticated. Covers could be drawn or collaged, the title is sometimes a primary element, sometimes secondary. McDonald's drawings are characterized by strong black outlines and vibrant colour, and, in fact, colour is the overwhelming impression. McDonald also designed several other book covers, including Picture Puffin 26, Janet Aitchison's *The Pirate's Tale* (1970), which had first been printed in *Puffin Post* in 1968.

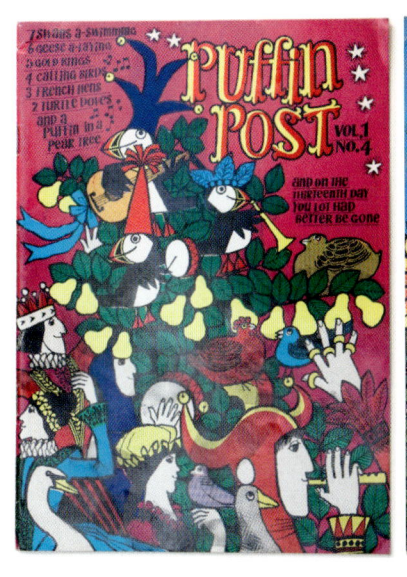

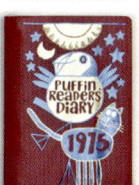

ABOVE: *Puffin Post,* volume 1, number 4, 1968; *Puffin Post,* volume 3, number 3, 1969; *Puffin Post,* volume 4, number 1, 1970. Cover illustrations and design by Jill McDonald

Puffin Readers' Diary, 1973, 1974, 1975 and 1976. Cover illustrations and design by Jill McDonald

Puffin book plate, 1972.

Puffin Club membership badge.

III. Expansion

Something to Do, 1968. Cover illustration by Shirley Hughes

Quizzes and activities

Puzzle books were part of the Puffin list from the start (see pp. 68–9, 82–3) and they continued to be produced alongside related titles. As with previous covers in the genre, those produced under Kaye Webb were an excuse for humour and visual play.

The two covers on this spread show clearly the change in style from the late 1950s to the early 1970s, from books that seem aimed at parents to books that are aimed directly at their readers.

Overleaf are covers by two illustrators whose work is synonymous with Puffin – Jill McDonald, whose distinctive work for *Puffin Post* has already been shown (pp. 122–3) – and Quentin Blake, who would go on to illustrate Roald Dahl titles from 1976.

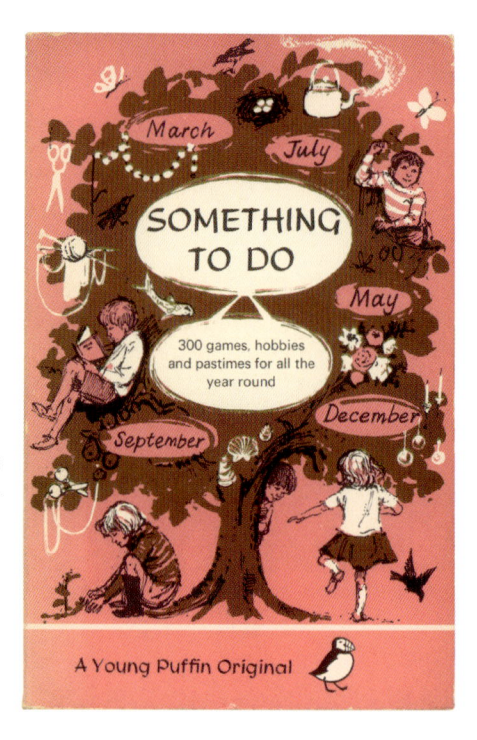

OPPOSITE:
Things to Do, 1978.

Hazel Evans
THINGS TO DO

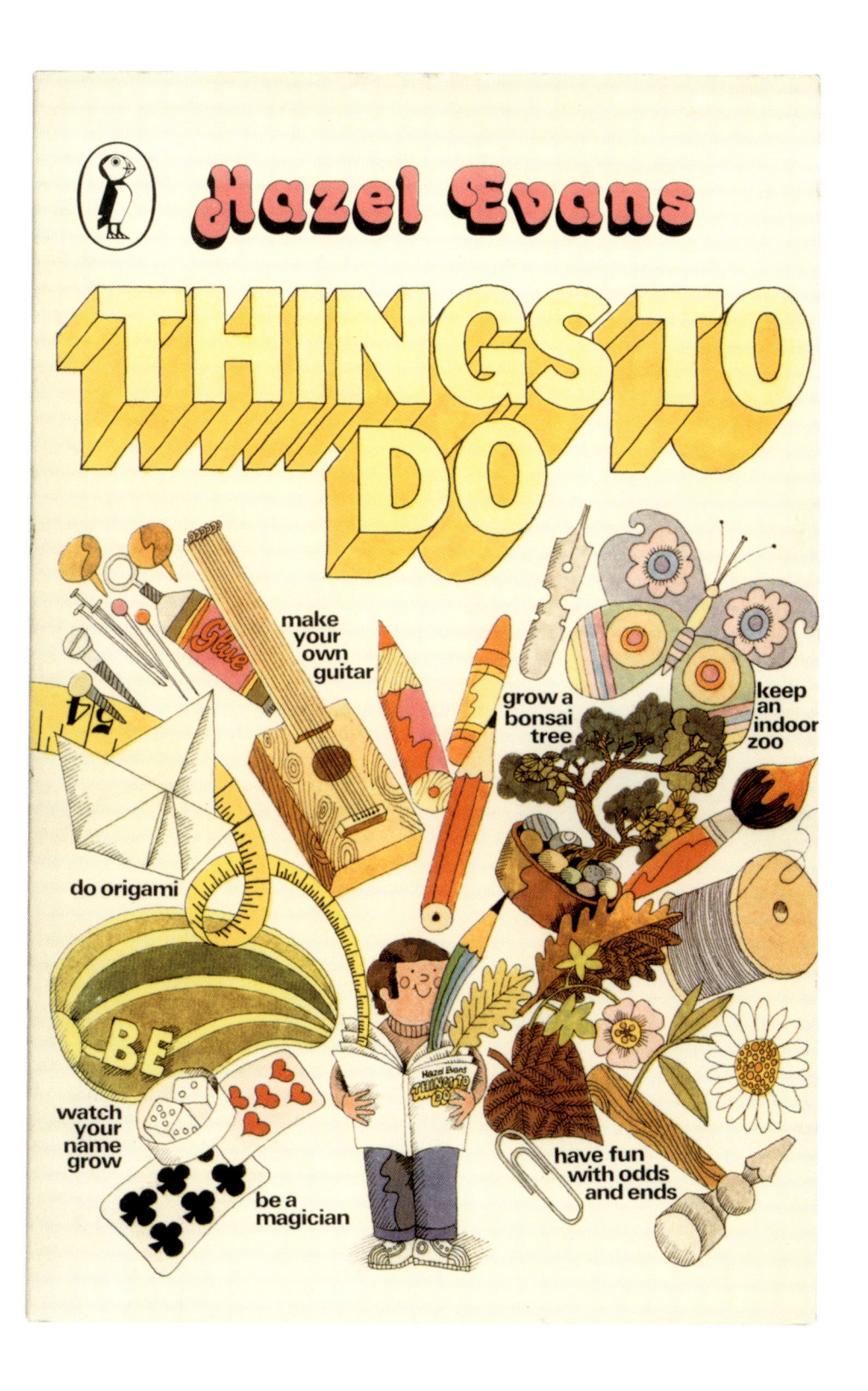

make your own guitar

grow a bonsai tree

keep an indoor zoo

do origami

watch your name grow

be a magician

have fun with odds and ends

The Puffin Crossword Puzzle Book, 1966. Cover illustration by Jill McDonald

The Puffin Quiz Book, 1969. Cover illustration by Jill McDonald

The Junior Puffin Quiz Book, 1966. Cover illustration by Jill McDonald

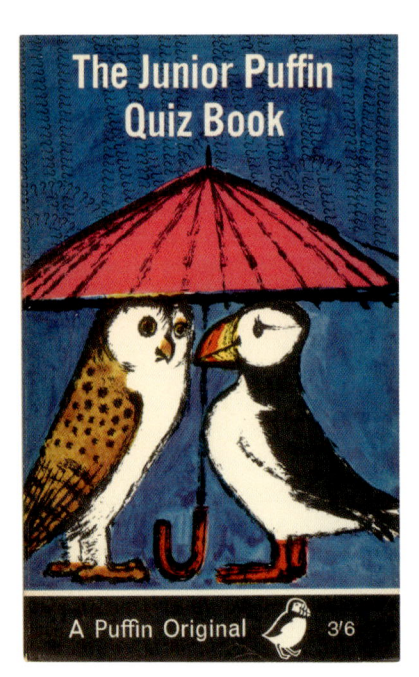

The Puffin Book of Magic, 1968. Cover illustration by Jill McDonald

OPPOSITE: *The Puffin Joke Book*, 1974. Cover illustration by Quentin Blake

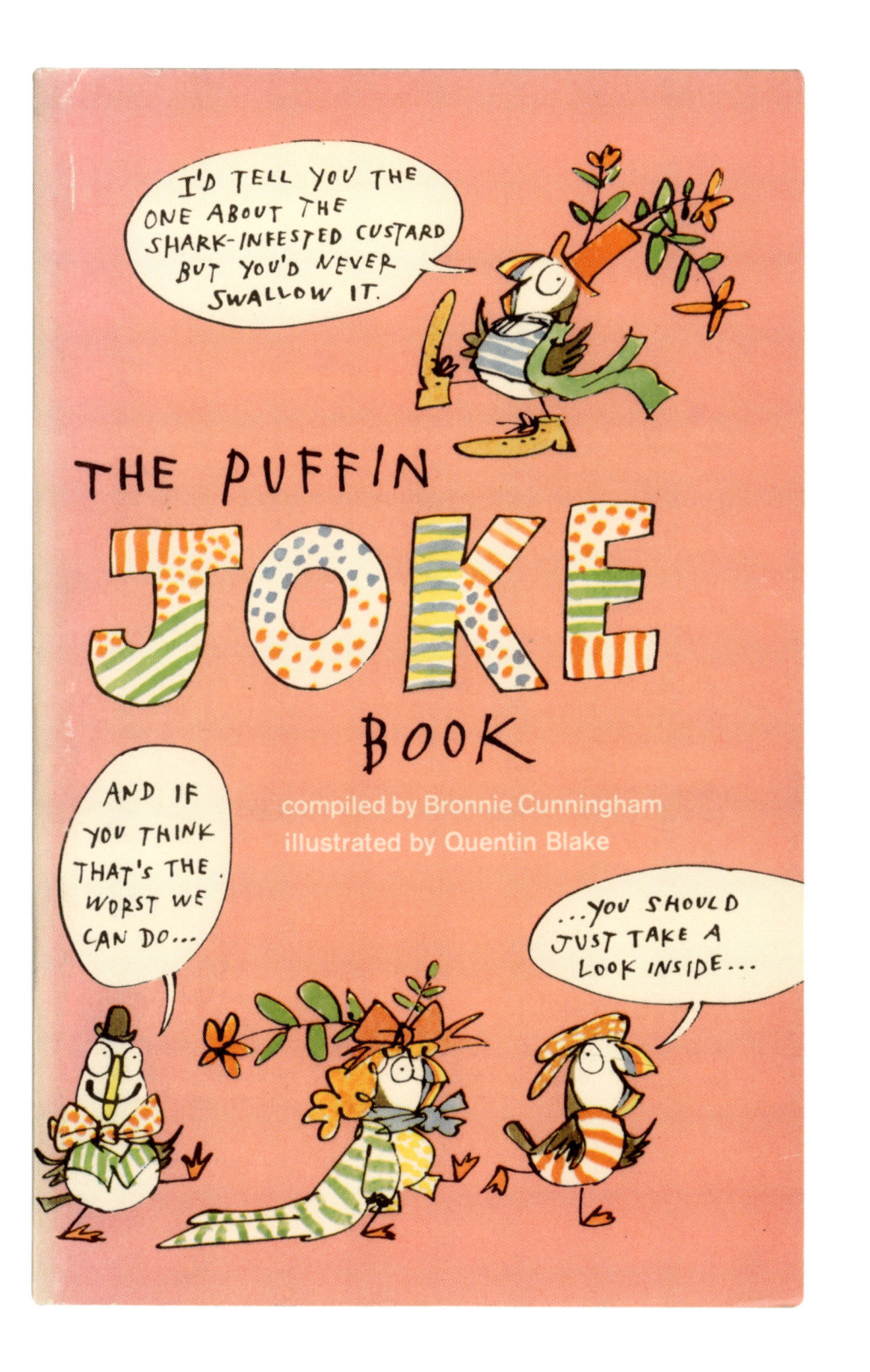

"I'd tell you the one about the shark-infested custard but you'd never swallow it."

THE PUFFIN JOKE BOOK

compiled by Bronnie Cunningham
illustrated by Quentin Blake

"And if you think that's the worst we can do..."

"...you should just take a look inside..."

The Puffin Book of Football, 1975. Cover design by Peter Barrett

The Puffin Book of Football, 1970. Cover illustration by Peter Barrett, showing an anonymous player of 1970 in England white, and a player of 1872 in Scottish colours

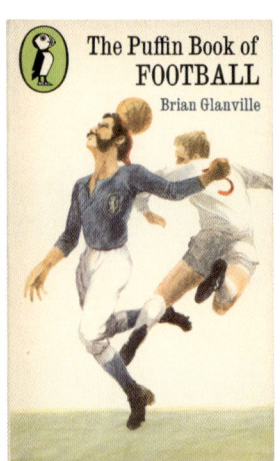

Sport

Puffin tried to provide the full range of titles that children might be interested in, both fiction and non-fiction. Hobbies and pastimes were prominent in the original Picture Books and books about similar subjects continued to be published.

Sadly, however, in the 1970s the covers fail to capture any of the magic of the sports concerned and do not have any visual relationship to each other.

The Puffin Book of Horses, 1975.

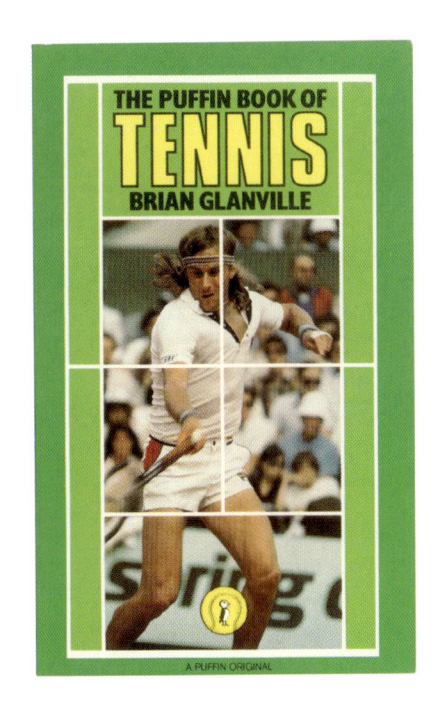

The Puffin Book of Athletics, 1980. Cover photograph by All-Sport, showing Sebastian Coe in Oslo setting a new world record for the mile in August 1979

The Puffin Book of Tennis, 1981. Cover photograph by Toby Glanville, showing five-times Wimbledon winner Björn Borg playing in the 1980 French championship

III. *Expansion*

In the Harbour, 1976.
Illustrated by Heinz Kurth
(cover and inside spread shown)

On the Road, 1977.
Illustrated by Peter Gregory
(cover and inside spread shown)

New Puffin Picture Books, 1975–7

Produced at a slightly smaller size (190 x 171 mm) than the first Picture Books, this series was an attempt to cover the non-fiction instructional aspects of their Carrington forebears. They are therefore interesting on several levels.

A comparison of parallel subjects between series reveals not only how much technology has moved on – see *On the Railway* overleaf with *The Book of Trains* on page 52, for example – but also a difference in what publishers assume children can take in – compare *Building a House* on pages 44–5 with *Build a House* overleaf.

And like the previous series, these books are also a record of their time: the optimism of the Advanced Passenger Train on the cover of *On the Railway* is similar to that surrounding the planes in *Airliners* of twenty years previously; while the double-page spread from *On the Road* is a real period piece, showing RT buses, Austin FX3 taxis and a mixture of old and new road signs, in addition to cars like the Mini, Morris 1000 and Rover 2000, which are now termed classics.

From a design point of view the series has a rather heavy-handed look, with the cover drawings marred by the insensitive black border and by the visual weight of the coloured panel above, which carries all the type. Also worth noting is the tightly spaced title type that had become particularly fashionable during this period, and the alternative 'a' and 'g' in the typeface used for the titles of *Harbour*, *Road*, *Print*, *Animals* and *Earth*, which was thought to be easier for (young) children to read.

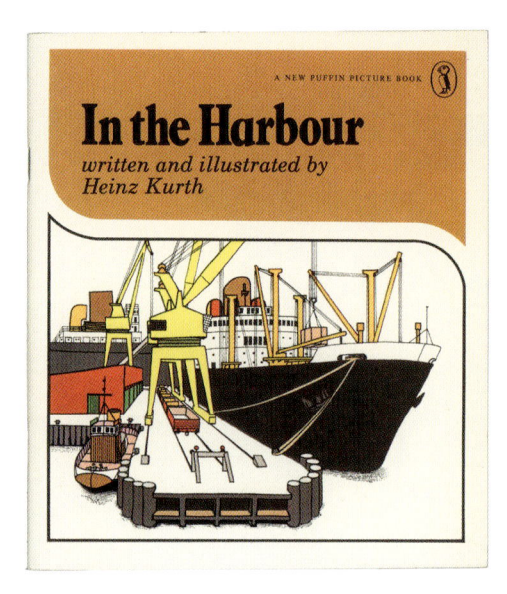

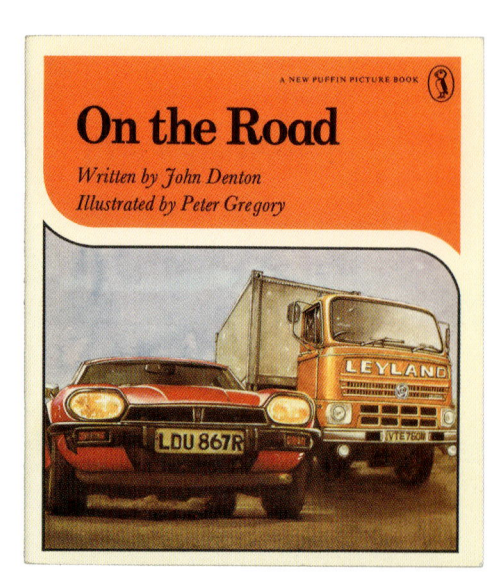

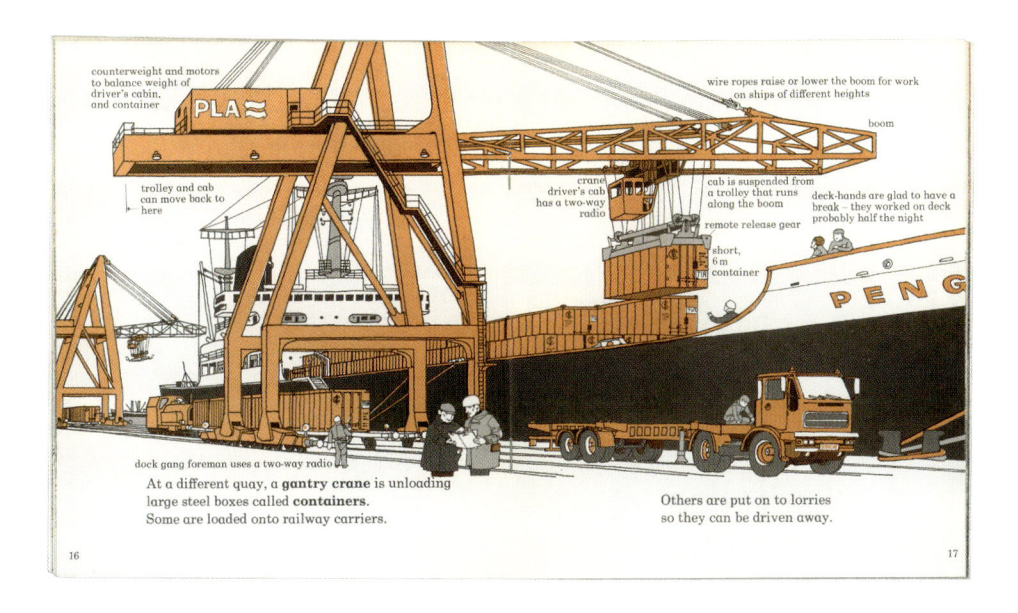

counterweight and motors to balance weight of driver's cabin, and container

wire ropes raise or lower the boom for work on ships of different heights

boom

trolley and cab can move back to here

crane driver's cab has a two-way radio

cab is suspended from a trolley that runs along the boom

deck-hands are glad to have a break – they worked on deck probably half the night

remote release gear

short, 6m container

dock gang foreman uses a two-way radio

At a different quay, a **gantry crane** is unloading large steel boxes called **containers**. Some are loaded onto railway carriers.

Others are put on to lorries so they can be driven away.

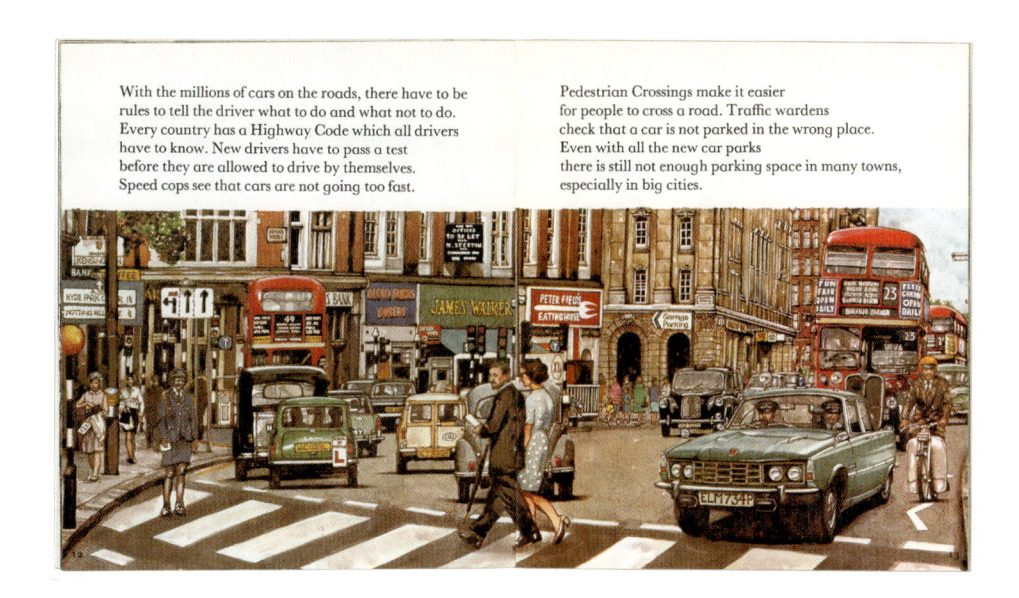

With the millions of cars on the roads, there have to be rules to tell the driver what to do and what not to do. Every country has a Highway Code which all drivers have to know. New drivers have to pass a test before they are allowed to drive by themselves. Speed cops see that cars are not going too fast.

Pedestrian Crossings make it easier for people to cross a road. Traffic wardens check that a car is not parked in the wrong place. Even with all the new car parks there is still not enough parking space in many towns, especially in big cities.

III. Expansion

Prehistoric Life, 1977.
Illustrated by Robert Gibson

The Vegetable Book, 1979.
Illustrated by Gillian Platt

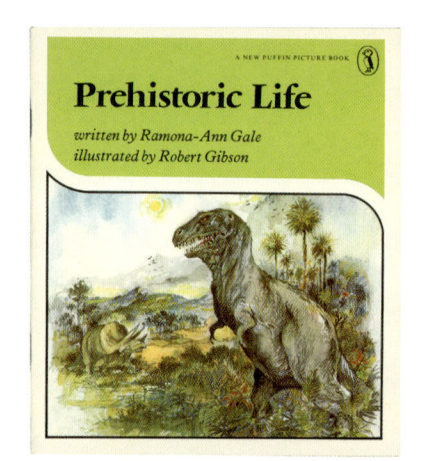

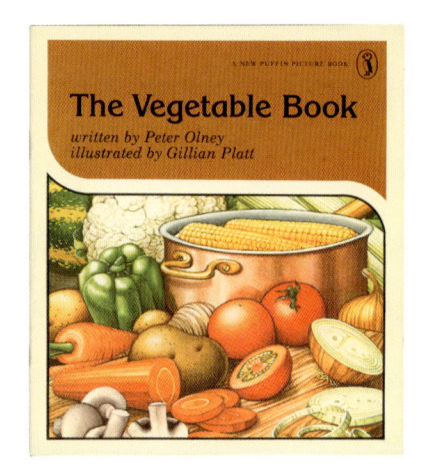

Household Machines, 1977.
Cover illustration by John Lobban

Machines on the Farm, 1975.
Illustrated by Val Biro

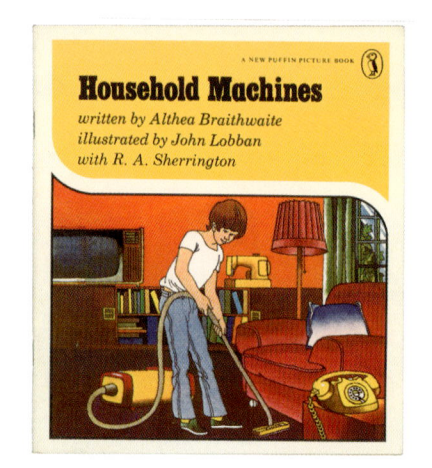

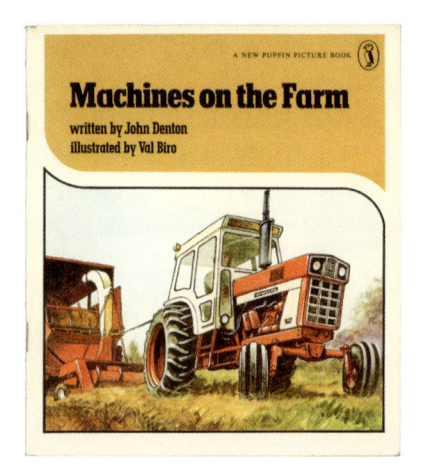

Print a Book, 1975.
Illustrated by Heinz Kurth

What's in a Pond?, 1976.
Illustrated by Peter McGinn

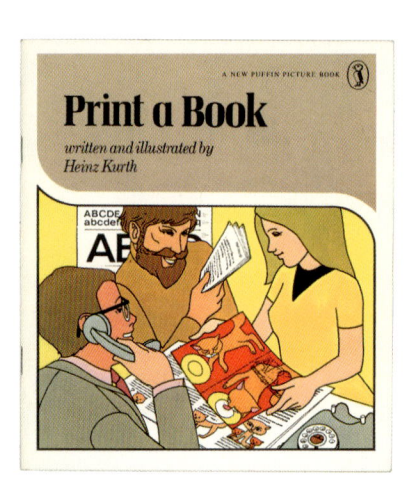

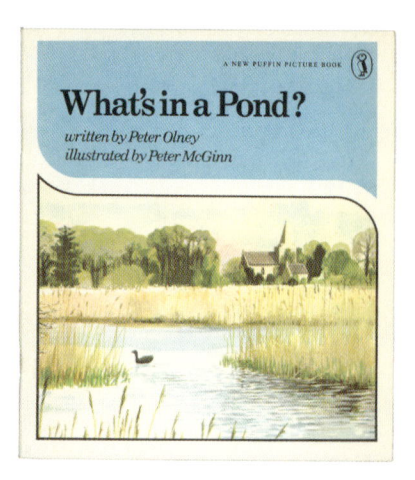

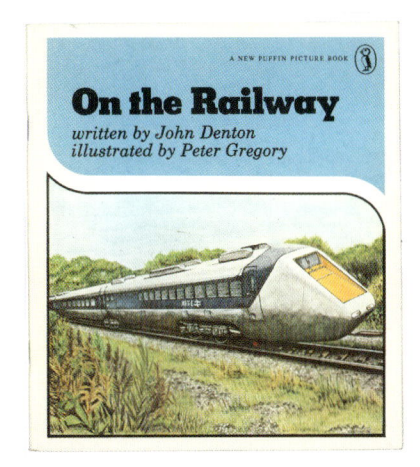

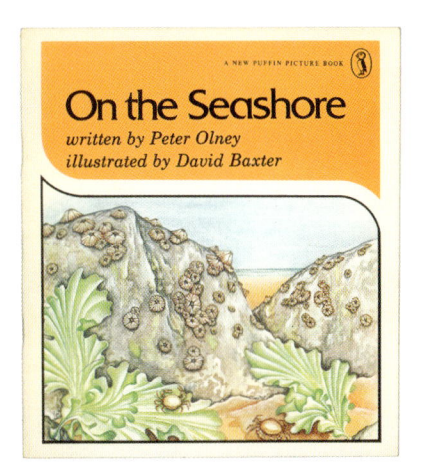

On the Railway, 1976.
Illustrated by Peter Gregory

On the Seashore, 1976.
Illustrated by David Baxter

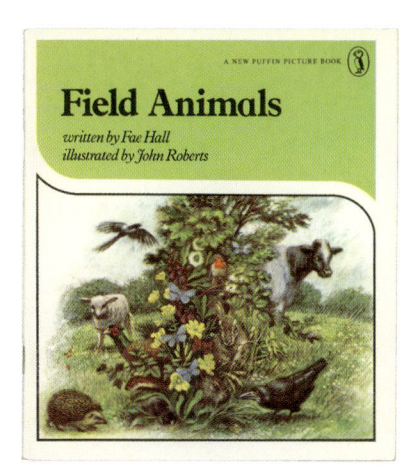

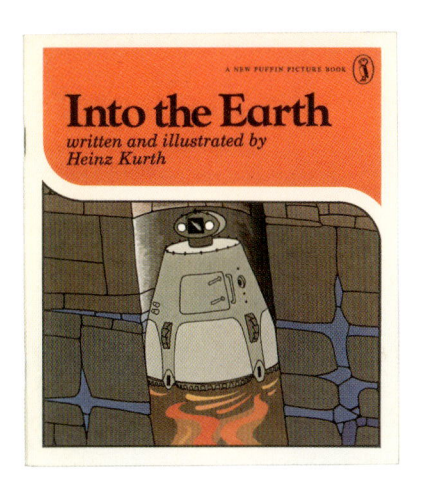

Field Animals, 1975.
Illustrated by John Roberts

Into the Earth, 1976.
Illustrated by Heinz Kurth

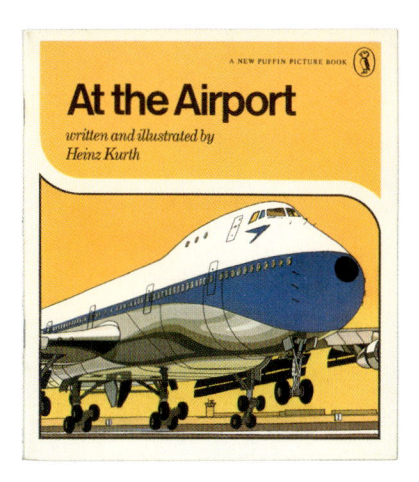

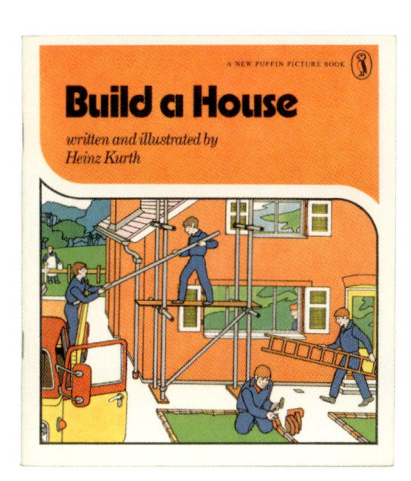

At the Airport, 1975.
Illustrated by Heinz Kurth

Build a House, 1975.
Illustrated by Heinz Kurth

Strange Things, 1976. Cover illustration by David Lancashire

Feasts, 1980. Cover illustration by David Lancashire

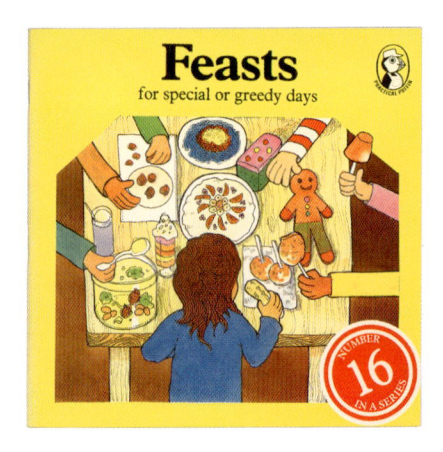

Bicycles, 1976. Cover illustration by David Lancashire

Creatures, 1980. Cover illustration by David Lancashire

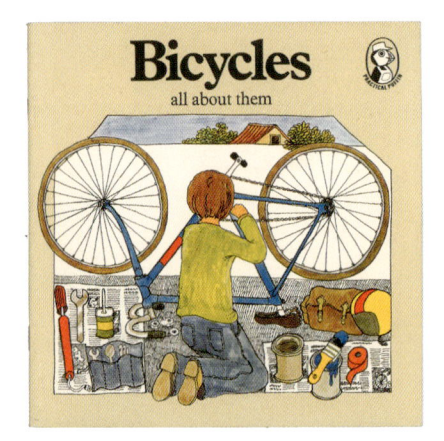

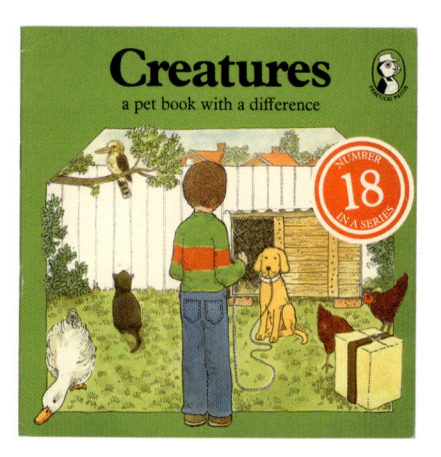

Body Tricks, 1976. Cover illustration by David Lancashire

Things to Fly, 1980. Cover illustration by Jack Newnham

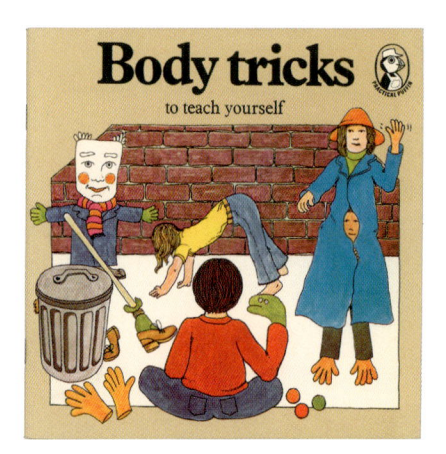

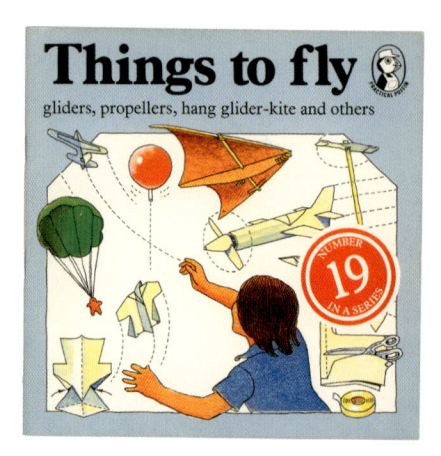

Practical Puffins 1978–80

Practical Puffins were an idea of John Hooker, Senior Editor of Puffin Australia, and were intended for independent-minded children aged 7 to 12. He sold the idea first to Kaye Webb, and then handed the job to Diana Gribble and Hilary McPhee, who worked with artist David Lancashire. The books were based on careful observation of what children did, and the demands of an international audience. From sample pages of six trial titles, Penguin offices in Britain, Canada and the USA ordered large quantities, and eventually there were Greek and Italian editions too.

They proved a great success and Australian profits became important in supporting the British company during a difficult financial period, but this in turn prevented Penguin Australia's own expansion plans. Other methods of raising money in Australia failed, Hooker was forced to resign, and the production of the books was organized differently, still by McPhee and Gribble, but working as publishers in their own right and co-publishing with Penguin. The series ended around 1980.

Visually they are a more unified series than New Puffin Picture Books and although the drawing style itself seems quite simplistic, the content is accurate and detailed for its purpose and intended audience.

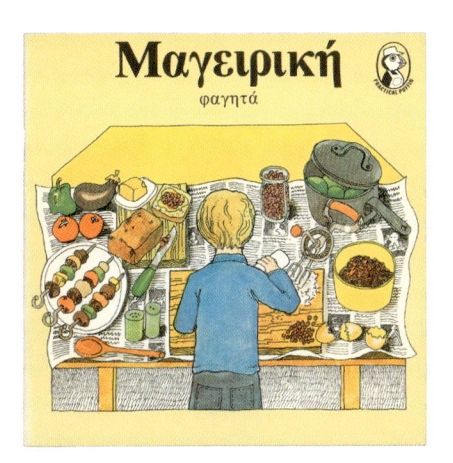

Cooking, 1980 (Greek edition). Cover illustration by David Lancashire

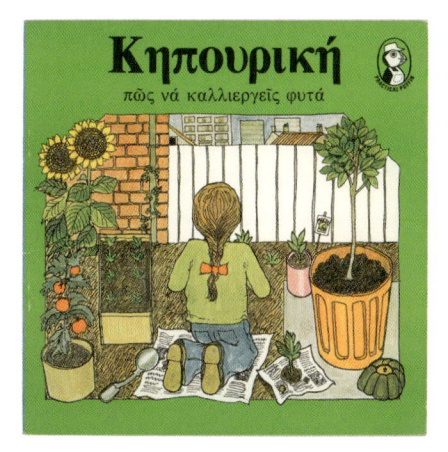

Gardening, 1979 (Greek edition). Cover illustration by David Lancashire

Carpentry, 1980 (Italian edition). Cover illustration by David Lancashire

National Velvet, 1962.
Cover illustration by Laurian Jones

Walkabout, 1967. Cover illustration by Richard Kennedy

Peacocks, 1962–79

To cater for a teenage market Kaye Webb chose to create a separate imprint that sat between Penguin and Puffin, and called it Peacock. The original cover design by Germano Facetti and John Sewell featured a coloured panel in the top centre, which contained the series and author name. This has echoes of the striped top that Facetti had introduced for Penguin's Peregrine imprint at the same time (see *Penguin by Design*: pp. 116–7). Covers were then illustrated, often wrapped round front and back as in the Graham period, and worked well as long as the coloured panel was taken into account (note the lost heads on the otherwise excellent *Suicide Club*).

In 1964, starting with PK33 *Last Year's Broken Toys*, a new design was introduced that mirrors the 'Marber grid' used for Penguin Crime and Fiction, and Pelican. With a completely white upper part to the cover, it was easier to commission illustration. Again, both front and back covers were used, either for one large image or in an episodic manner.

From 1965, however, and in line with the adult list, Peacock abandoned a clearly defined series look and illustrated its covers with whatever seemed appropriate for each title. Alongside more established styles, photorealism, photography, collage and airbrush were all featured and are shown on the following pages. During this latter period, the Peacock was re-drawn to make it sit more comfortably alongside the Penguin and Puffin logos. While easier to integrate into a cover it is far less satisfying visually.

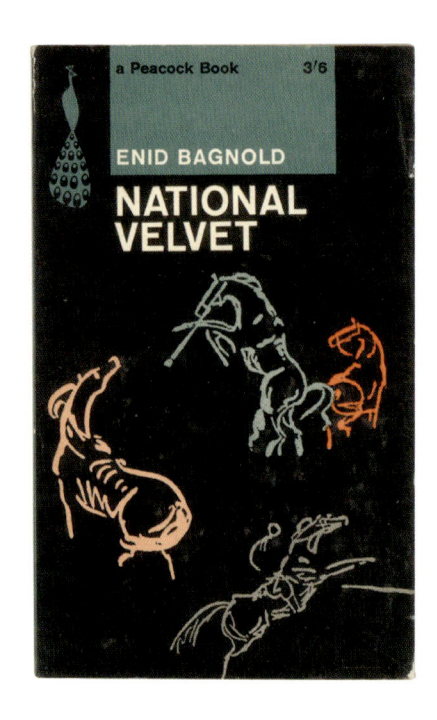

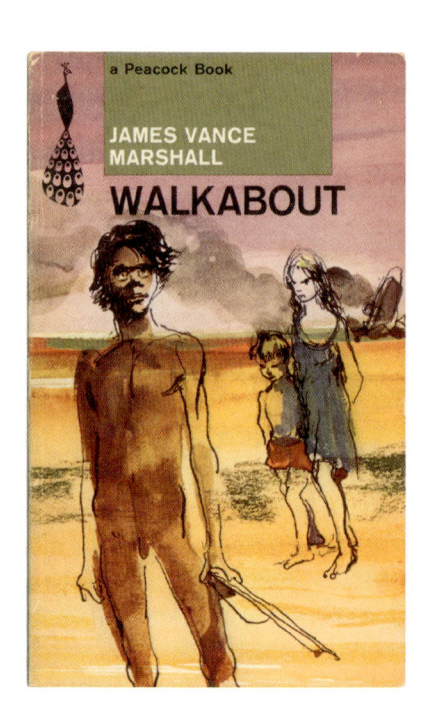

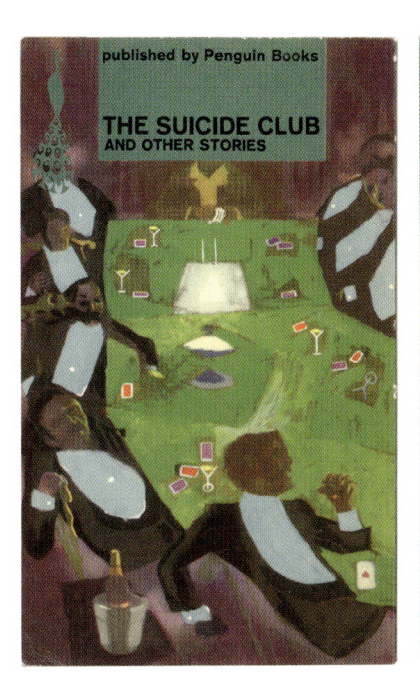

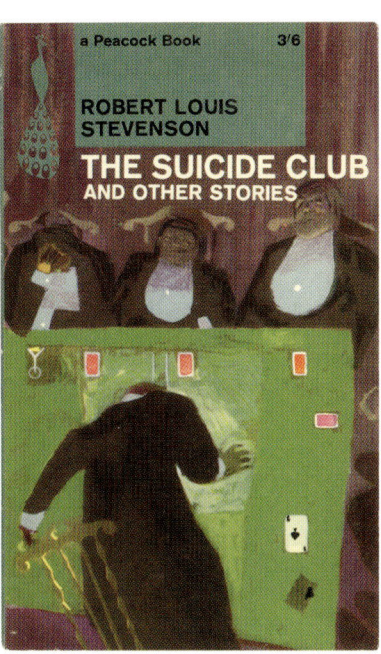

The Suicide Club and Other Stories, 1963. Cover illustration by Peter Edwards

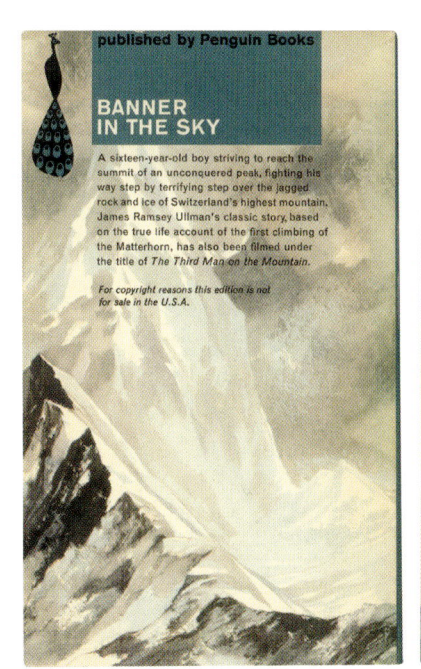

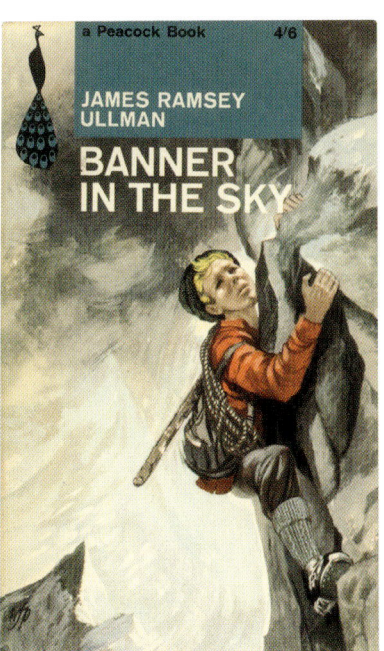

Banner in the Sky, 1963. [Cover illustration by W. Francis Phillips]

III. Expansion 137

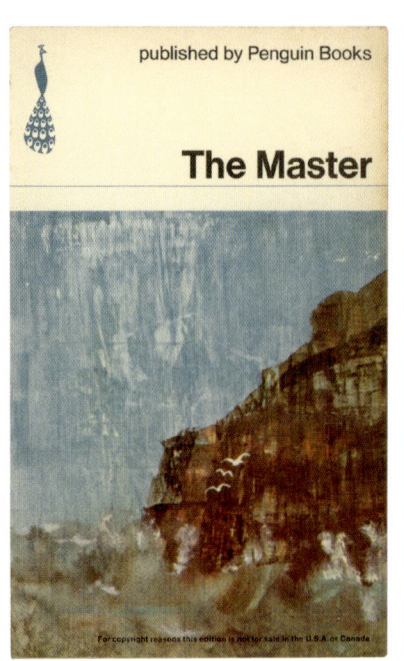

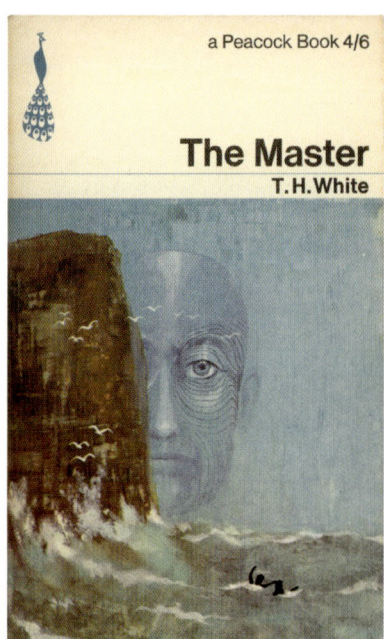

The Master, 1964. Cover illustration by Peter Le Vasseur

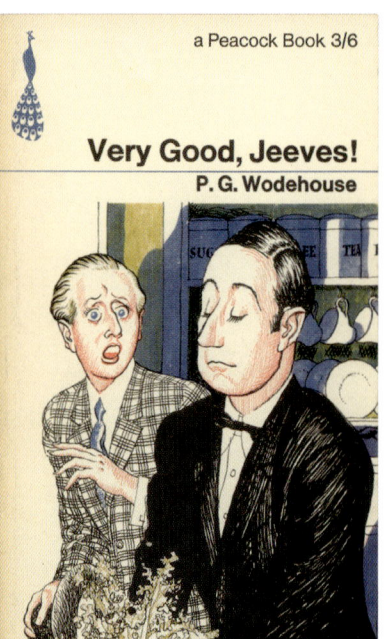

Very Good, Jeeves!, 1964. Cover illustration by Leslie Illingworth

138 Puffin by Design

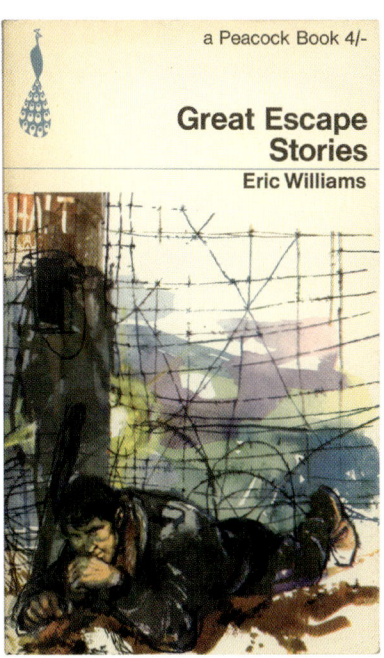

Great Escape Stories, 1964.
Cover illustration by Victor Ambrus

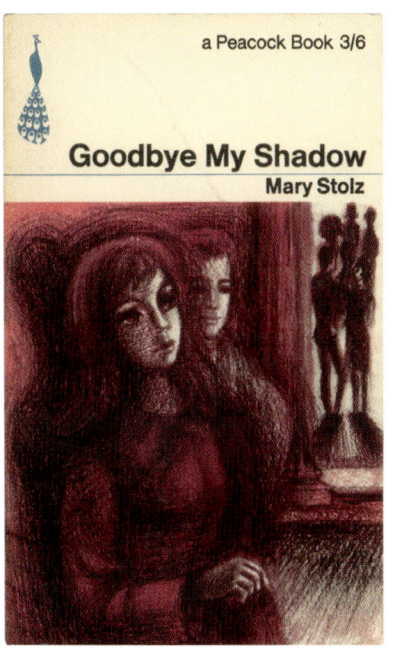

Goodbye My Shadow, 1964. Cover illustration by Patricia Hamilton

III. Expansion

A Working Life, 1973.
Cover illustration by
Madelon Vriesendorp

Citizen of the Galaxy, 1972.
Cover illustration by
Madelon Vriesendorp

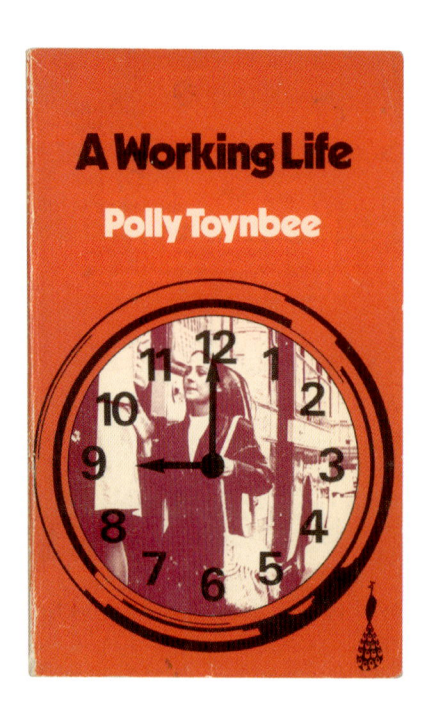

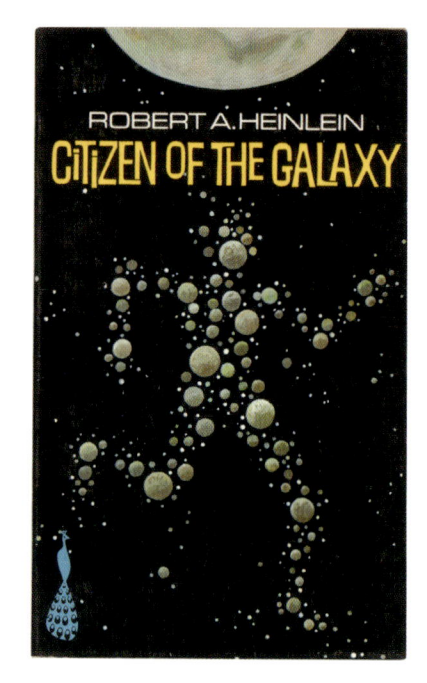

The Owl Service, 1972.
Cover illustration by
Charles Keeping

The House on the Brink, 1972.
Cover illustration by
Madelon Vriesendorp

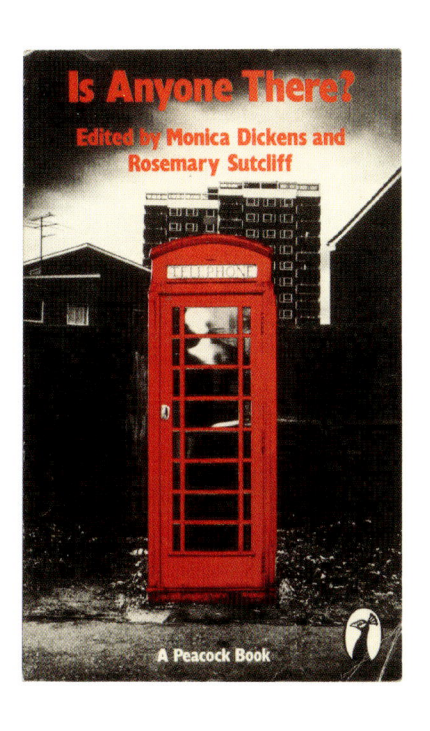

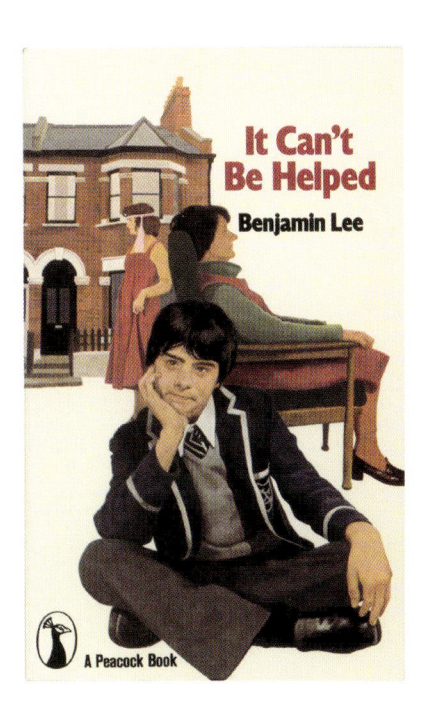

Is Anyone There?, 1978.
Cover illustration by Simon John

It Can't Be Helped, 1978.
Cover illustration by
Allan Manham

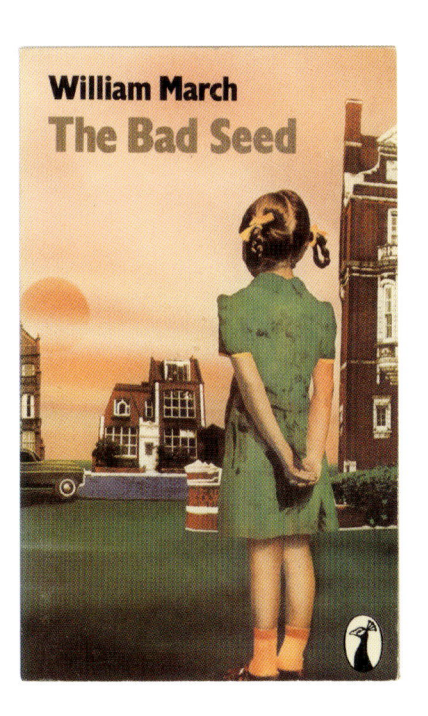

A Bad Lot and Other Stories, 1977.
Cover illustration by Paul Bawden

The Bad Seed, 1978.
Cover illustration by Philip Hale

III. Expansion

Immortality Inc., 1978.
Cover illustration by
Peter Goodfellow

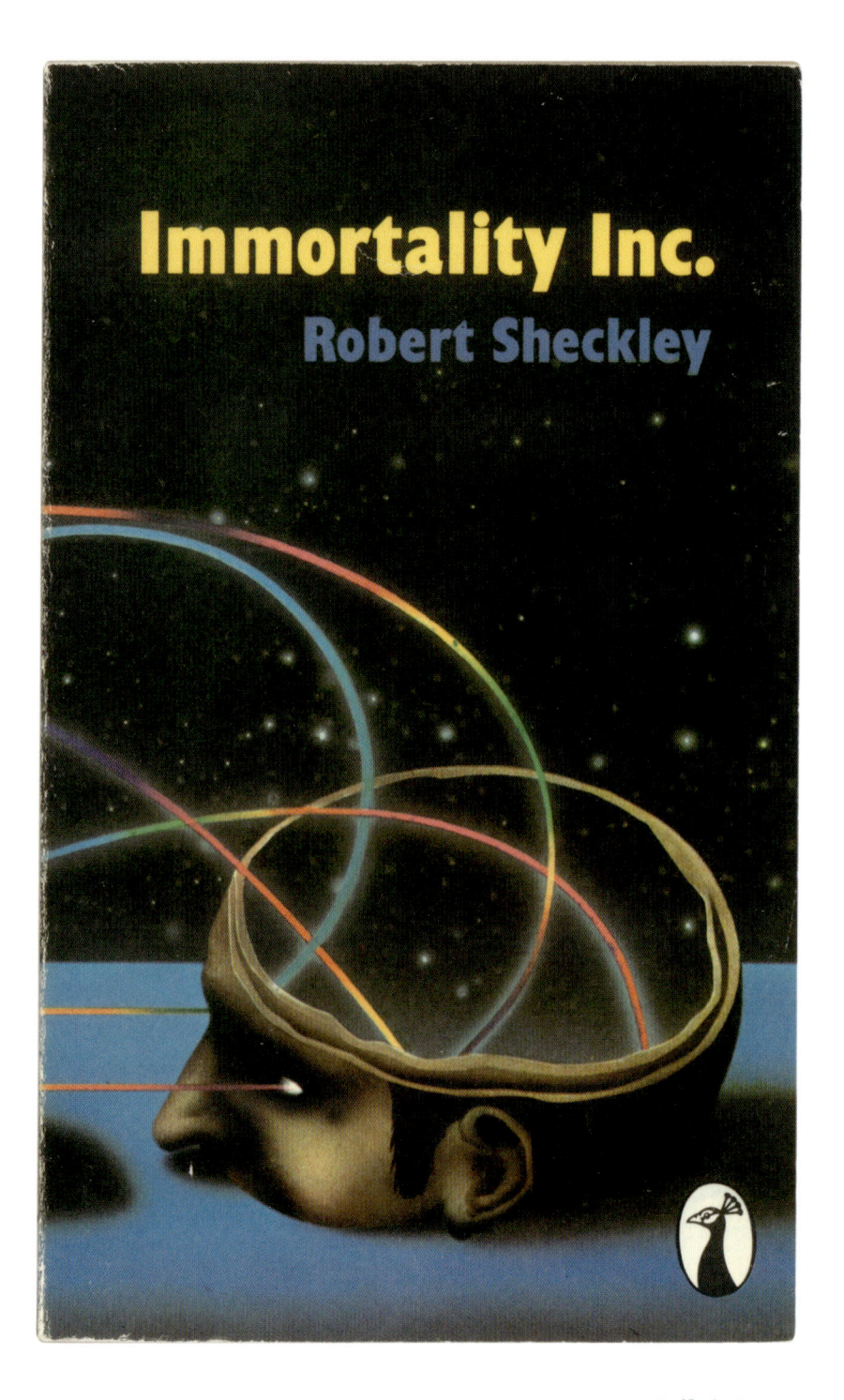

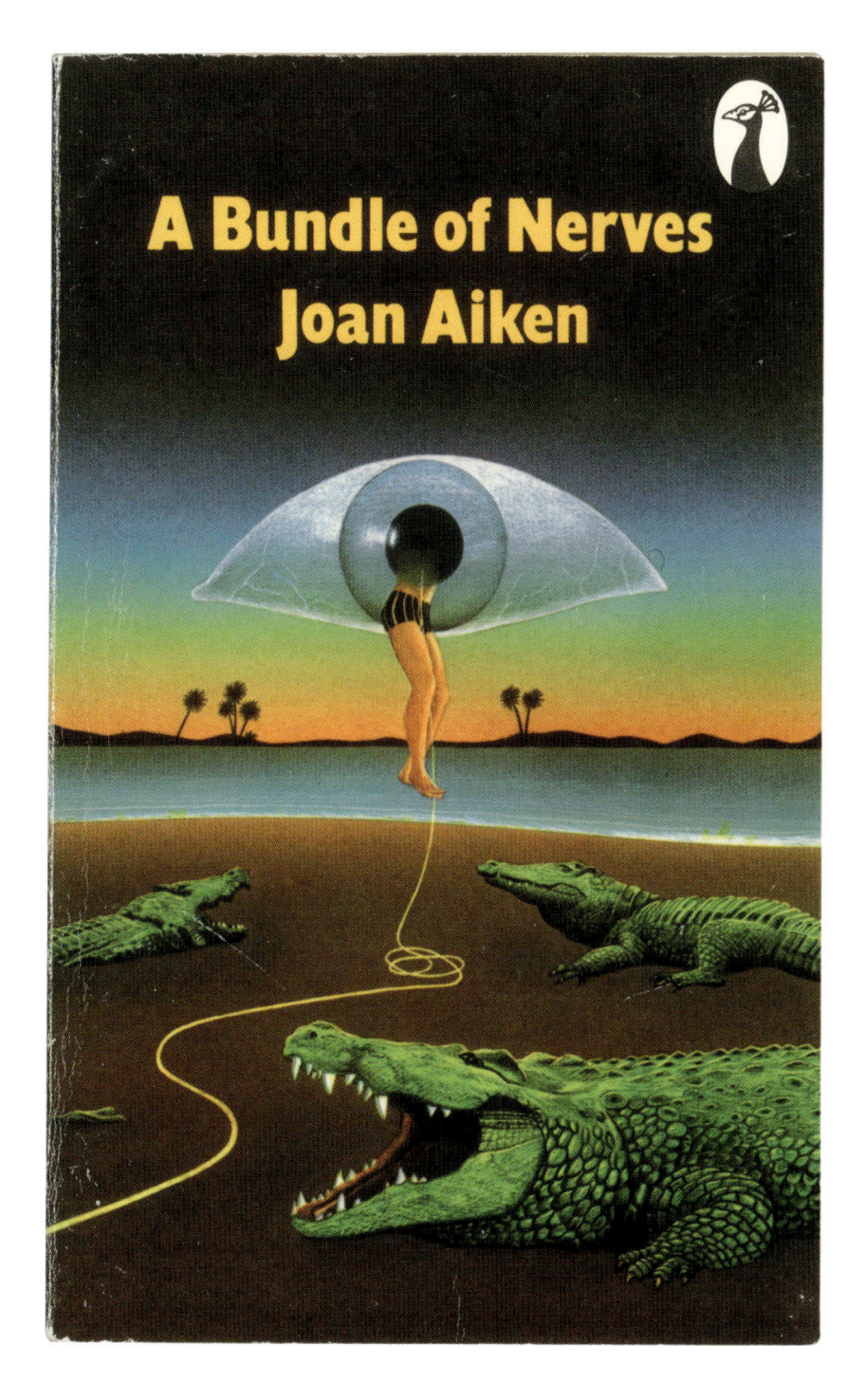

A Bundle of Nerves, 1978.
Cover illustration by
Peter Goodfellow

IV. Consolidation

On Monday he ate through one apple. But he was still hungry.

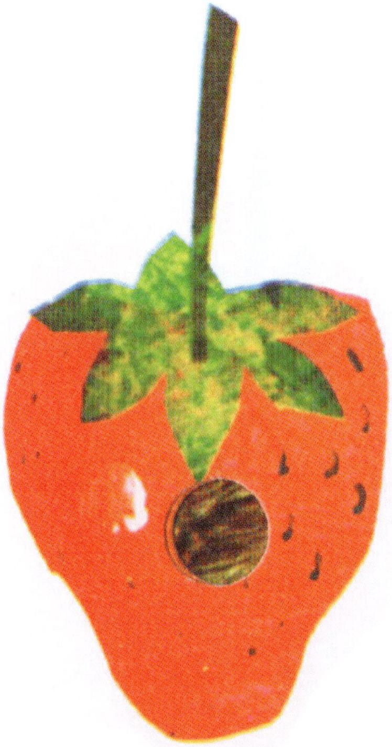

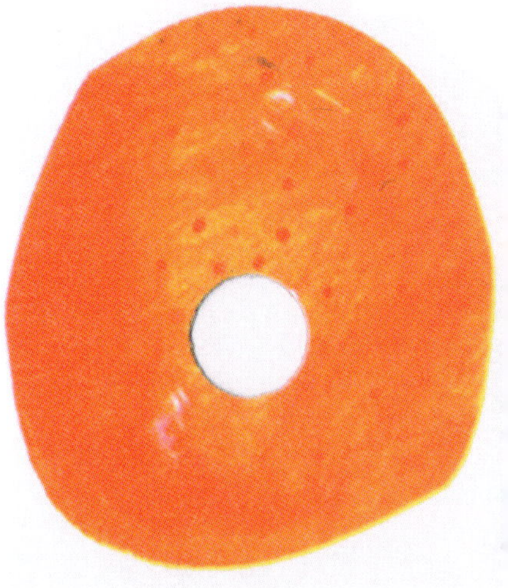

We would be mad to throw away a reputation that distinguishes us from the many competing imprints. (in Gritten, 1991, p. 25)

The importance of Puffin, 1979–95

Kaye Webb retired in 1979 and was succeeded by Tony Lacey, and in the same year the editorial offices moved from Grosvenor Gardens to larger premises on the New King's Road in Chelsea.

Lacey had previously worked for Penguin Education before moving over to Kestrel, Penguin's children's hardback imprint. Run by Patrick Hardy, who was answerable to Webb, Kestrel had grown out of Longman's children's publishing and fed titles to the Puffin paperback list. While there, and as an extension of his role, Lacey edited the Peacock titles during their flurry of activity in 1977 before he left the company to set up a children's division at Granada. However, in 1979 he was invited back to Penguin by Managing Director Peter Mayer to become Puffin's Publishing Director. Lacey's experience at Kestrel had put him in a good position for this new role.

The company had made a loss in 1979 and Mayer's solution was new practices, including more aggressive marketing of fewer titles. Although his presence was felt strongly by both editorial and design departments throughout the company it had far less impact at Puffin. Lacey describes his inheritance from Webb as 'wonderful' and Mayer allowed him to build on her success – Puffin was in a much stronger position than many other parts of the company.

Lacey consolidated Puffin's place in the market and, like Webb, pursued authors and titles that would sell well and underpin the stability of the division. Some of these, such as Eric Hill's *Where's Spot?* and Rod Campbell's *Dear Zoo*, quickly became bestsellers in Picture Puffin and have remained hugely popular ever since. When, in 1983, Frederick Warne was

Tony Lacey

PREVIOUS PAGE: detail from the original Puffin edition of *The Very Hungry Caterpillar*, 1974. Written and illustrated by Eric Carle put up for sale, Lacey saw the possibilities of the Beatrix Potter books and advised senior management of their worth.

Although Lacey had previously been Editor of the Peacock series, it was decided that a separate imprint was not essential for reaching the teenage market and in 1981 Peacock titles were re-branded as Puffin Plus (see pp. 168–73) in order to bring the series closer to Puffin and to reduce the number of imprints within the Penguin group.

Other new series that were developed during his editorship included Puffin Classics in 1983 (see pp. 180–3). While the Penguin Classics series took a longer, historical view of literature, and published titles or translations of works that Penguin did not already publish, Puffin Classics instead highlighted the very best from its own list. Flagging titles in this way meant that many appeared in two covers and could potentially appeal to a wider buying public.

Books for boys also took a more prominent role during Lacey's editorship as demonstrated by a rise in football-related titles; publication of the opportunistic *You Can Do the Cube* by Patrick Bossert; and in 1982 the launch of the interactive gamebook series Fighting Fantasy by Steve Jackson and Ian Livingstone. The series was a huge success with the first title, *The Warlock of Firetop Mountain* (see p. 149), quickly selling its 50,000 print run. The importance of Puffin to the main company at this period can be seen by the sales figures – by 1983 one in every three Penguin books sold was a Puffin.

Liz Attenborough took over the Puffin editorship in September 1983 when Lacey became Publishing Director of the new Viking list, Penguin's adult hardback division. Attenborough had worked at William Heinemann and Piccolo before becoming Commissioning Editor for Kestrel in 1977, then Chief Editor two years later. Her role at Puffin expanded in 1984 to become Editorial Director of all Penguin children's imprints.

Attenborough built on previous achievements, and like her predecessor, introduced further sub-series or brandings such as Read Aloud, Read Alone, Fantail and Young Puffin in 1985; Pocket Puffin in 1987; and branched out into audio in 1988. Throughout this period, the influence of other Penguin territories became increasingly important. The Australian input with the McPhee/Gribble titles was discussed in the last chapter and continues into the 1980s. The United States, too, became important with many Picture Puffins being re-branded as Puffin Pied Piper for their market, and many titles that originated there were imported and re-priced for the British market. Stylistically, the American titles heralded a visual change, for it was there that the first significant changes in artwork and design methods and production occurred (see pp. 160–1).

The Puffin Club continued to grow but, of more lasting importance perhaps, the Puffin School Book Club was improved. Begun in parallel with the club, this method of selling directly to schools and organizations continues to this day.

With Penguin's acquisition in 1985 of the Michael Joseph and Hamish Hamilton publishing companies, the editorial offices needed to expand once more and moved to Wrights Lane, Kensington. There were further management changes too. Peter Mayer felt he needed to spend more time with Penguin's American operation, and so in 1987 Trevor Glover returned from Penguin Australia and took over as Managing Director. Liz Attenborough continued as Editorial Director until leaving in 1998 to work for the National Literacy Trust.

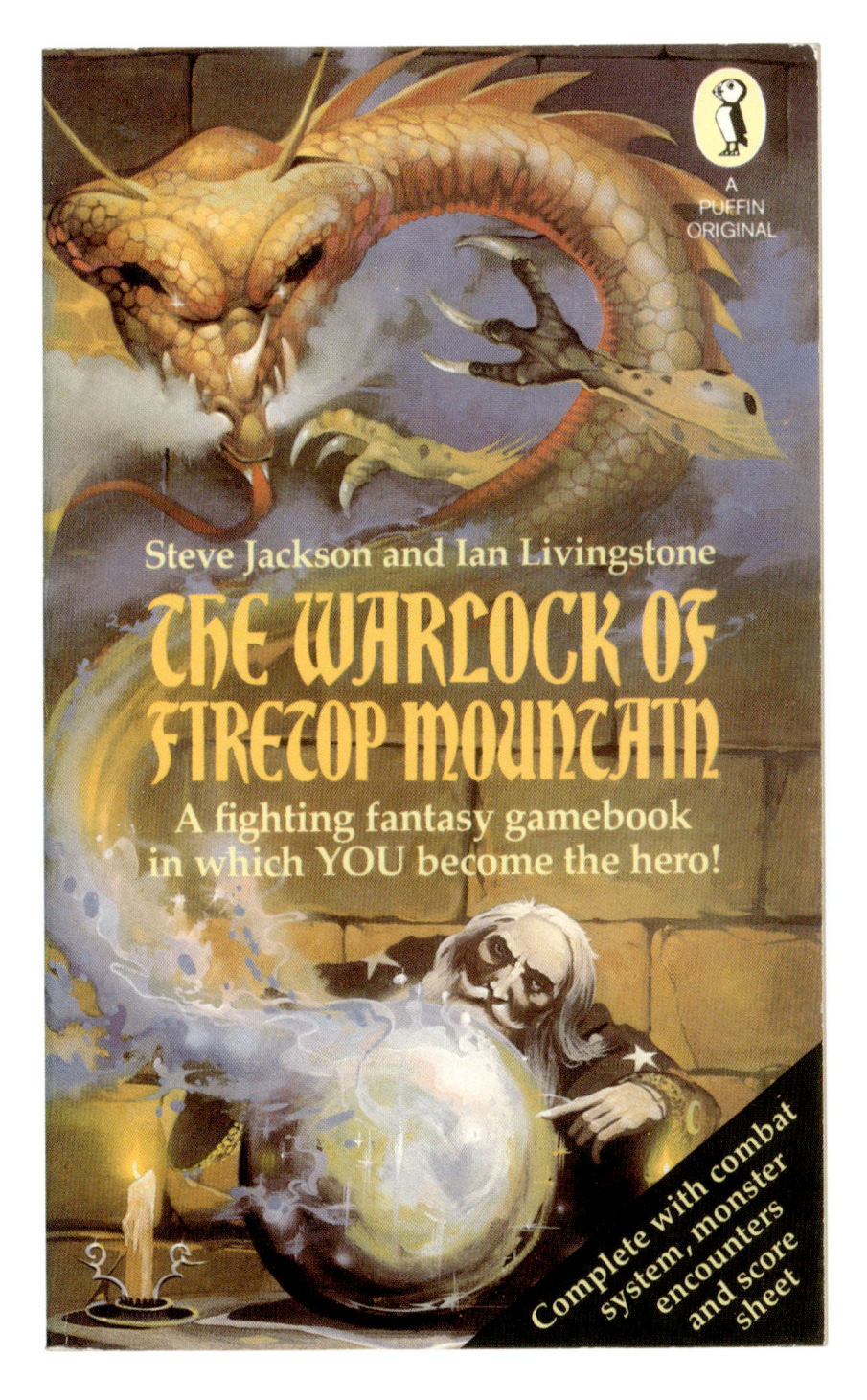

The Warlock of Firetop Mountain, 1982. Cover illustration by Peter Jones. Commissioned by Penguin but published by Puffin, *The Warlock of Firetop Mountain* was the first of the hugely successful Fighting Fantasy series, which eventually numbered fifty-nine titles published between 1982 and 1995

OPPOSITE: *Where's Spot?*, 1983. Illustrated by Eric Hill (cover and inside spread shown)

Picture Puffins, from 1968

Picture Puffins had been introduced by Kaye Webb in 1968 and picked up the baton of fiction from Carrington's original series. During Tony Lacey's editorship the series continued to develop and a number of significant illustrators were published by Puffin. The following pages show a range of these, from books to delight small children, to books that cross over to an adult audience. Around 1980 the 'happy Puffin' is moved to the corner in a yellow quadrant bordered by an orange band containing the series name.

Eric Hill (b. 1927) worked as a cartoonist, visualizer in the advertising industry and freelance designer and illustrator before – like many other Puffin authors – he created a character from stories he read to his child at bedtime. *Where's Spot?* first appeared as a Puffin in 1980, and with its innovative lift-the-flap concept, simple story and charming illustrations became a bestseller in a matter of weeks. Spot has remained hugely popular ever since, with titles now in Warne and Ladybird, as well as Puffin.

Jan Pieńkowski's work with Joan Aiken has already been seen on pages 114–5. Meg and Mog and the nursery books were developed from the early 1970s with Helen Nicoll, whom he had got to know through working for her, producing titles for the BBC's *Watch!* Much of the work on these books was done in Membury Service Station on the M4, midway between both their homes. Meg and Mog first appeared as Puffins in 1975, and the nursery titles in 1983. The strong simple drawings and bright colours made them instantly successful.

Another example of books for the very young are those by Eric Carle (b. 1929). Carle was born in New York, but moved to Germany aged six. He returned to the USA in 1952 and worked in advertising and graphic design. He was asked by Bill Martin Jr. to illustrate his *Brown Bear, Brown Bear: What Do You See?* and the result was an instant hit, encouraging Carle to put forward his own ideas for books. The first of these was *The Very Hungry Caterpillar*, published by Puffin in 1974. Carle creates the illustrations from tissue paper he paints himself; they are put together very quickly, but only after a long time has been spent drafting and refining every detail of the story itself.

A different visual feel characterizes the work of Janet Ahlberg (1944–94). She met her future husband, Allan (b. 1938), while he was training to be a teacher, and they married in 1969. Janet later studied graphic design when she realized her talent for illustration, and later still, when wanting something to illustrate, she asked Allan to write for her. That accident was the beginning of a great and productive partnership, where ideas for books were bounced backwards and forwards between them as text and image developed. *Peepo!* is a mixture of influences, from memories of their childhoods in the 1940s and 1950s, to the comics and artefacts that they carefully researched. Because Allan wrote faster than Janet could illustrate, he collaborated with other illustrators and has continued to do so since her death.

Raymond Briggs (b. 1934) attended the Wimbledon School of Art and the Central, and after his National Service studied painting at the Slade School of Fine Art before turning to illustration. Although sceptical of children's illustration at first, he soon warmed to its challenges and his first book was published in 1961. Briggs is perhaps best known for *The Snowman*, the wordless, magical Christmas story that became a film some years later, but the comic-strip narrative of *Father Christmas* (winner of the Kate Greenaway Medal 1973) and *Fungus the Bogeyman* are more typical of his work.

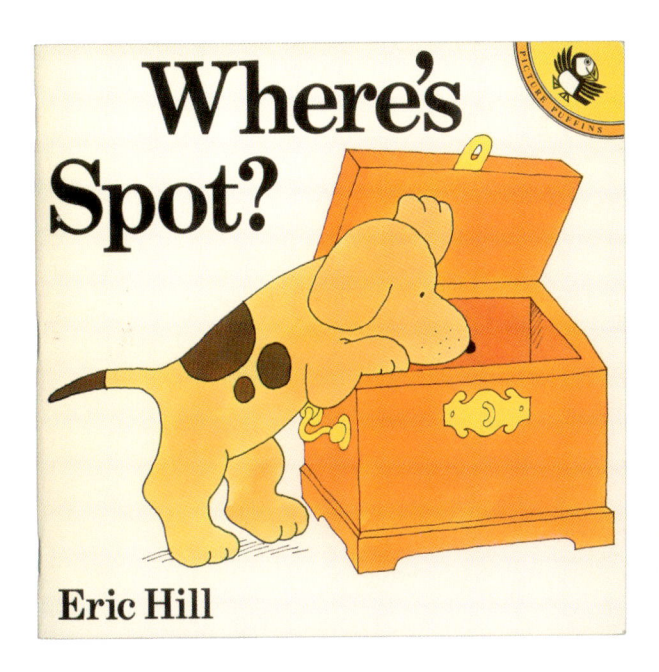

Time, 1985. Illustrated by
    Jan Pieńkowski

Numbers, 1984. Illustrated by Jan Pieńkowski

ABC, 1983. Illustrated by Jan Pieńkowski

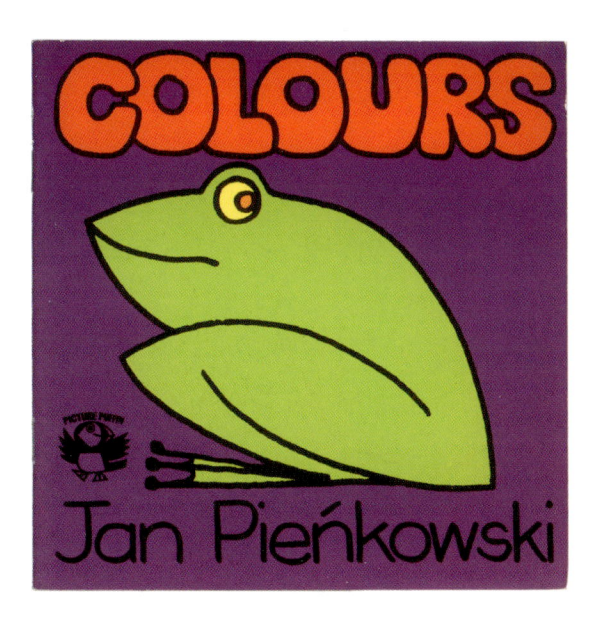

Colours, 1985. Illustrated by Jan Pieńkowski

Homes, 1983. Illustrated by Jan Pieńkowski

The original Puffin edition of
The Very Hungry Caterpillar, 1974.
Illustrated by Eric Carle

The Bad-Tempered Ladybird, 1982.
Illustrated by Eric Carle

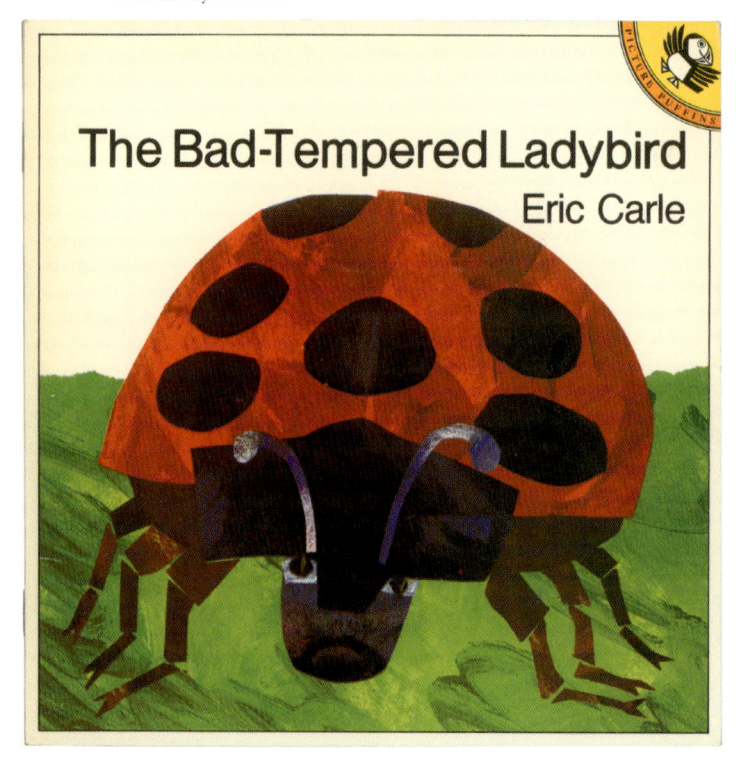

THE VERY HUNGRY CATERPILLAR

by Eric Carle

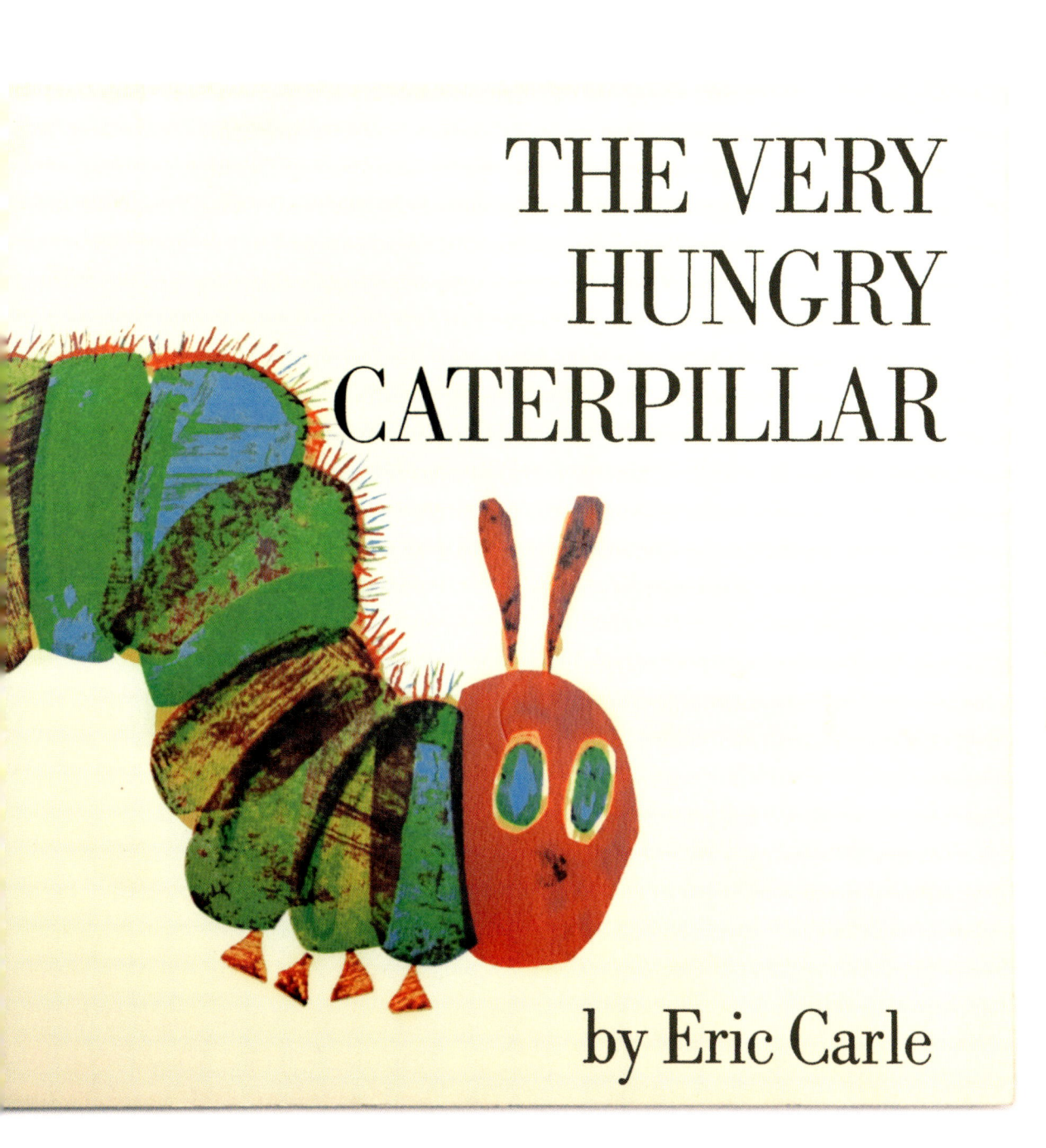

Each Peach Pear Plum, 1989.
Illustrated by Janet Ahlberg

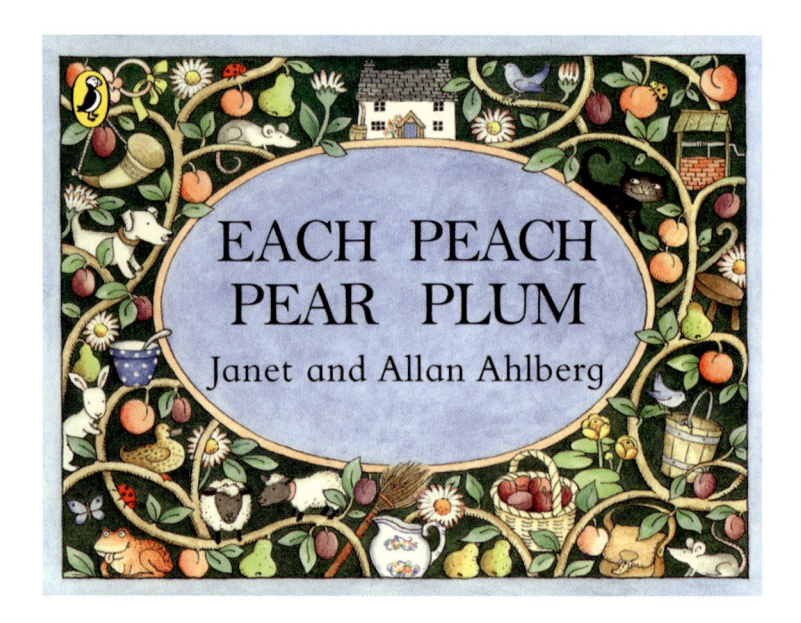

*The Jolly Postman or Other
People's Letters*, 1997.
Illustrated by Janet Ahlberg

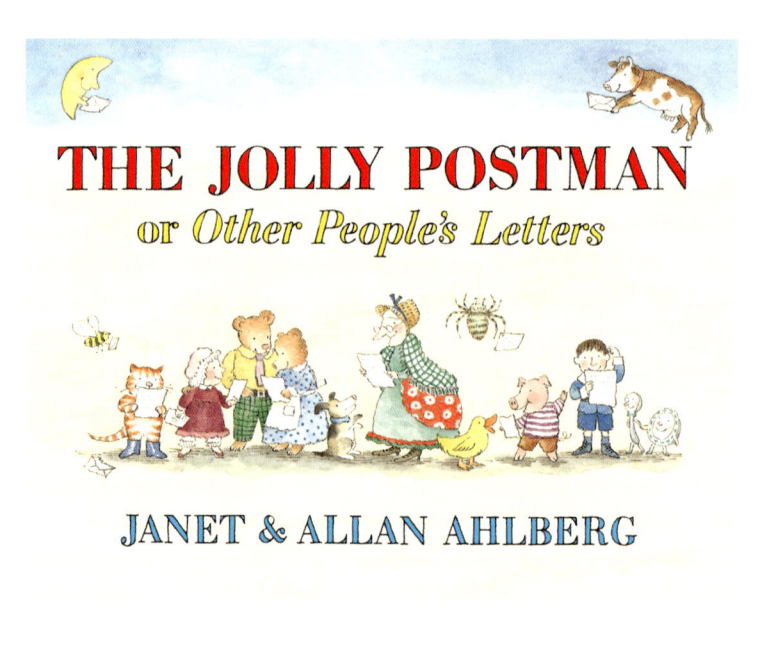

OPPOSITE: *Peepo!*, 1983. Illustrated
by Janet Ahlberg

PEEPO!

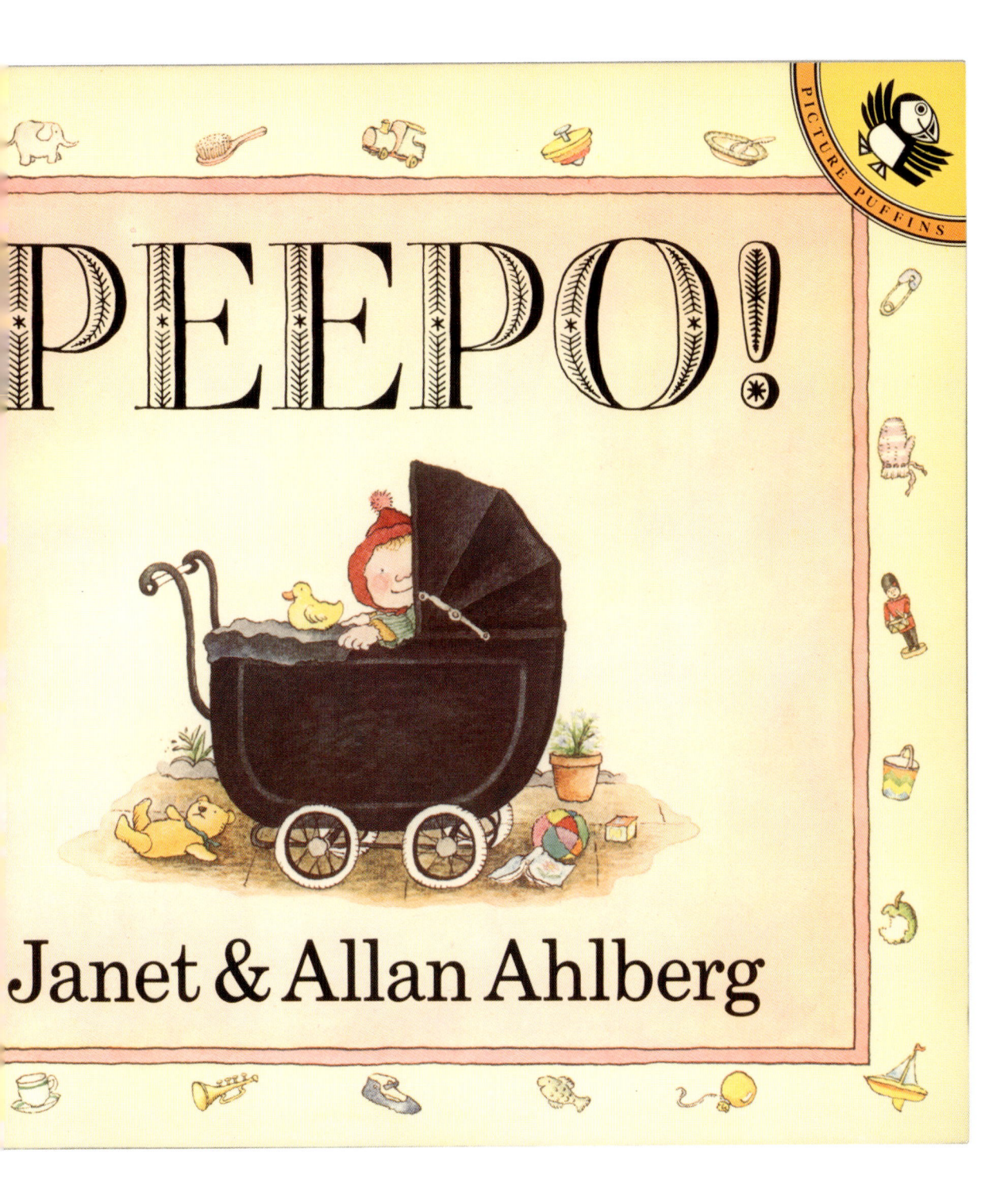

Janet & Allan Ahlberg

IV. Consolidation

The Snowman
RAYMOND BRIGGS

Fungus the Bogeyman
RAYMOND BRIGGS

That was a nice rotten shaddock.*
There's three eggs, drear.. not quite ready yet. Only one really ripe and green.
Daily Midden SLIME SHORTAGE
DEFALCATION AT ARSENAL
FLAKED CORNS
Golden WAXY BITS
GRIPE NITS
GUTTER
These flaked corns are still a bit crisp, Mum – not mouldy yet at all.
shaddock: citrus decumana – grapefruit
DEFALCATION: embezzlement
Chauffeur: one addicted to warmth – a Bogey pervert
The outside lavatory is working again, drear.
I know Mildew, drearest, I must get it blocked.
Close the window, please Mould – There's a good boy. The fresh air is getting in again – I can hardly smell myself.
Bogeyboy found clean
I could hardly smell you when you came in from work yesterday.
Well, you know what it's like Up Top. A good stench wears off in no time. Oh listen! – Sssssh.....
THE FOLLOWING WARMTH WARNING WAS ISSUED BY THE BOGEYOLOGICAL OFFICE AT 0700 BMT TODAY – WARMTH FORCE 8 GUSTING TO FORCE 9...
BOGEY WIRELESS (BBC)
Bogey wireless speaks in a near-whisper and has no music. Bogeymen cannot bear music or noise of any kind.

Hear that, son? Mind you wrap up well or you'll get dry – Here Mildew, look. This milk's not solid yet – it's still white.
I must speak to that milkman.
OK Dad.
BOGEY NEWSPAPERS
All Bogeys are misoneists (those who hate anything new.) Consequently, they do not like "news". They prefer "olds". All the information in Bogey oldspapers is guaranteed to be at least one year old. The older the information the more highly Bogeys value it.
However, Bogeys are usually too apathetic to take an interest in important events, no matter how old, so their oldspapers are filled with "strip cartoons" – (a form of entertainment for the simple-minded) which has a large and devoted following in Bogeydom, and "stick-ups".*
Bogey stick-ups present an interesting contrast to "pin-ups," as Bogeymen like their stick-ups to be pictures of fat, ugly, heavily-clothed, old Bogey women.
* stick-ups: pin-ups. Bogey newspapers are so wet, and Bogey walls so mucky, no pins are needed.
Sully Sloven: (88-93-99) Grey-haired Sully is 84. Her favourite colour is bile green and her favourite pets are her twenty-seven sewer-rats.
LATER
Oooh! What a lovely egg, drear! Really ripe and fuscous* Mmmm, the smell!
Well, I'd better be off, Mildew my love.
Take care, Fungus my darkling. Try not to get your feet dry.
Give us a nice slimy kiss, drear.
* fuscous: brown tinged with black or grey
* Bolbye, Sourheart. Bolbye, Fungus love....
SMELL THIS HOUSE
Bolbye Mould.
I'll glaur* the bar muffs on the Bogeybike, Dad.
* Bolbye: corruption of "Boils be with you"
* glaur: to make muddy
1 polygastric: having many stomachs 2 poephagus: subsisting on grass 3 poleys: hornless (of cattle)

OPPOSITE: *The Snowman*, 1980. Illustrated by Raymond Briggs

Fungus the Bogeyman, 1977. Illustrated by Raymond Briggs (cover and inside spread shown)

THIS PAGE: *Father Christmas*, 1975. Illustrated by Raymond Briggs (cover and inside spread shown)

American imports

A feature of the Picture Puffin list throughout this period was the increasing number of US-originated books. The three shown here are among the most visual and striking.

Donald Crews's *Freight Train* conjures up the immensity of the States with its repetitive, chunky typography and layered, airbrush illustrations, which show the different kinds of scenery an American freight train might pass through on its journey. Crews followed this with two other books *Truck* and *School Bus*. *Freight Train* and *Truck* were Caldecott Honor Books (an American award for illustration similar to the British Kate Greenaway Medal).

THIS PAGE: *Truck*, 1985.
Illustrated by Donald Crews

School Bus, 1985.
Illustrated by Donald Crews

OPPOSITE: *Freight Train*, 1985.
Illustrated by Donald Crews

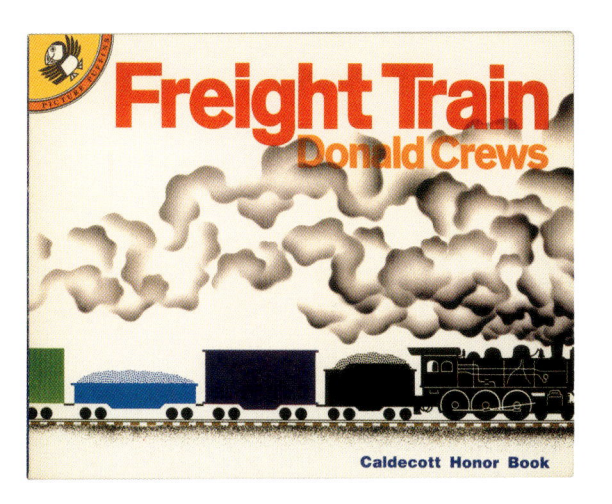

Freight Train
Donald Crews

Caldecott Honor Book

Moving in daylight. Going, going...

Crossing trestles.

Going by cities

Stories for Five-Year-Olds, 1973. Cover illustration by Shirley Hughes

Branding by giftwrap

The problems of correctly highlighting an intended audience are the subject of perennial discussion among children's publishers. At Puffin, Young Puffins started to be discreetly flagged as such in the early 1960s (see pp. 104–6) and Peacocks were created in 1962 to cater more obviously for a teenage market. However, the idea of more overt visual branding for the Puffin sub-series really took hold in the 1980s.

These collections of stories aimed at very specific age groups first appeared in 1976 (this page), but underwent a severe facelift in 1985. The original illustration is lost and everything fights for attention on these covers where the target age group is mentioned no less than fifteen times.

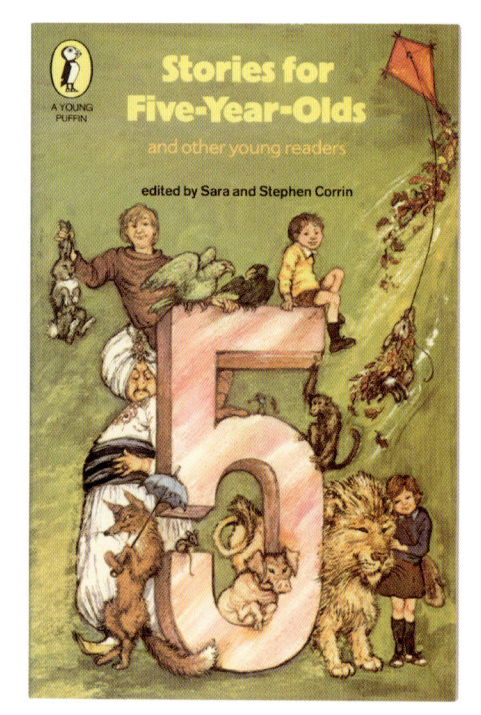

Stories for Six-Year-Olds, 1996. Cover illustration by Steve Cox

OPPOSITE:

Stories for Seven-Year-Olds, 1988. Cover illustration by Shirley Hughes

Stories for Eight-Year-Olds, 1986. Cover illustration by Shirley Hughes

Stories for Nine-Year-Olds, 1987. Cover illustration by Shirley Hughes

Stories for Tens and Overs, 1986. Cover illustration by Shirley Hughes

IV. Consolidation

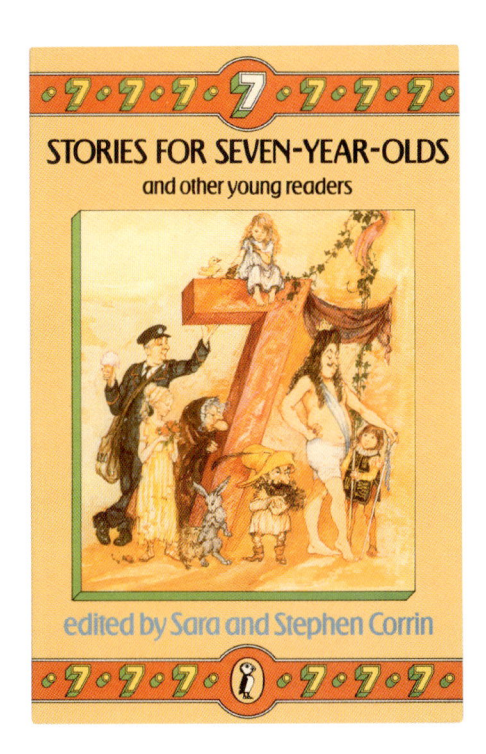

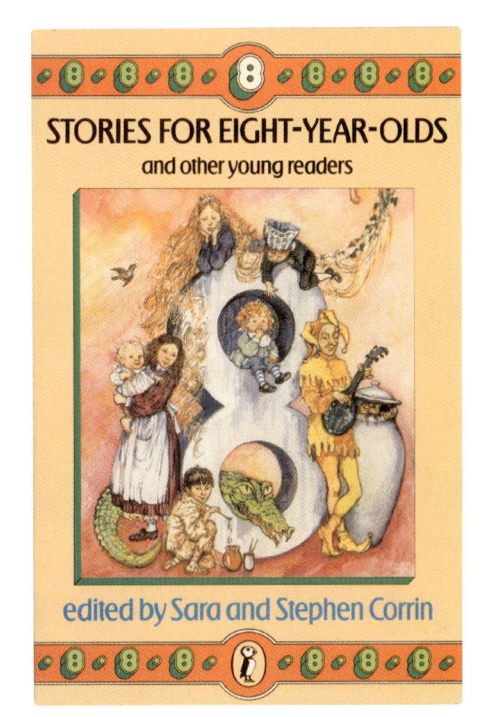

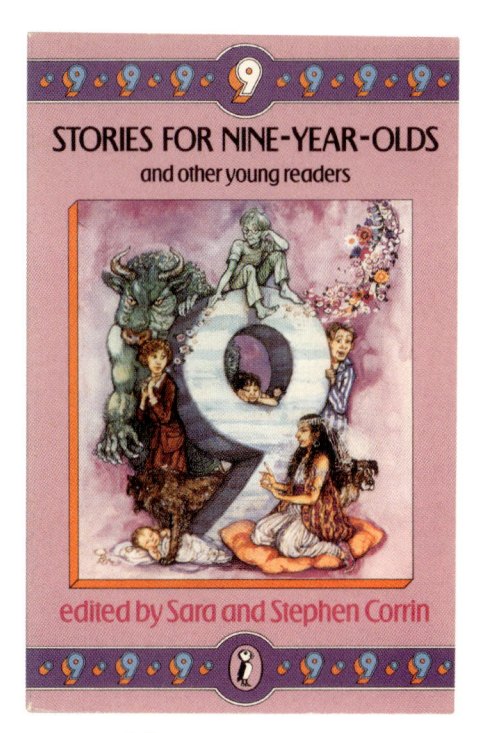

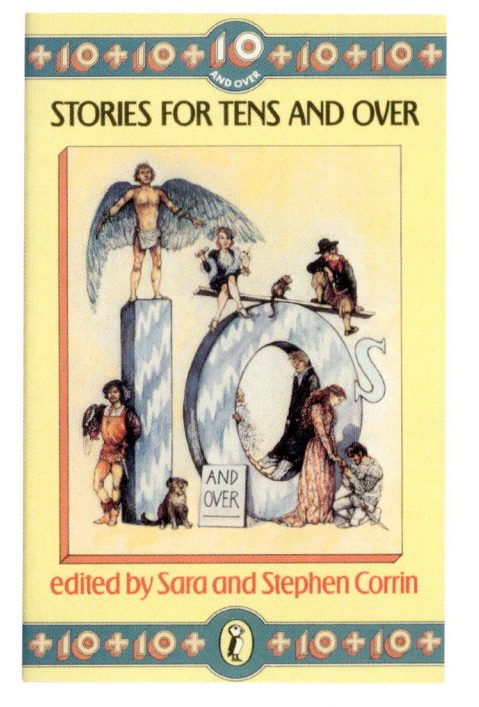

The Young Puffin Book of Crosswords, 1977. Cover illustration by Stuart Kettle

Young Puffins, c.1985

The discreet typographic annotation that had identified Young Puffins since 1961 was abandoned in the mid-1980s when they too underwent a facelift. Thankfully this was not as severe as the giftwrap covers on the previous spread, but one that upsets the visual balance of the covers nonetheless. A comparison of *Albert* from the previous look with *The Little Girl and the Tiny Doll* or *Adventures of the Little Wooden Horse* makes it clear how the additional elements of the boxes across the top and the 'read aloud' flash detracts from the lovely illustrations.

Albert, 1983. Cover illustration by Margaret Gordon

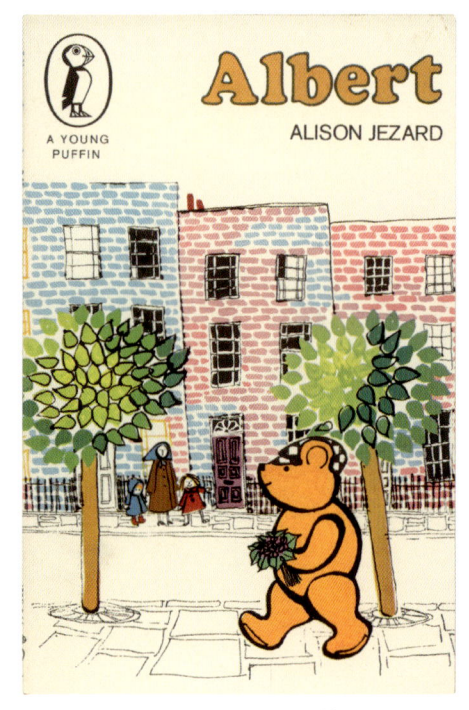

OPPOSITE:
The Young Puffin Book of Crosswords, 1988. Cover illustration by Derek Matthews

The Little Girl and the Tiny Doll, 1979. Cover illustration by Edward Ardizzone

Adventures of Sam Pig, 1985. Cover illustration by Lyndie Wright

Danny Fox, 1985. Cover illustration by Rowan Clifford

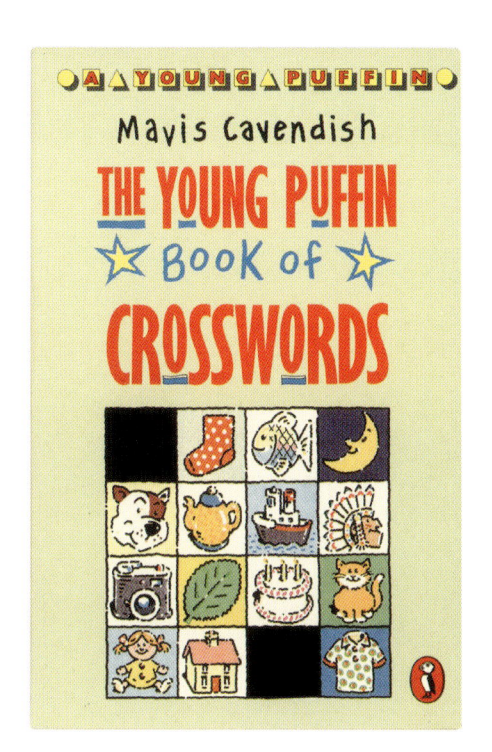

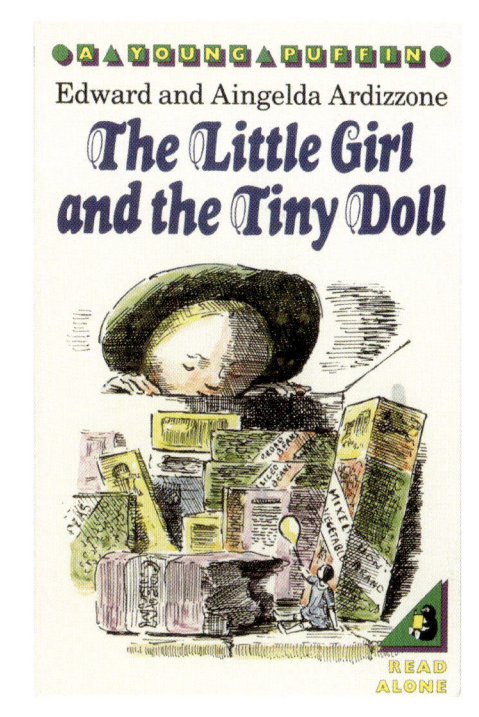

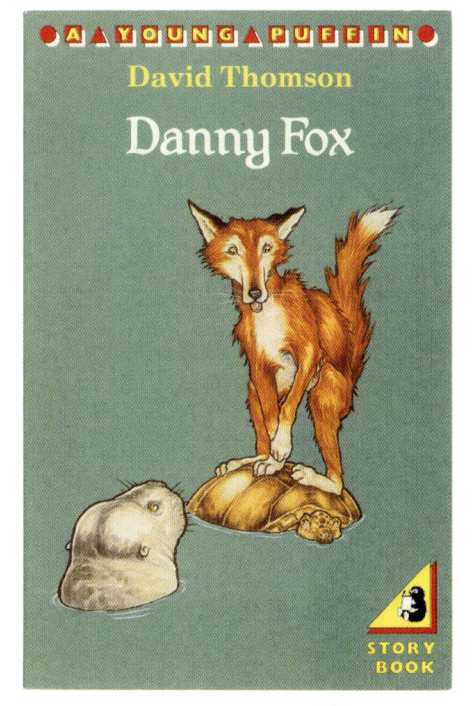

IV. Consolidation

A YOUNG PUFFIN

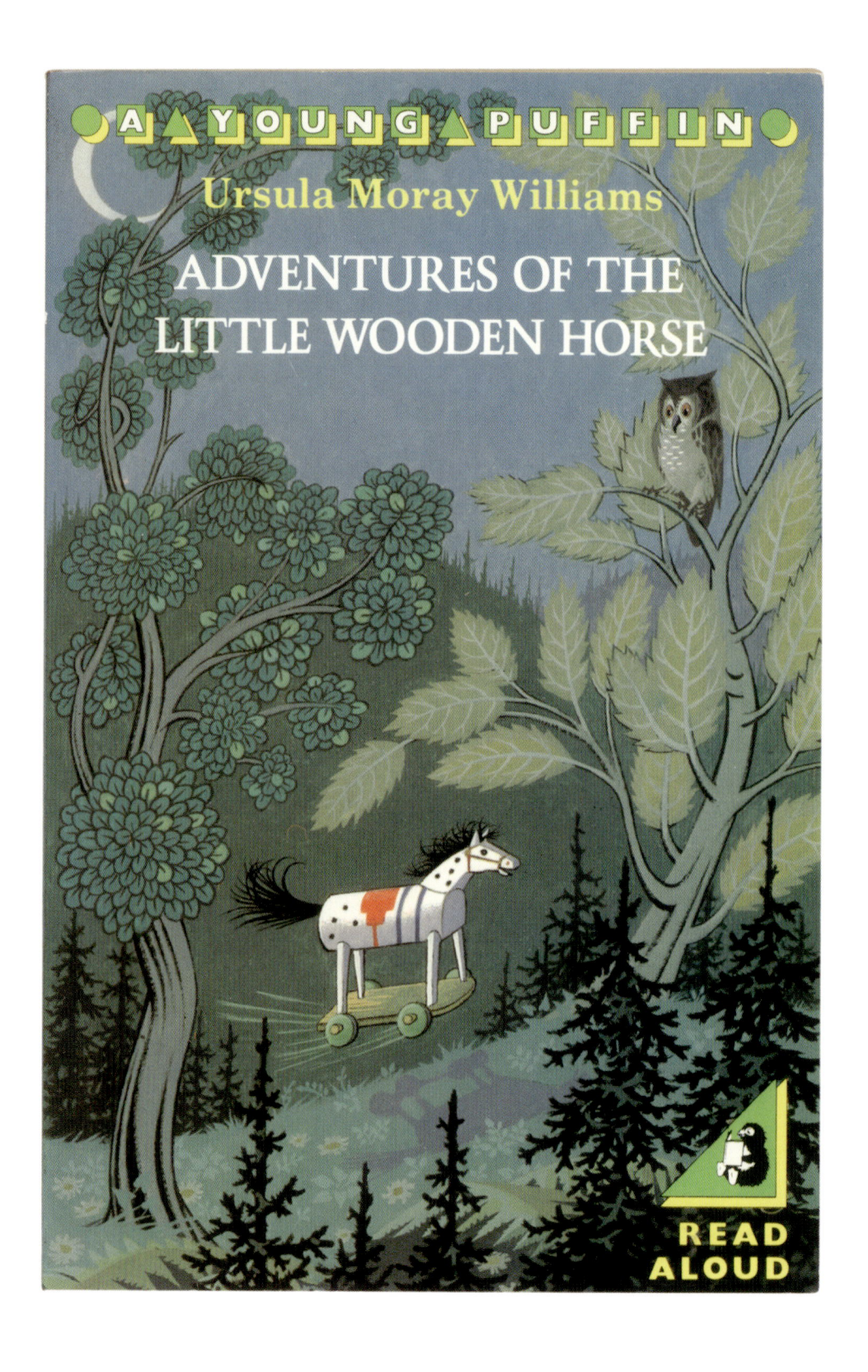

Ursula Moray Williams

ADVENTURES OF THE LITTLE WOODEN HORSE

READ ALOUD

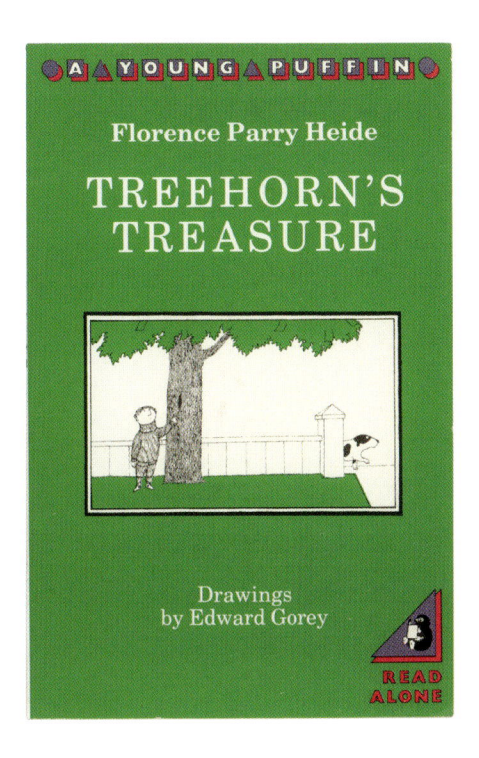

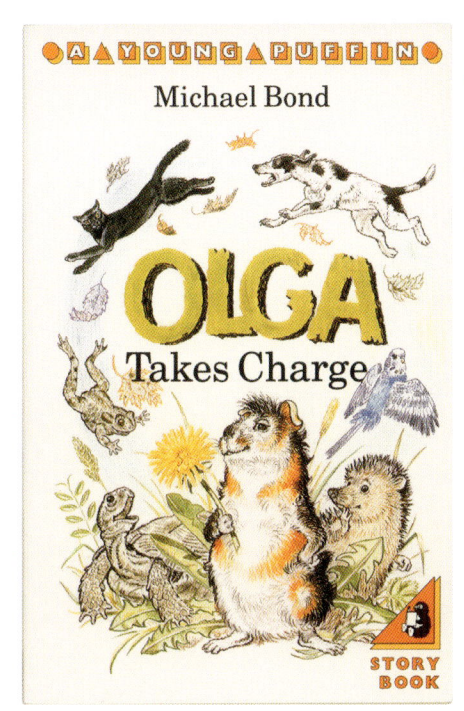

Treehorn's Treasure, 1984.
Cover illustration by
Edward Gorey

Olga Takes Charge, 1987.
Cover illustration by
Hans Helweg

Clever Polly and the Stupid Wolf,
1985. Cover illustration by
Sally Holmes

*The Elephant Party and Other
Stories*, 1985. Cover illustration
by Sally Holmes

OPPOSITE: *Adventures of the Little
Wooden Horse*, 1985. Cover
illustration by Pauline Baynes

IV. Consolidation

ABOVE: *Fifteen*, 1977.

RIGHT: *Fifteen*, 1984.
Cover photograph by
Peter Chadwick

Puffin Plus, 1981, 1988, 1992

Soon after Tony Lacey took over the decision was made to cease publishing teenage titles under the Peacock imprint and to revert to Puffin with the suffix Plus.

Over a period of twelve years or so Puffin Plus had three distinct series styles, all of which can be seen here with *Fifteen*. In 1981 the series was branded discreetly by the repetition of the name across the bottom of the cover and set in American Typewriter. The author and title could change for each cover to suit the subject and image.

By 1988 the look changed, and the series began to be identified by a coloured flash, which also contained genre information, placed in a corner. Again, this is not too distracting.

For the final look the coloured flash is retained and echoed by a vertical stripe down the left-hand side of the front cover. Distracting enough, the author and title information were then set in arbitrarily shaped coloured panels rather like the graphics from teenage music magazines of the mid 1980s.

It is interesting to see the original version of *Fifteen* alongside these three Puffin Plus designs and the various ideas of what a fifteen-year-old looks like.

Fifteen, 1988.
Cover photograph by Helen Pask

Fifteen, 1988.
Cover photograph by Helen Pask

IV. Consolidation

The Wave, 1982.
Cover photograph copyright
T.A.T., 1981

Cloudy Bright, 1985.
Cover photograph by
Peter Greenland

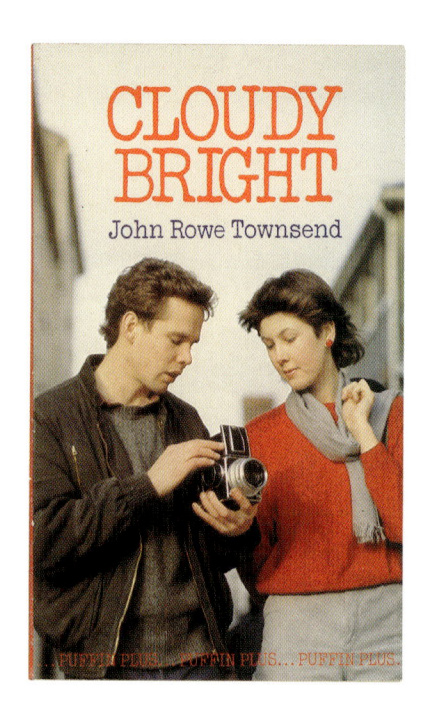

Max in Love, 1987.
Cover illustration by Richard Dunn

Feet and Other Stories, 1984.
Cover illustration by Bert Kitchen

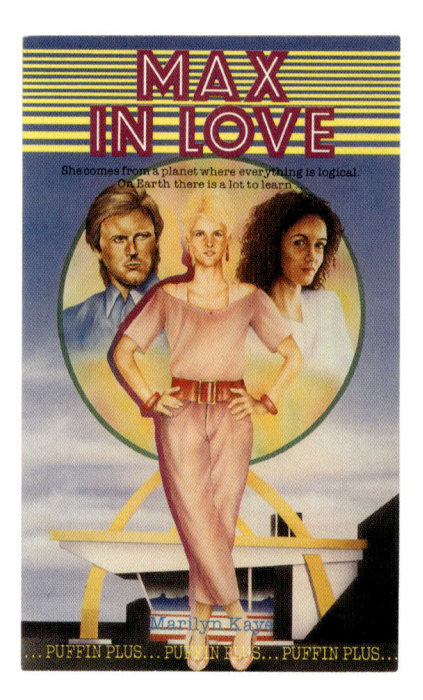

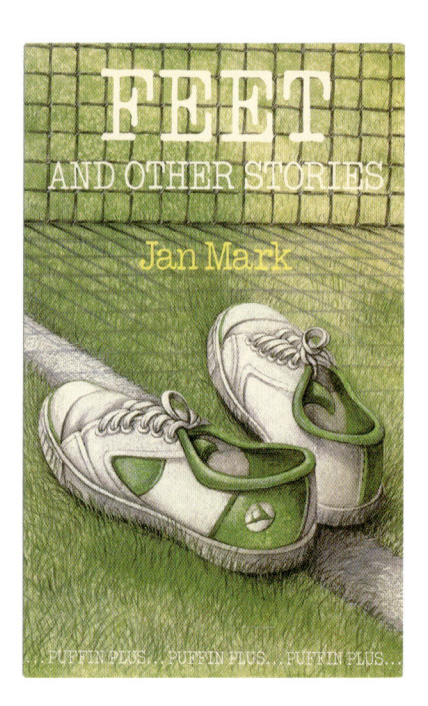

Girls are Powerful, 1991.

To Be a Slave, 1992.
Cover illustration by Alun Hood

Collision Course, 1990.
Cover illustration by Richard Jones

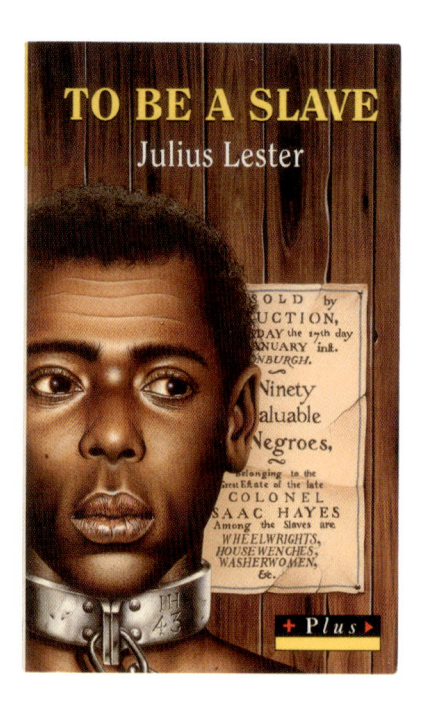

Buddy, 1988.
Cover photographs by Sally Humphreys (copyright BBC Enterprises Ltd) show Wayne Goddard and Roger Daltrey in the BBC School TV production of *Buddy* by Nigel Hinton, produced and directed by Roger Tonge

Dear Jo Plus, 1991.

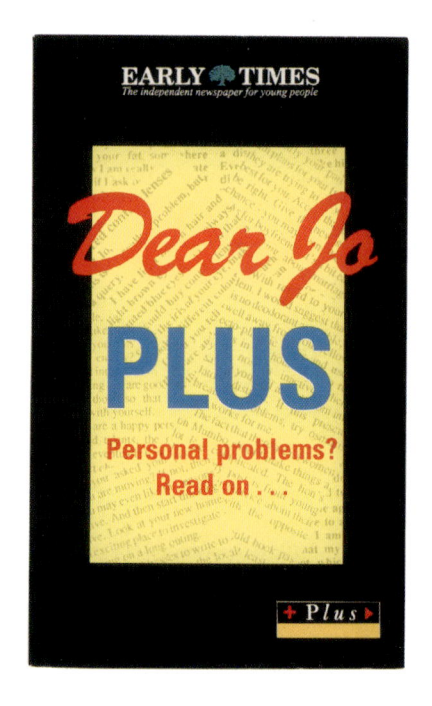

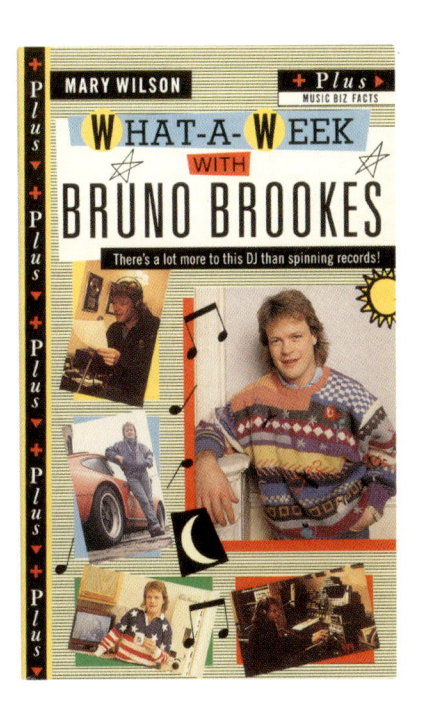

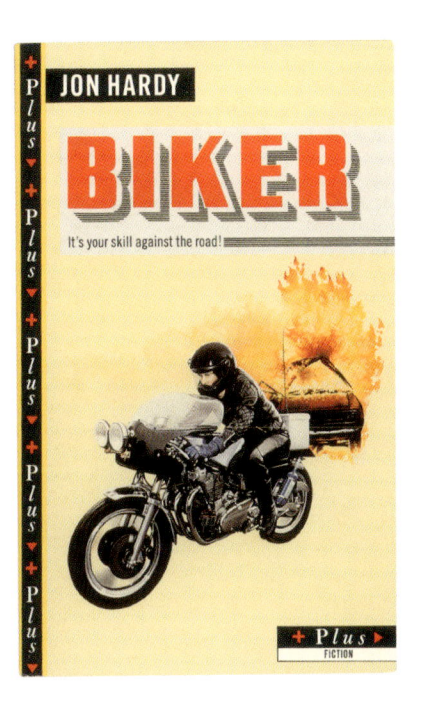

What-a-Week with Bruno Brookes, 1988. Cover photograph by Tony Hutchings

Biker, 1982. Cover illustration by David McAllister

Chartbreak, 1988. Cover photograph by James Walker

See You Thursday, 1988. Cover photograph by John Knights

IV. Consolidation

You Can Do the Cube, 1981.
Cover photograph by Geoff Howes

You Can Do the Cube, 1981

When the Rubik's Cube craze first hit Britain it was clear that there was a marketing opportunity waiting for a publisher who could react quickly. Puffin heard about a schoolboy in Richmond who was drawing diagrams and selling them to his schoolmates, so Tony Lacey went to visit him and his parents. Lacey asked the schoolboy – Patrick Bossert – to draw up a sample set of instructions and, on receipt of these, Lacey immediately offered him a contract with a significant advance.

Because the whole book was produced so quickly, little time was left for the cover shot, so Tony asked a neighbour, glamour photographer Geoff Howes, to help out. The shoot took place one Saturday at Geoff's studio off Oxford Street, with Patrick accompanied by his mother and a friend, and with Geoff's other work out of sight.

The book sold a million copies between its July publication and Christmas that year, and was re-published by Puffin in 2008.

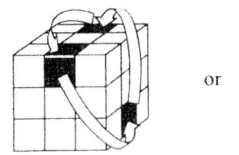

For this situation, use trick D3

For this situation, use trick D4

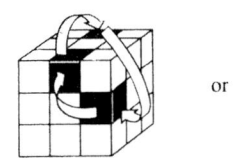

For this situation, use trick D5

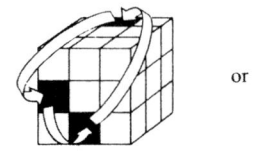

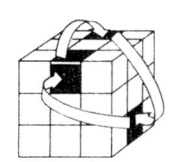

You Can Do the Cube, 1981.
Diagrams by Patrick Bossert

IV. Consolidation

Fighting Fantasy, 1984.
Cover illustration by Duncan Smith

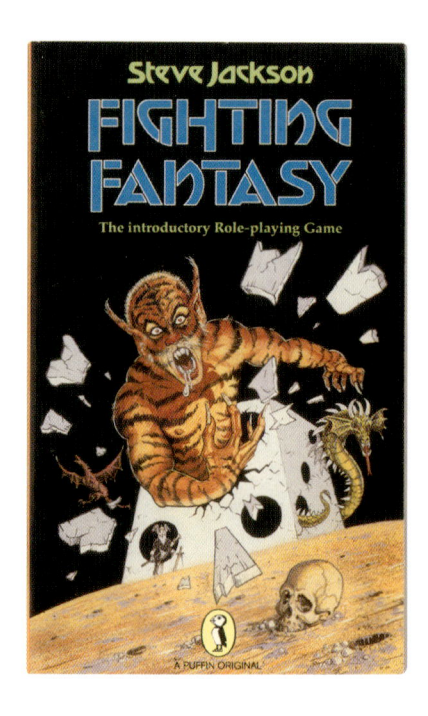

Starship Traveller, 1983.
Cover illustration by
Peter Andrew Jones

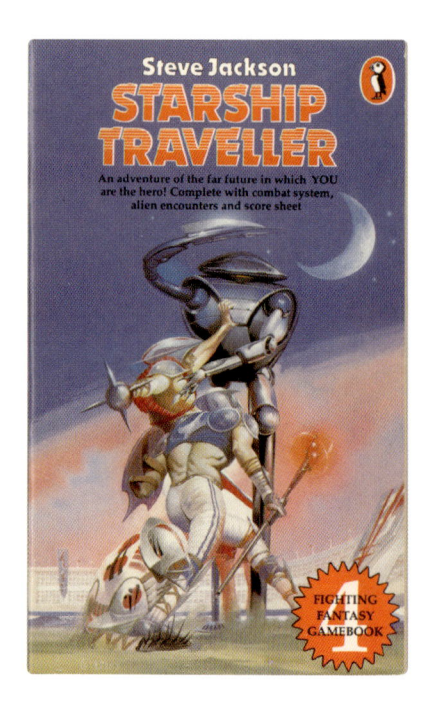

Fighting Fantasy, adventures and role play

The Fighting Fantasy series grew out of the Dungeons and Dragons craze and was the idea of Steve Jackson and Ian Livingstone. Invited by Geraldine Cooke at Penguin to present a synopsis for a book about the fantasy-role-playing hobby, they countered with the idea of a solo role-playing game within a book format: the reader becomes the hero of his own adventure, using the mechanics of jumbled paragraphs and a simple dice-based combat system. When worked up into a manuscript it became *The Warlock of Firetop Mountain* (see pp. 147, 149).

Penguin was unsure of what to make of it and it was some time before it was decided to publish it as a Puffin. Although initial sales were slow, word spread and it was reprinted twenty times in its first year. The first title was jointly written but after that, partly to speed up the process, and partly to avoid a mix of styles, Jackson and Livingstone wrote separately, and other contributors wrote later titles. The covers for the series were illustrated by the leading figures in British fantasy art from the period. Initial covers are free from distraction, but as the series takes off numerical badging starts to appear and is followed later by an incongruous version of the giftwrap branding seen on other Puffin series.

The role-playing idea was extended to other areas too by the moody-looking Starlight Adventures series, which dealt with mystery and romance (see p. 179).

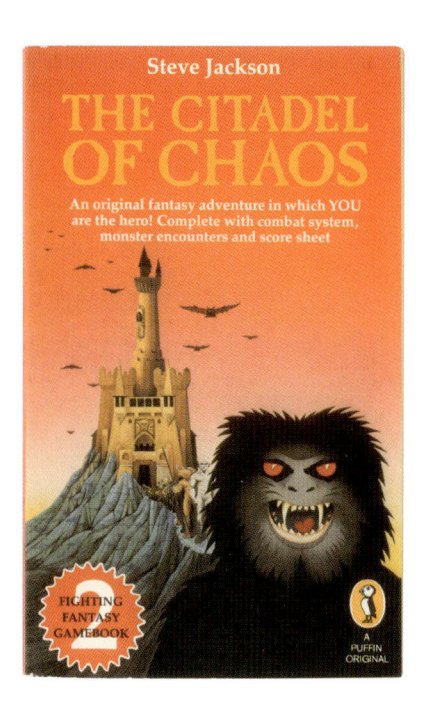

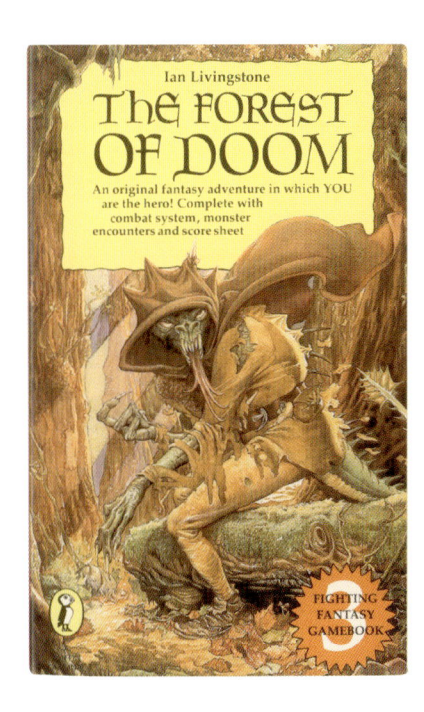

The Citadel of Chaos, 1983. Cover illustration by Emmanuel

The Forest of Doom, 1983. Cover illustration by Iain McCaig

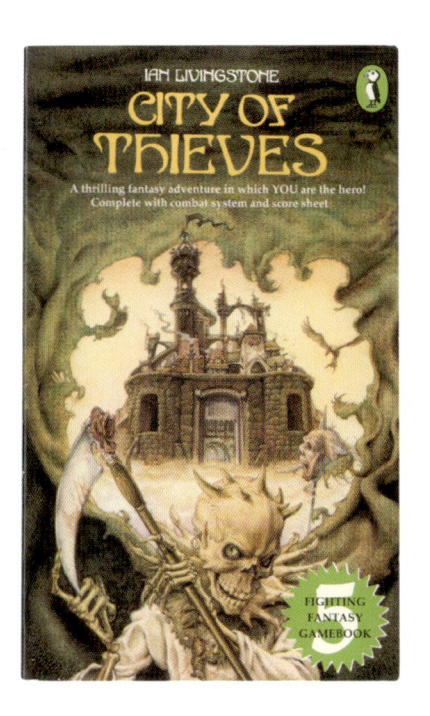

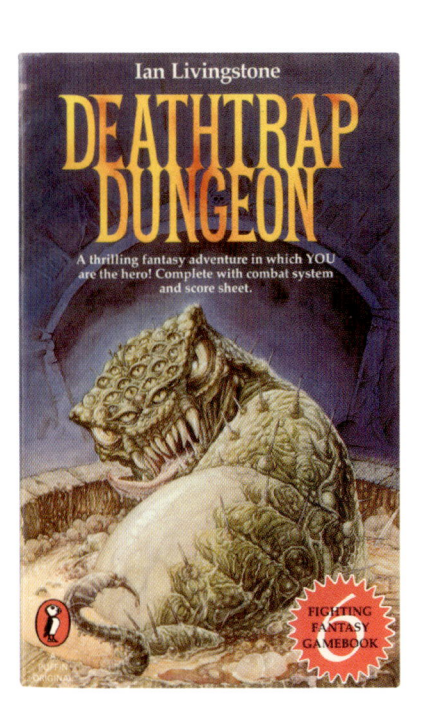

City of Thieves, 1983. Cover illustration by Iain McCaig

Deathtrap Dungeon, 1984. Cover illustration by Iain McCaig

IV. Consolidation

House of Hell, 1984.
Cover illustration by Ian Miller

Space Assassin, 1985.
Cover illustration by
Christos Achilleos

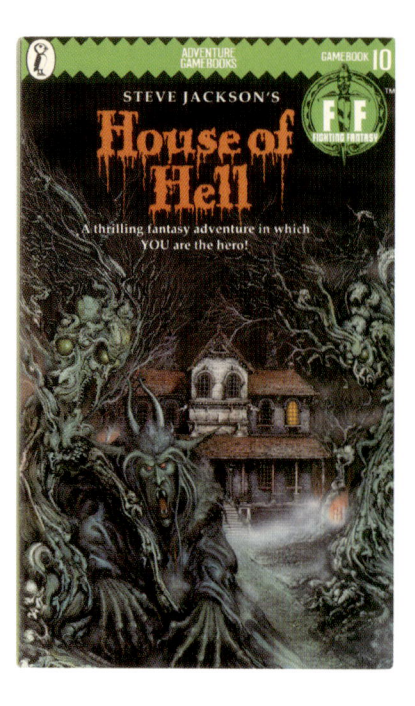

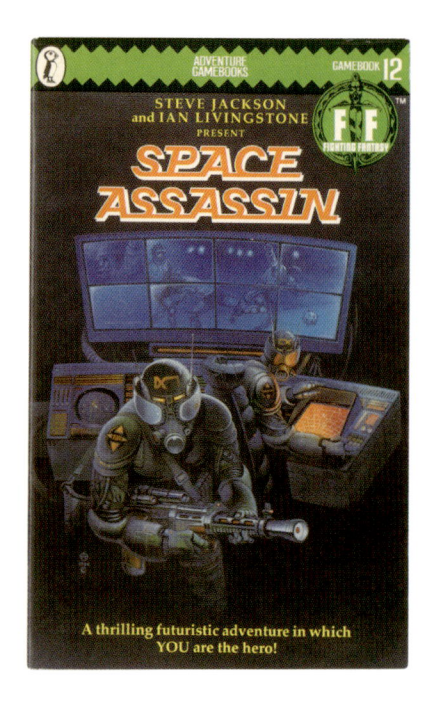

Freeway Fighter, 1985.
Cover illustration by Jim Burns

Temple of Terror, 1985.
Cover illustration by
Christos Achilleos

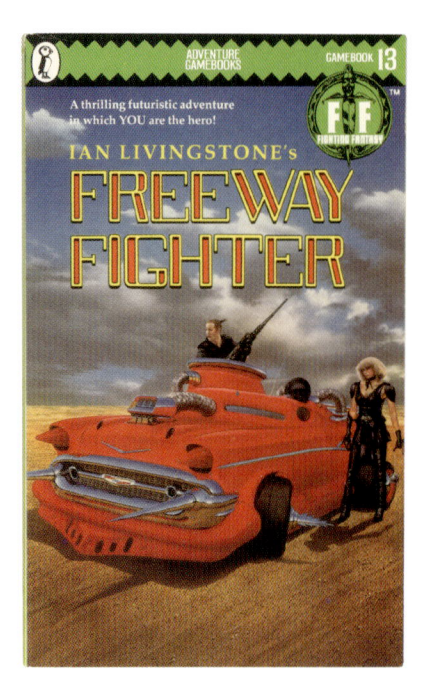

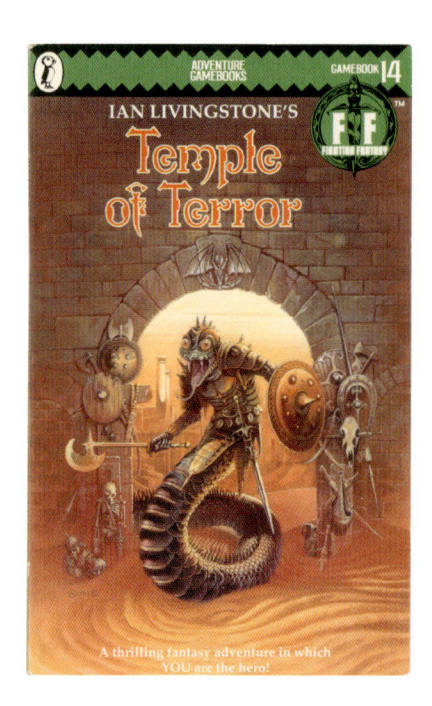

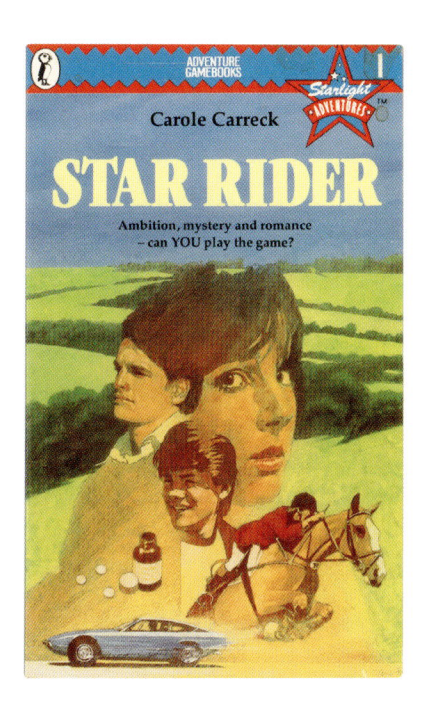

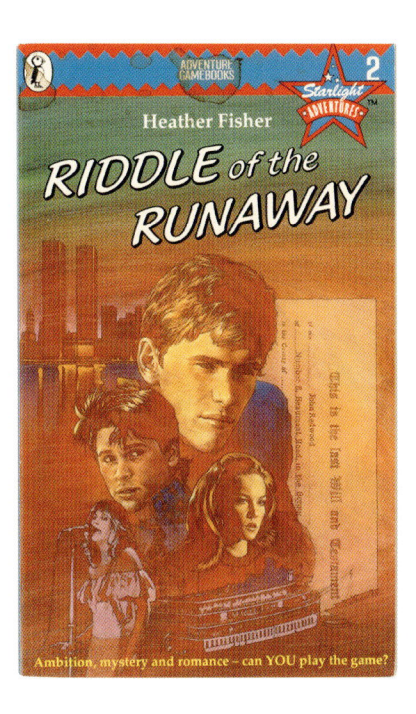

Star Rider, 1985.
Cover illustration by Steve Jones

Riddle of the Runaway, 1985.
Cover illustration by
James Bareham

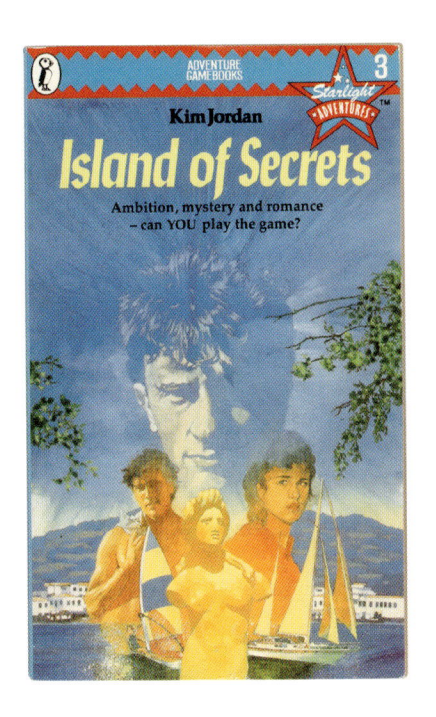

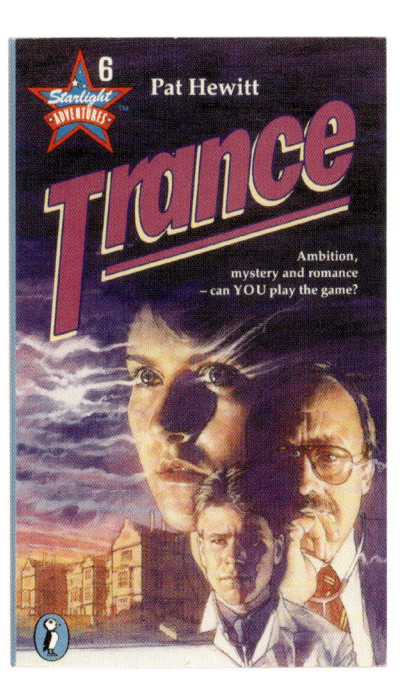

Island of Secrets, 1985.
Cover illustration by Steve Jones

Trance, 1985. Cover illustration by
James Bareham

IV. Consolidation 179

Around the World in Eighty Days, 1990. Cover illustration by Iain McCaig

The Strange Case of Dr Jekyll and Mr Hyde and The Suicide Club, 1985. Cover illustration by Alun Hood

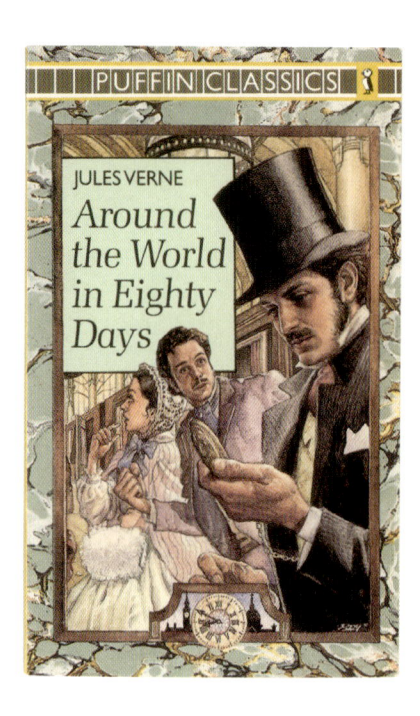

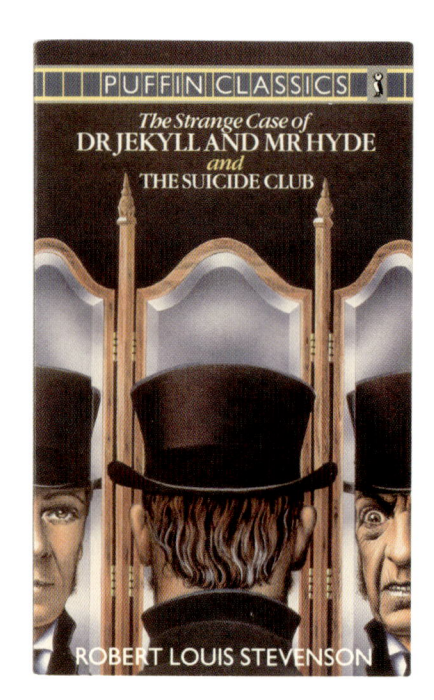

The Adventures of Tom Sawyer, 1982. Cover illustration by Geoff Taylor

What Katy Did, 1982. Cover illustration by Coral Guppy

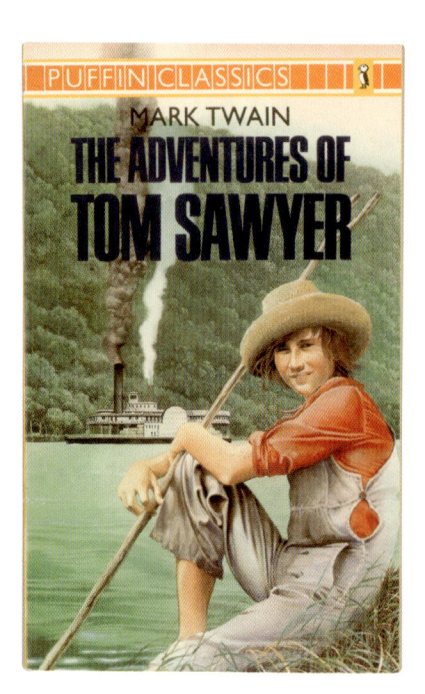

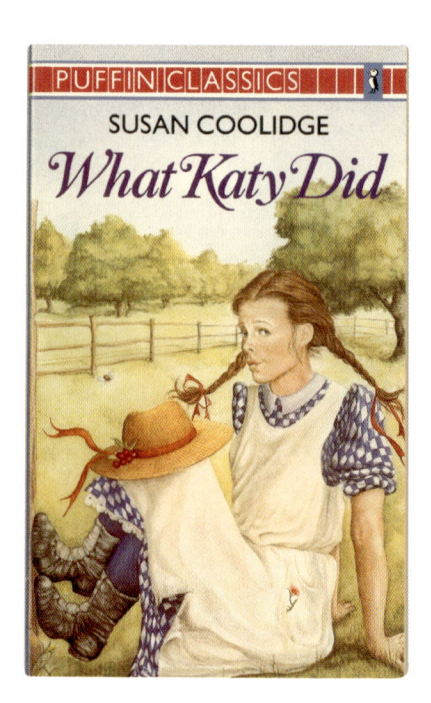

Puffin Classics, 1983: giftwrap

The Puffin Classics series differs from the Penguin version by being more limited in its historical range, but it has the same general principle: namely, to acknowledge and present the very best in established fiction. First appearing in 1983, the original design featured the series name set in Gill Cameo in the giftwrap-branding manner featured on many series at Puffin at this time.

The dilemma with a series look is how to balance the identification of the series with the identification of the individual title. Here the giftwrap is generally coloured to reflect the image, which helps unify the cover, and on the better ones – *Around the World in Eighty Days* and *Dr Jekyll and Mr Hyde* – it is toned down and clearly takes a secondary role.

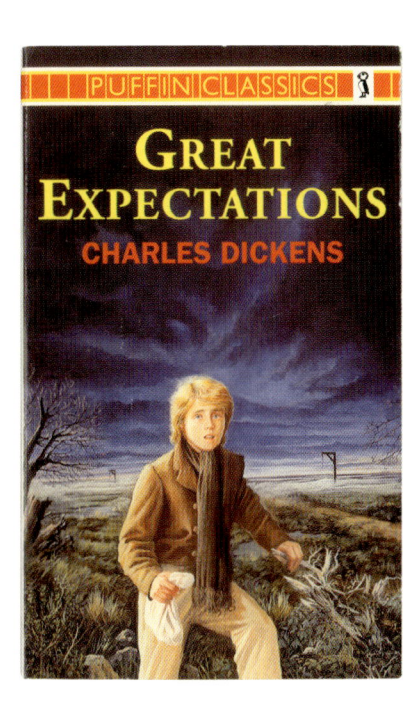

Great Expectations, 1991.
Cover illustration by Mark Viney

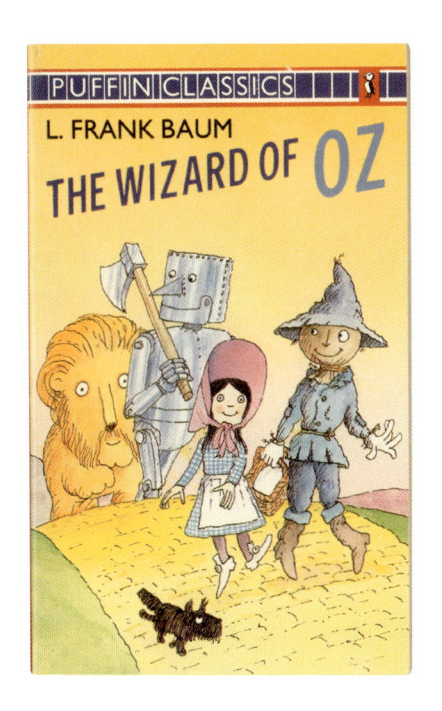

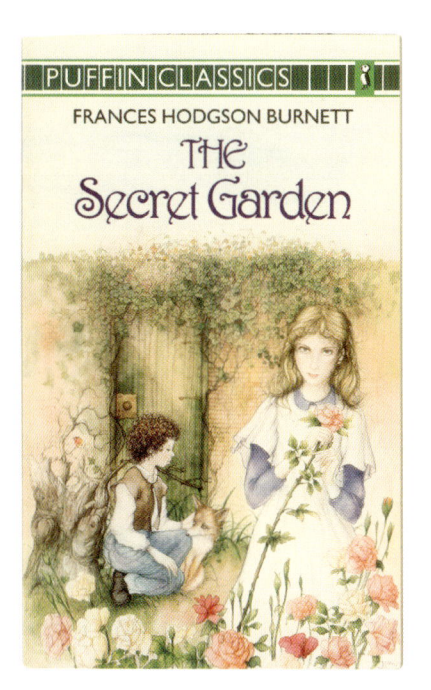

The Wizard of Oz, 1982.
Cover illustration by David McKee

The Secret Garden, 1982.
Cover illustration by Johnny Pau

IV. Consolidation

A Child's Garden of Verses, 1994. Cover illustration by Alan Cracknell

Puffin Classics, 1994: label

For the 1993 redesign Puffin went with a more obviously 'classic' look, and one that had some similarity to the Penguin Classics of 1985–2005, and indeed to several Penguin series from the 1950s. All type and the logo are grouped in a single panel that has the appearance of a label over an image. The image itself is always carefully arranged to work around this label and, on occasion, parts of the image are allowed to appear in front, giving the illusion of three dimensions.

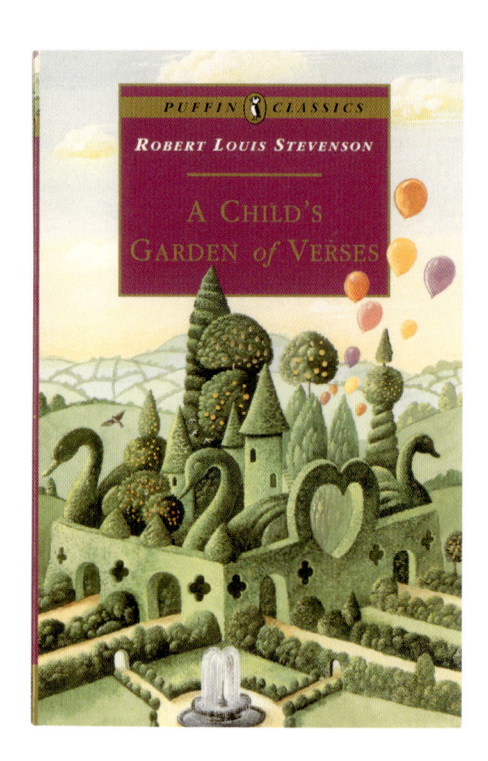

Alice's Adventures in Wonderland, 1994. Cover illustration by James Marsh

Through the Looking Glass, 1994. Cover illustration by James Marsh

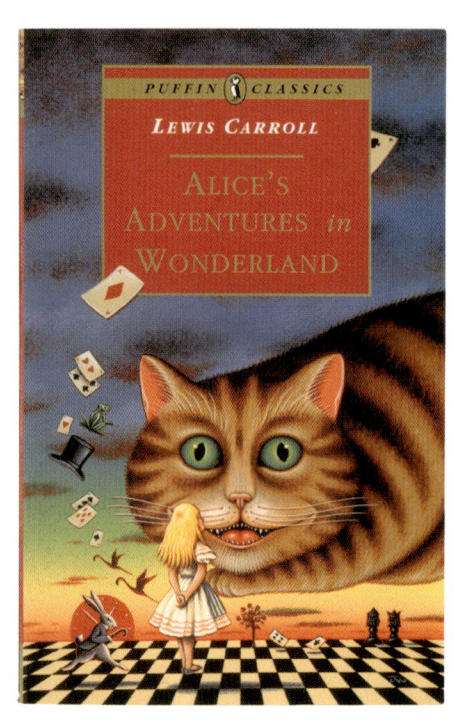

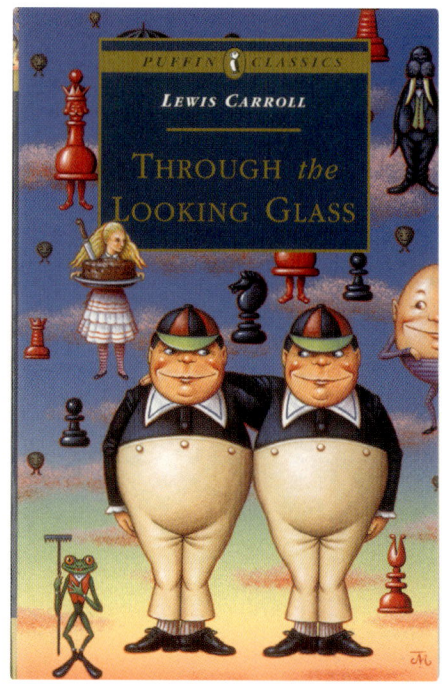

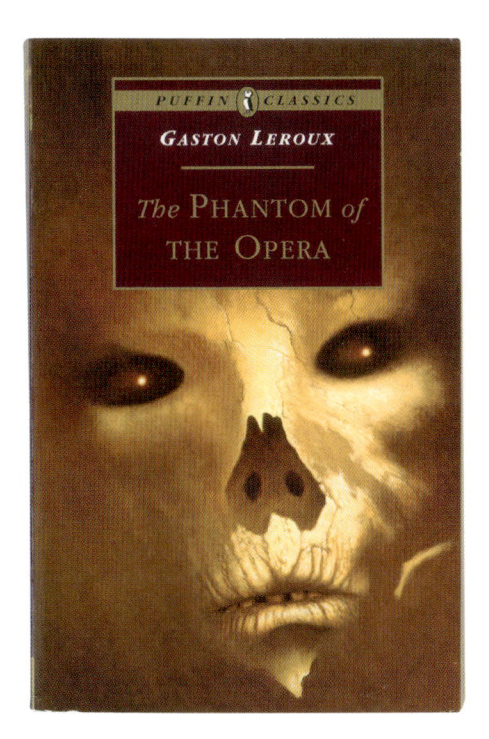

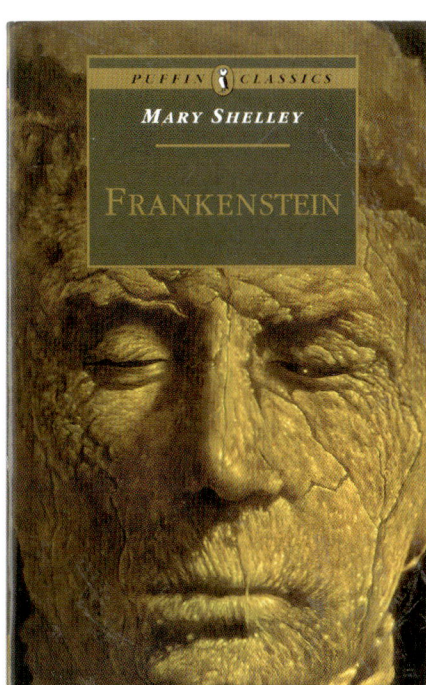

The Phantom of the Opera, 1994.
Cover illustration by
David Bergen

Frankenstein, 1994.
Cover illustration by
David Bergen

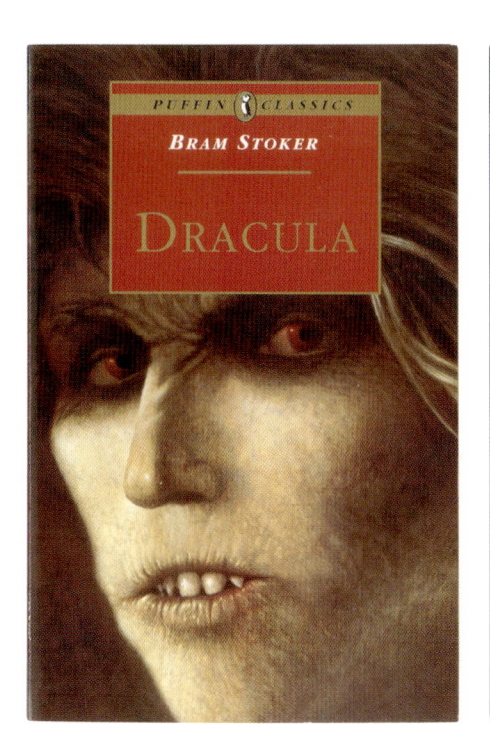

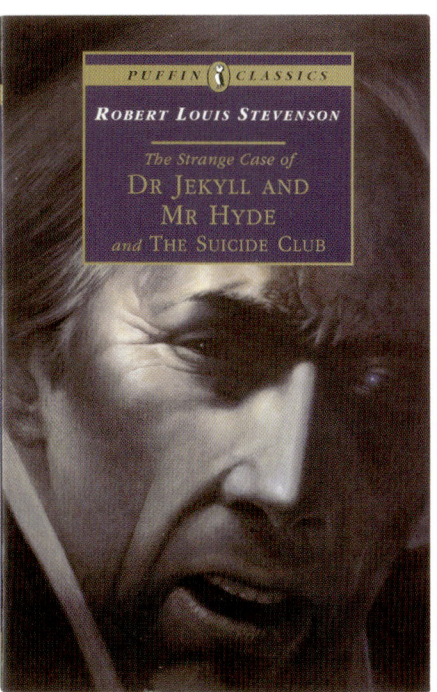

Dracula, 1994.
Cover illustration by
David Bergen

The Strange Case of Dr Jekyll and Mr Hyde and The Suicide Club, 1997. Cover illustration by David Bergen

The Sheep-Pig, 1999.
Cover illustration by Mike Terry

Puffin Modern Classics, 1993: two-tone band

This Puffin Modern Classics design pre-dates the latest Penguin Classics and Puffin Classics design and so, if success is measured by imitation, can be regarded as successful. The series name, author and title are all grouped in the lower four-ninths, giving a clearly defined area for the image, which is only marred by the logo.

However, although very practical and easy to manage as a template, the area given to the type seems unnecessarily large, which is accentuated in two of the examples shown by its strong colour. Typographic details, such as the vertical bar in the series name, look fussy and the letter-spaced title lacks presence.

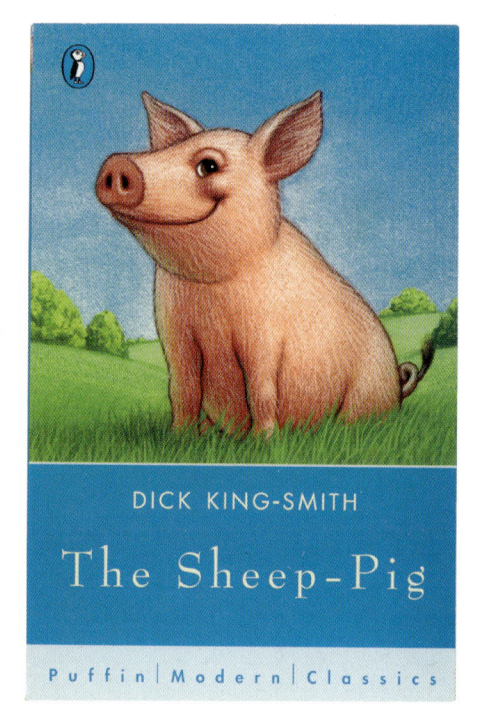

The BFG, 1999.
Cover illustration by Quentin Blake

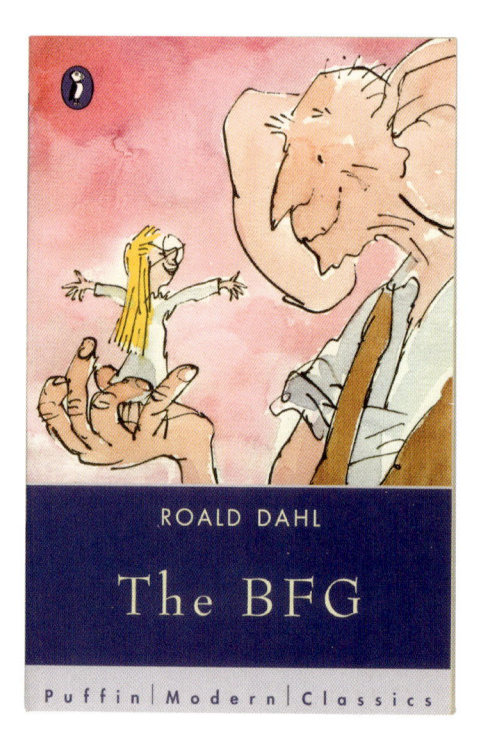

OPPOSITE: *The Haunting*, 1999.
Cover illustration by Mark Preston

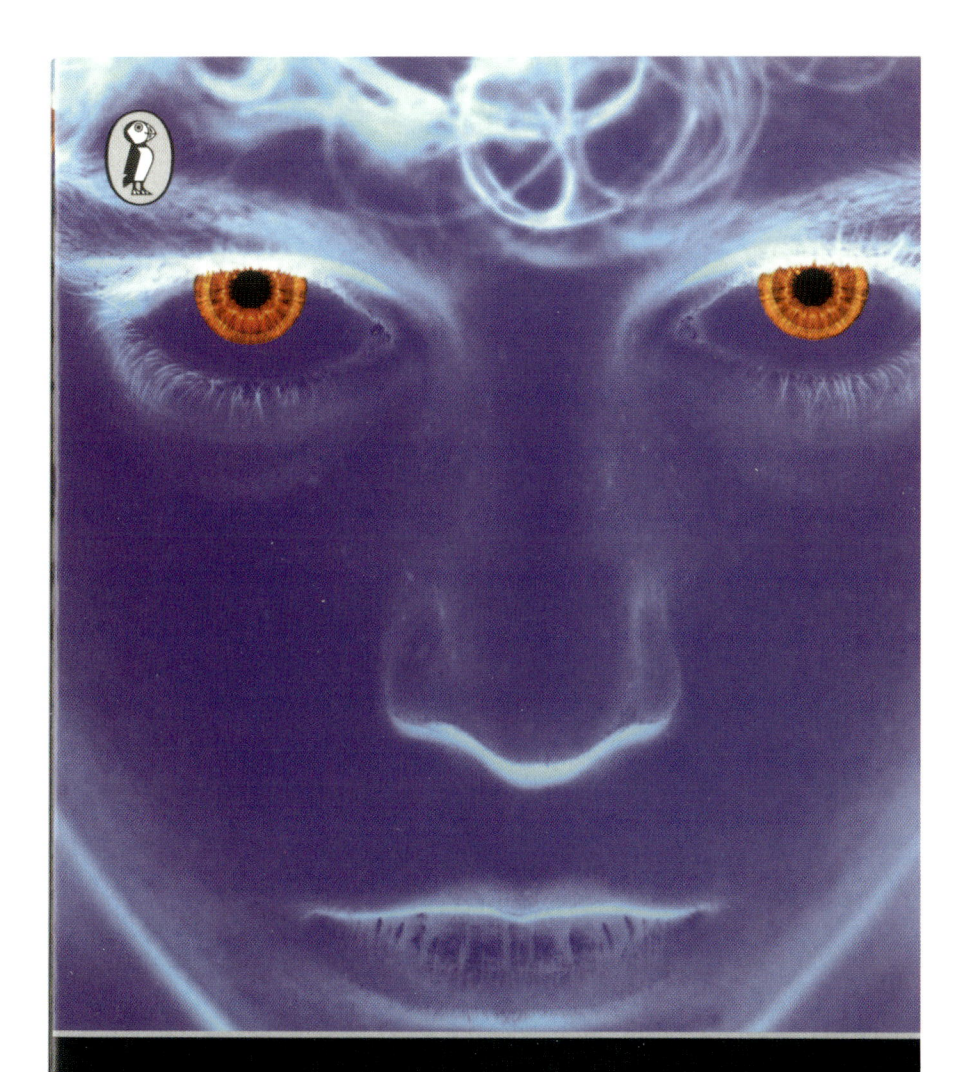

MARGARET MAHY

The Haunting

Puffin | Modern | Classic

ANNE FINE

Madame Doubtfire

Puffin Modern Classics

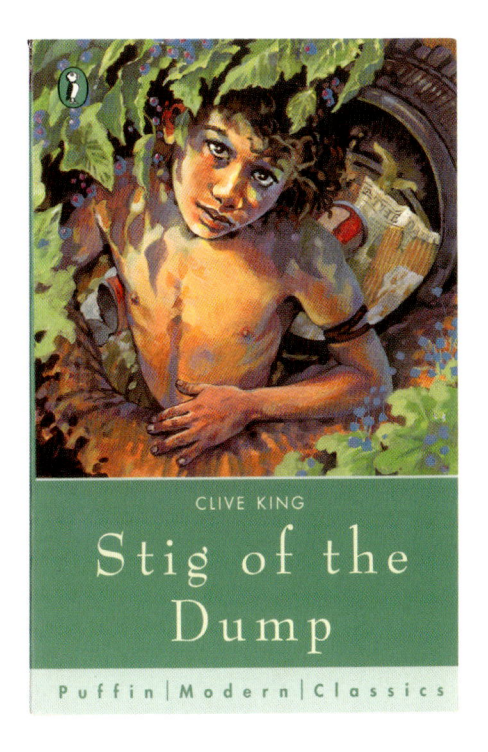

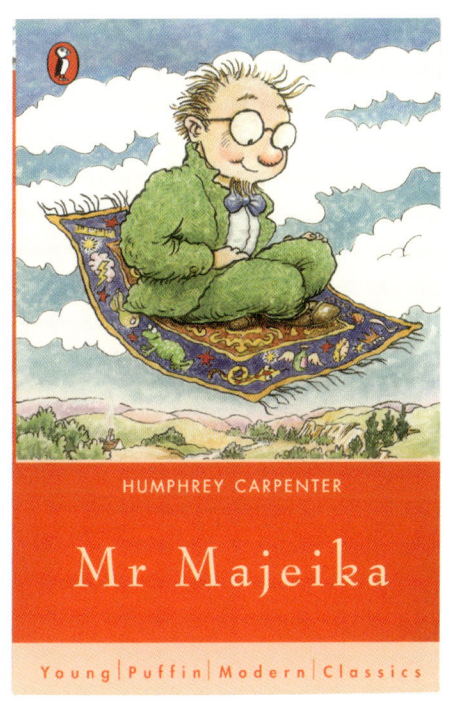

Stig of the Dump, 1993. Cover illustration by Dick van der Maat

Mr Majeika, 1999. Cover illustration by Frank Rodgers

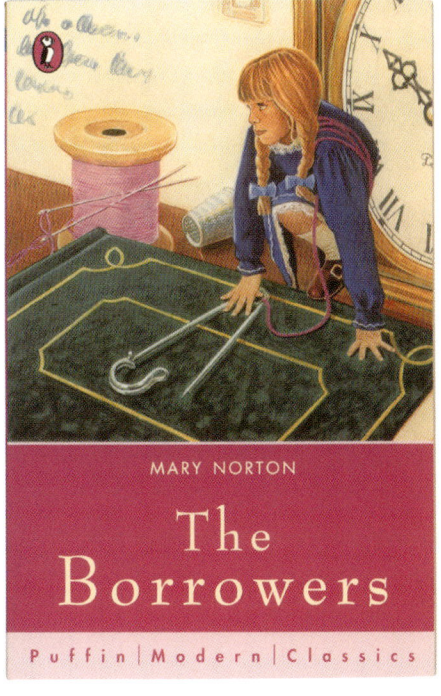

Charlotte's Web, 1993. Cover illustration by Garth Williams

The Borrowers, 1993. Cover illustration by David Kearney

OPPOSITE: *Madame Doubtfire*, 1998. Cover illustration by Stuart Williams

V. Reinvention

rework buildings					car det

Good design is absolutely crucial. A book will only succeed if it looks really good. Children are such sophisticated judges and they are the first to reject a book because of its cover. Format, typeface, blurb and, of course, the cover design play a crucial role in our success. We spend a lot of time talking about how a book should look – as much time as we do thinking about whether we should acquire it in the first place. I love this crucial, creative part of the business. (Francesca Dow, 2009)

Francesca Dow

History and innovation, 1995–

The most recent period of Penguin's history has been characterized partly by another change of editorial premises and partly by restructuring within the company. But it's been characterized too by the significant changes in the market, with the birth of the Internet and online retailing and, of course, online marketing.

In 2001 the company's editorial and art departments moved from Wrights Lane, Kensington, to central London and the former Shell-Mex House, now known as 80 Strand. At the same time, the Harmondsworth site was sold, and the warehouse and distribution of Penguin books was united with Pearson at Central Park in Rugby.

In 1998 at Puffin, Philippa Milnes-Smith succeeded Liz Attenborough as Managing Director. Like her two immediate predecessors, Milnes-Smith continued to develop the legacy of Kaye Webb, nurturing new titles and authors while developing existing successes, and making brands out of authors. Between 1995 and 1999 Puffin had grown strongly, but sales of the backlist fell away sharply the following year. The imprint re-focused efforts on its frontlist and in 2001, despite falling sales throughout the sector, Puffin returned to the number one position.

An important acquisition during Milnes-Smith's time was that of Angelina Ballerina, a tie-in with the CITV animated series, which first aired in 2001. The publishing went on to become an international success and still sells extremely well today. For the fiction list, Eoin Colfer, an unknown young Irish author with the first of his now bestselling Artemis Fowl series, was won by Puffin in a hotly contested auction.

Anthony Forbes Watson had taken over as Penguin's Chief Executive in

PREVIOUS PAGE: Lauren Child's original collaged artwork for pp. 30–1 of *Who Wants to be a Poodle – I Don't*, 2009

1996 and he brought in Helen Fraser from Reed to run the publishing. With her new team she set about rekindling the excitement of Penguin's heyday for a contemporary market. John Makinson became Chairman of the Penguin Group in 2001, and CEO in 2002. When Milnes-Smith left in 2001 to become Managing Director at LAW (Lucas Alexander Whitley) Fraser hired Francesca Dow as Puffin's new Managing Director. Dow began her publishing career at Collins before joining Orchard Books, where she became Editorial Director in 1993 and published the young Lauren Child, who went on to win the prestigious Kate Greenaway Medal. Coming to Puffin (in 2002) was, Dow said, in a way like coming home, 'having been brought up on Puffin books'. But at the same time, with backlist sales dropping and a small frontlist, her mission was to re-invigorate the division. 'Puffin's list is something of a curate's egg – good in parts. Puffin's treasure trove of a backlist feels neglected and we need some more new authors. Today's most talented authors should be Puffin authors,' said Dow when she started her role.

Since taking up the position Dow has focused with her team on acquiring new authors for the fiction list, and building them into today's top-selling brands – authors such as Charlie Higson, Cathy Cassidy, Meg Rosoff, Rick Riordan and Jeff Kinney – and on modernizing the picture-book list with Lauren Child's extraordinarily successful Charlie and Lola series (a tie-in with the award-winning BBC series created by Tiger Aspect), Ian Whybrow's Harry and the Dinosaurs, Ed Vere, Jan Pieńkowski and Jeanne Willis. Developing the legacy of Kaye Webb, Dow and her team have also been conscious of nurturing the strong evergreen backlist authors who are so central to Puffin's profile and sales – Eric Carle with his *The Very Hungry Caterpillar*, Raymond Briggs's *The Snowman*, Lynley Dodd with Hairy Maclary, and Janet and Allan Ahlberg's picture-book classics. Both Puffin Classics and Puffin Modern Classics have been relaunched, and Roald Dahl's books, with new branding and strong marketing, continue to underpin an extremely strong list. Sales of Puffin books have grown significantly since Dow's arrival, as has market share and Puffin's profile. Puffin is now once again the publisher many authors and agents turn to – the golden list in a highly competitive market.

A belief in the importance of good design sits absolutely at the heart of Dow's publishing philosophy. Dow hired Anna Billson as Puffin's Art Director soon after arriving in 2002 and Billson has played a key role in giving the Puffin list a design identity. 'Children are increasingly bombarded

Anna Billson

by more and more visual imagery and this, coupled with the rise of authors as brands in children's publishing, means we have had to be more focused on creating a distinct brand look for each author. This look must be instantly recognizable and tap into the right audience and excite them, but it also needs updating and refreshing regularly to keep the look vibrant and ahead of the competition. It is about building on what we have, breaking boundaries, to create tomorrow,' says Billson.

Puffin believes in the importance of marketing itself to its young consumers and the role good design plays in this. Everyone at Puffin understands that nothing will sell a book more effectively – or less if it is a bad one – than its cover. Design connects all parts of the business: Puffin's marketing materials link to the books, whether this is websites, catalogues, blogs or printed matter, such as postcards and bookmarks. Kaye Webb's remarkable legacy lives on in this way – she understood the value of strong design that links books and marketing better than most. With the Internet age and the birth of digital books, the challenge will be to create print books that are truly irresistible, while continuing to innovate in design for the new digital age.

Since Webb's editorship, the link between Puffin and its readers has always been understood as critical to success. The Puffin Club and associated magazine *Puffin Post* (which closed in 1982) were key elements of that, and today putting the reader at the very heart of each of Puffin's marketing campaigns, and creating links between Puffin authors and their fans, is central to their strategy. In 2008 the Puffin Club was re-launched by The Book People with support from Puffin. Available bimonthly for a subscription, readers can choose a free book with each issue. Following Webb's model, this very much echoes her aim of creating life-long readers. The Book People has also taken over management of the Puffin Book Club, which is Puffin's direct route into schools, where millions of children every term can interact with Puffin books and the Puffin brand.

Puffin is confident of the future. 'Penguin and Puffin are companies that innovate and lead the way – you have only to look at our histories to see that. And as long as creativity and innovation remain right at the heart of the business, Puffin will continue to excite and to succeed,' says Dow.

The trick, which Puffin has managed to pull off for seventy years now, is to know how to reach the spectrum of buyers that they sell to, and to offer the best of children's literature presented in the most appealing way.

OPPOSITE: *The Princess and the Pea*, 2006. Cover illustration by Lauren Child; photography by Polly Borland

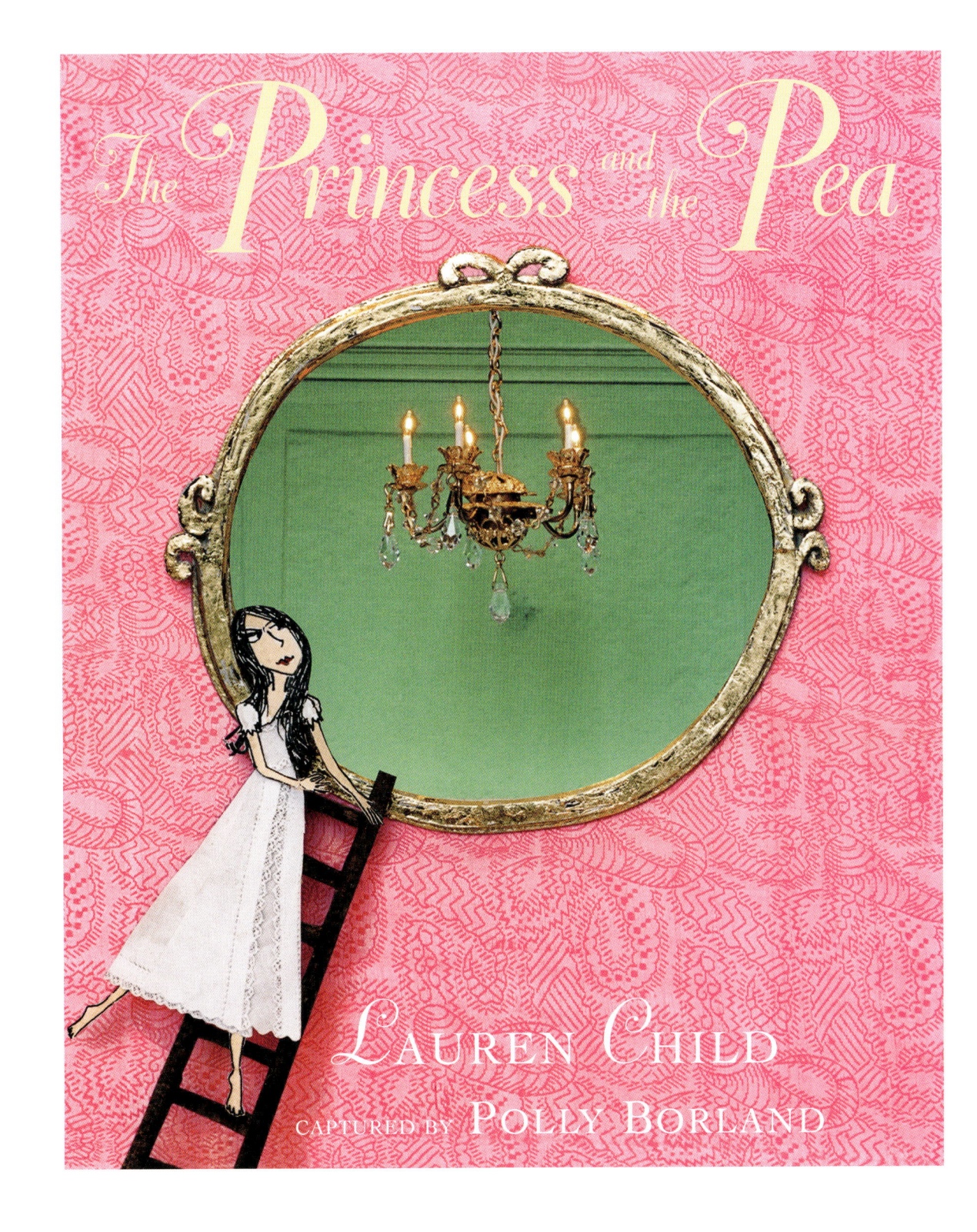

The Princess and the Pea

Lauren Child
captured by Polly Borland

Ruby, 1995. Cover illustration by Caroline Birch

Summer of My German Soldier, 1994. Cover illustration by Charles Lilly

Identity through variety

Puffin Story Books, like Penguin, began as an imprint publishing existing works in paperback. A key to the success of the imprint has been in maintaining a high-quality list of published titles and ensuring that the list contains a balance of established and new authors, and titles that appeal to a range of readers, from the very young to teenagers. Approaches to the design of covers for these titles has varied from the ninth book onwards (see p. 68) and that practice continues.

The covers shown from the early part of the period under review seem to reflect some uncertainty about how they should be marketed. Those that follow are much more resolved: the typography and images seem relaxed, and there appears to be a confidence that the title and its reputation obviates the need for excess or overstatement.

Lionboy (see p. 196) illustrates something of a contemporary tendency – across all sectors of publishing – to try to make both text and image work in equal measure. The cover is really two designs combined: one with lettering that uses the 'O' as a lion's face, the other pictorial with its pouncing lions. As it is, neither truly owns the cover.

A few books appear in more than one Puffin edition, such as *The Sheep-Pig*, which also exists as a Modern Classic with a different cover design (albeit with the same illustration) and for sale at a different price.

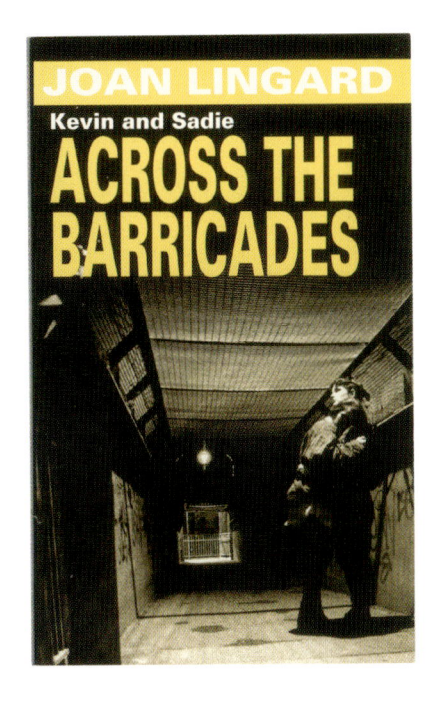

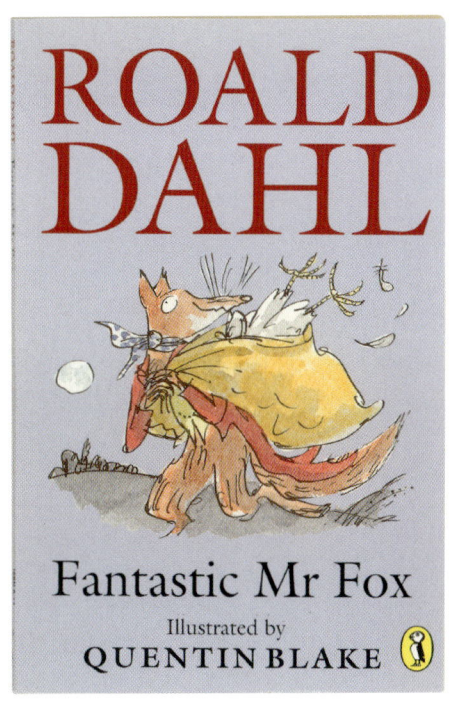

Across the Barricades, 1995.
Cover illustration by Richard Ivey

Fantastic Mr Fox, 1996.
Cover illustration by Quentin Blake

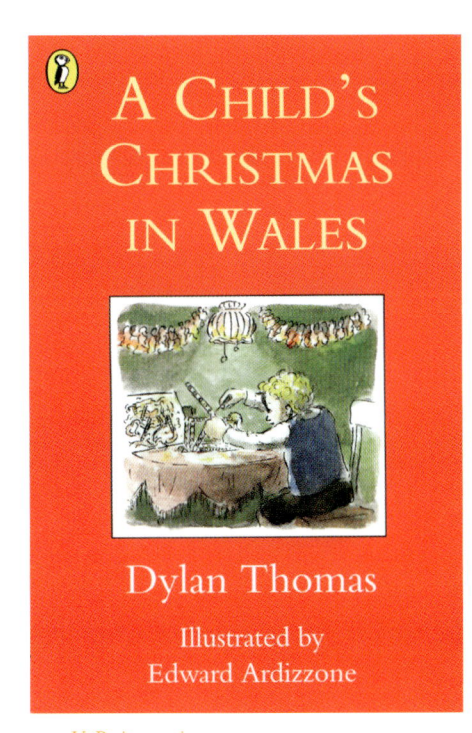

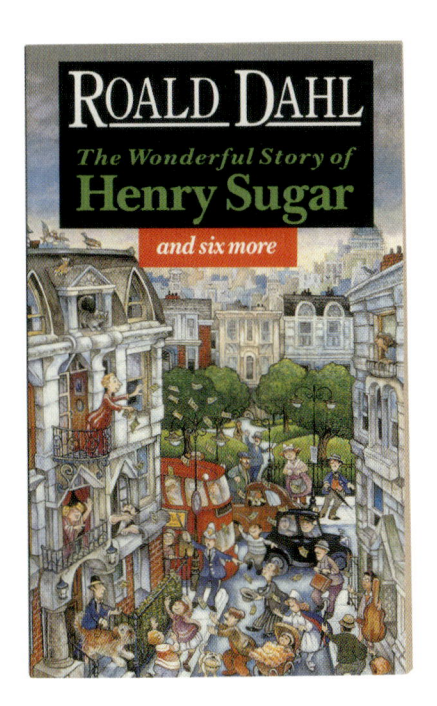

A Child's Christmas in Wales, 1996.
Cover illustration by
Edward Ardizzone

The Wonderful Story of Henry Sugar and Six More, 1995. Cover illustration by Bill Bell

FOLLOWING PAGES:
Lionboy, 2003. Cover illustration by Fred Van Deelan

Skin and Other Stories, 2001.
Cover illustration by
Bill Gregory

V. Reinvention

He can speak Cat. But can he smell danger?

LION BOY

'LIONBOY DESERVES A ROAR OF APPROVAL' – *Observer*

ZIZOU CORDER

ROALD DAHL

SKIN
AND OTHER STORIES

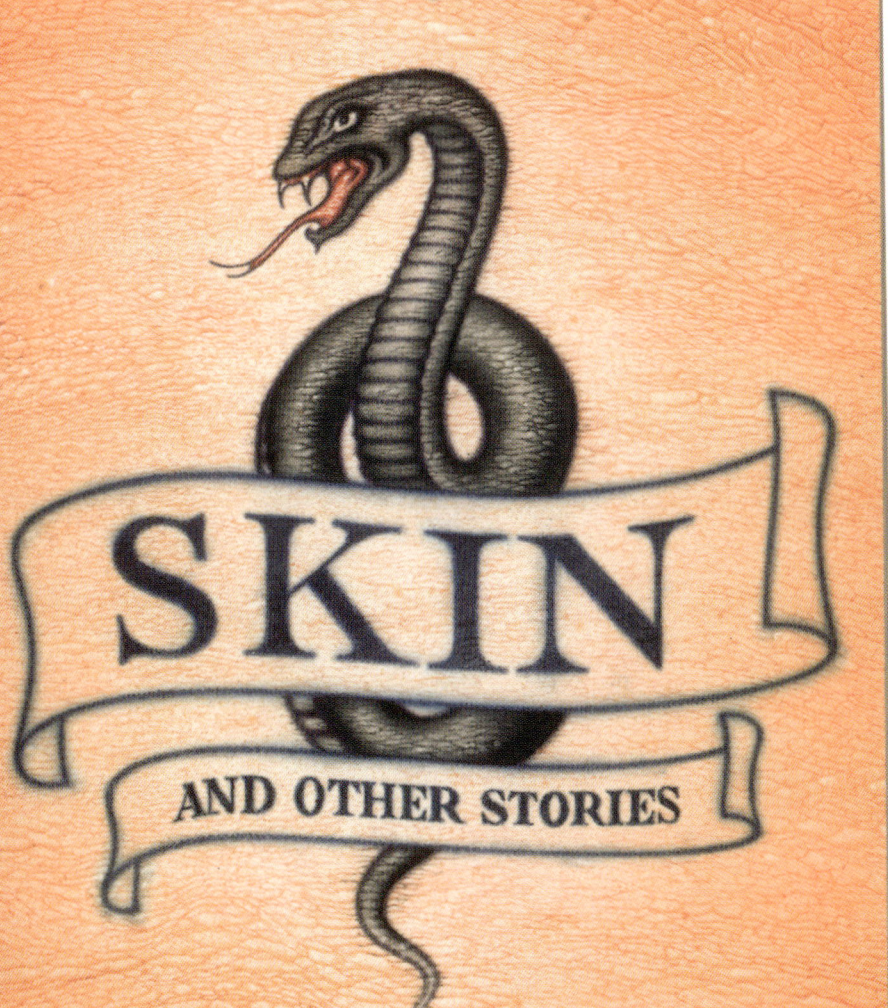

The Last Gold Diggers, 1998.
Cover illustration by Harry Horse.

The Improbable Cat, 2003.
Cover illustration by Peter Bailey.

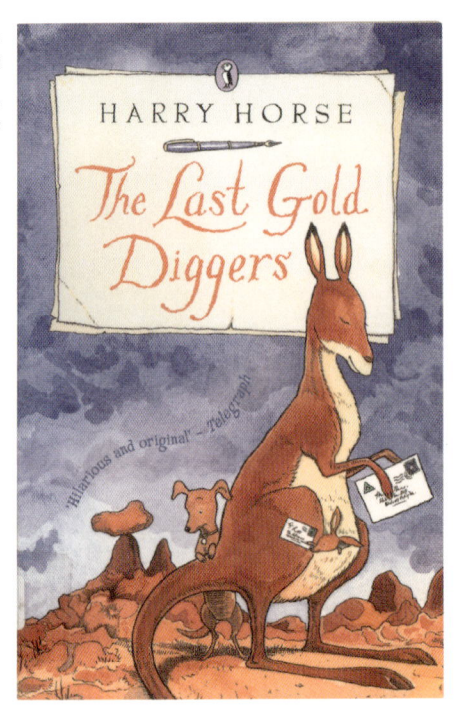

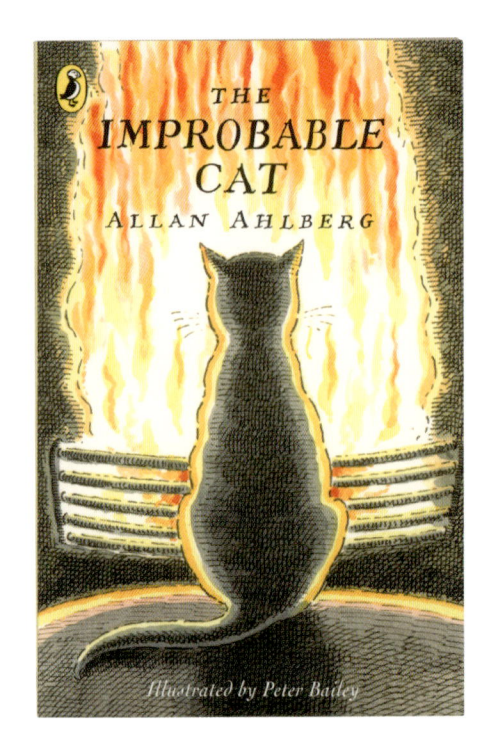

My Brother's Ghost, 2001.
Cover illustration by Gill Tyler.

The Boyhood of Burglar Bill, 2007.
Cover illustration by Jessica Ahlberg; cover photograph from Getty Images

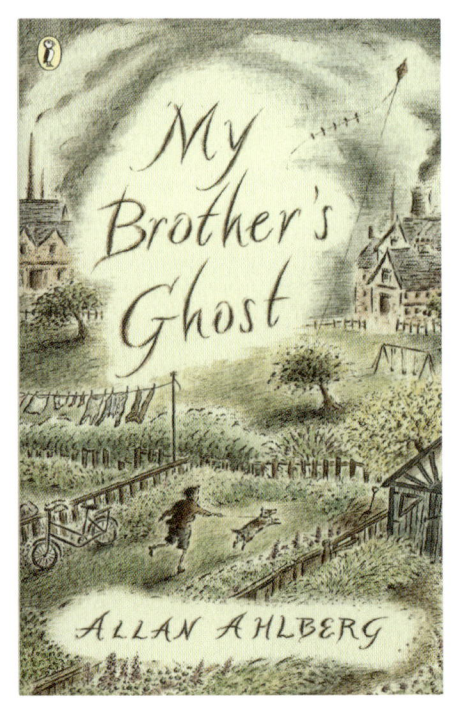

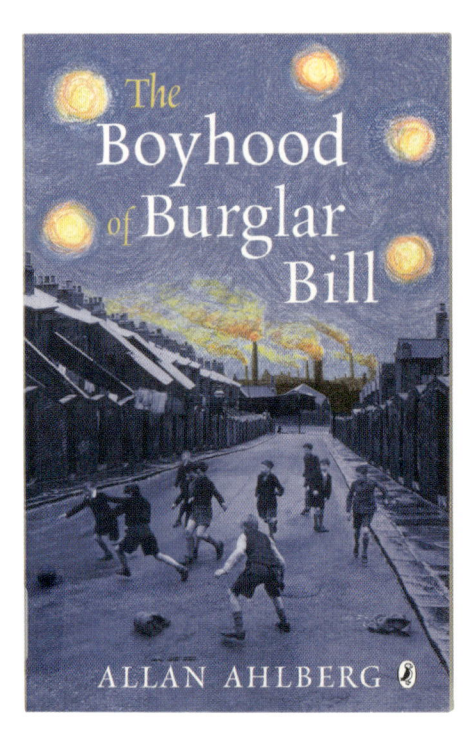

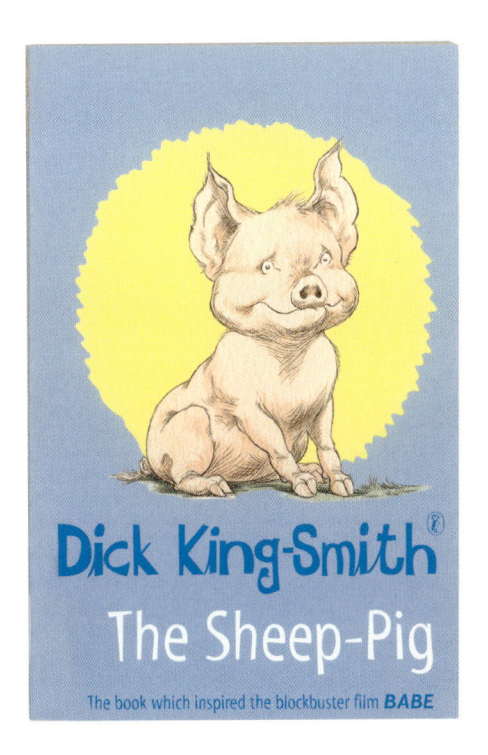

The Sheep-Pig, 2003.
Cover illustration by Chris Riddell

The Diary of a Young Girl, 2002.
Cover photograph copyright
Anne Frank-Fonds Basle; cover
background and signature
copyright AFF/AFS, Amsterdam

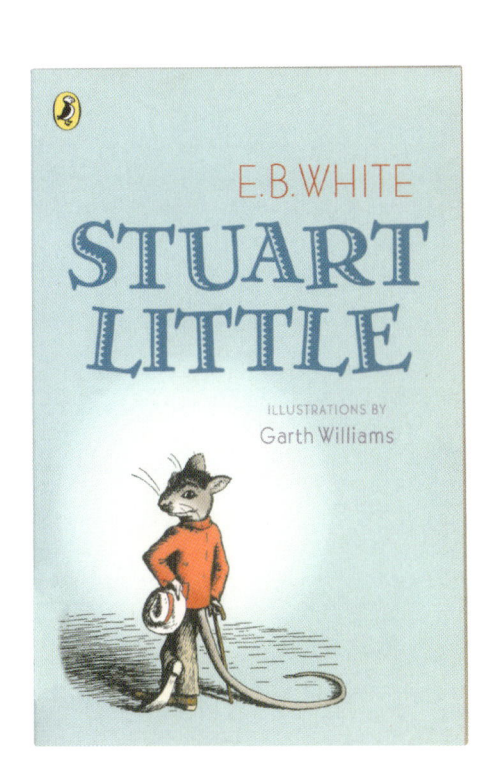

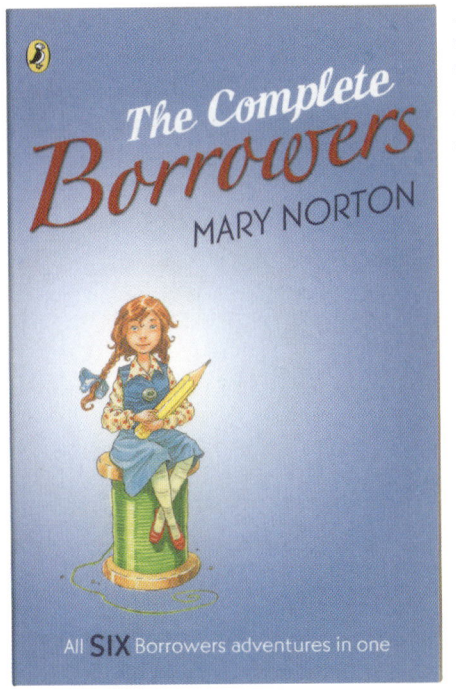

Stuart Little, 2007.
Cover illustration by
Garth Williams

The Complete Borrowers, 2007.
Cover illustration by Adam Stower

PUFFIN CLASSICS

JUST SO STORIES

RUDYARD KIPLING

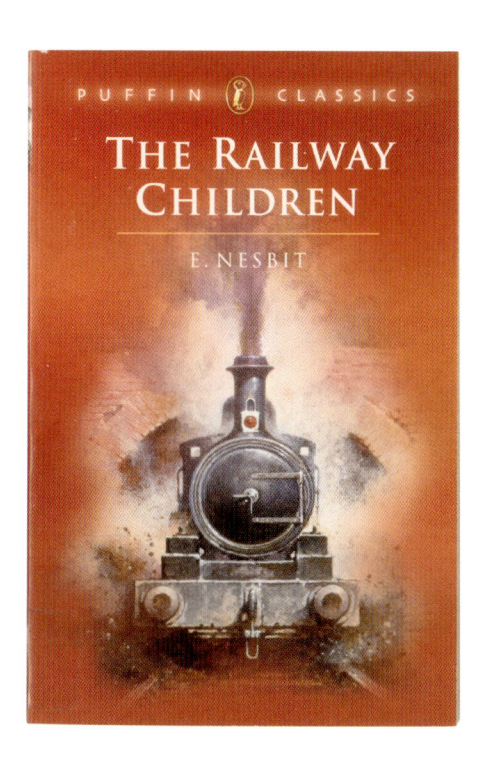

Puffin Classics, 2003

The Puffin Classics received a facelift in 2003. This was a subtle rather than a radical overhaul and images commissioned for the previous design (see pp. 182–3) were retained. While this allowed a sense of continuity – and avoided too many extra costs – much of the image's impact was lost by the resultant cropping.

The typography was freed from the label in this redesign and featured the typeface Trajan. Based on Roman inscriptional lettering, the font has now become so widely used it is divorced from its classical roots and is a staple of British publishers for subjects as varied as war, history, serious fiction and classics.

The Railway Children, 2003. Cover illustration by Gino D'Achille

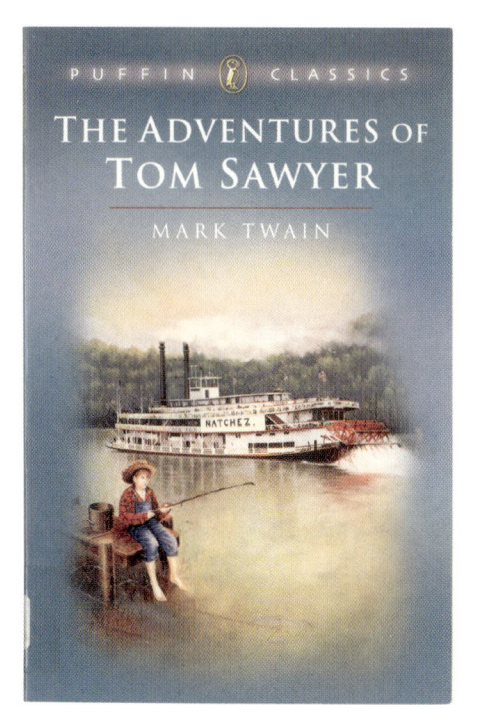

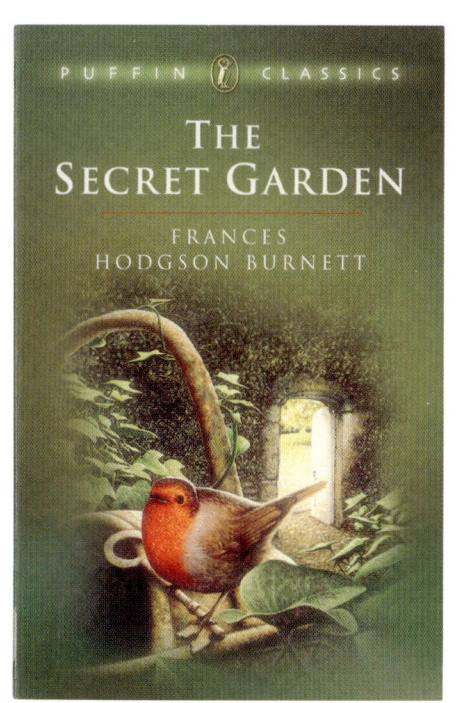

The Adventures of Tom Sawyer, 2003. Cover illustration by Gavin Dunn

The Secret Garden, 2003. Cover illustration by Angelo Rinaldi

OPPOSITE: *Just So Stories*, 2004. Cover illustration by Sally Taylor

Junk, 2003.
Cover illustration by
Robert Harding

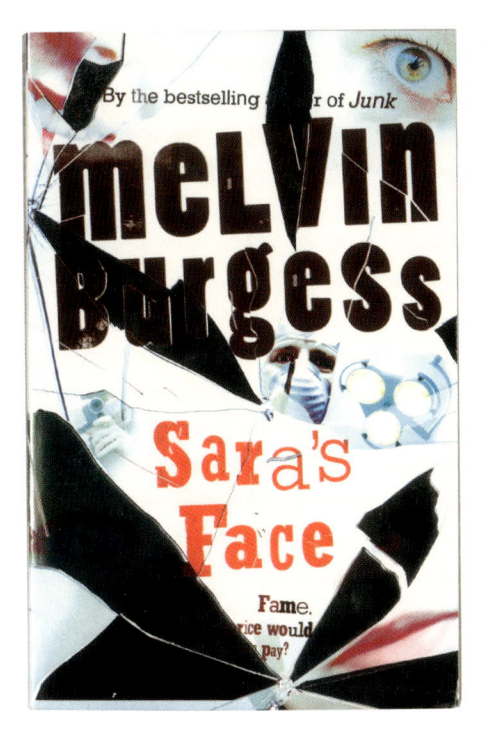

Teenage fiction

Puffin, like any publisher, needs to keep an eye on the market carefully and to make sure that the appearance of its books meets the approval of its readership. Exposed to visual stimuli through television and the Internet in ways that older generations can barely comprehend, children today have arguably more divergent tastes than ever before, and this is reflected in Puffin's more recent covers for teenage fiction. These are often virtually indistinguishable from adult titles in terms of subject matter and appearance, and this marks a shift from the carefully filtered look of the Peacocks in the sixties as seen on pages 136–43.

A children's imprint publishing teenage fiction, however, faces problems of perception and prejudice, and in the covers shown all omit the Puffin logo on the front in case it misleads or puts off the intended readership.

Lady: My Life as a Bitch, 2003. Cover design by Nick Stearn

Sara's Face, 2008. Cover design by Tom Sanderson

FOLLOWING PAGES:
Being, 2007. Cover design by Tom Sanderson

Black Rabbit Summer, 2008. Cover design by Tom Sanderson

Kevin Brooks
Being

Can you ESCAPE from WHAT you REALLY ARE?

'A cracking story... grips like a vice'
Guardian

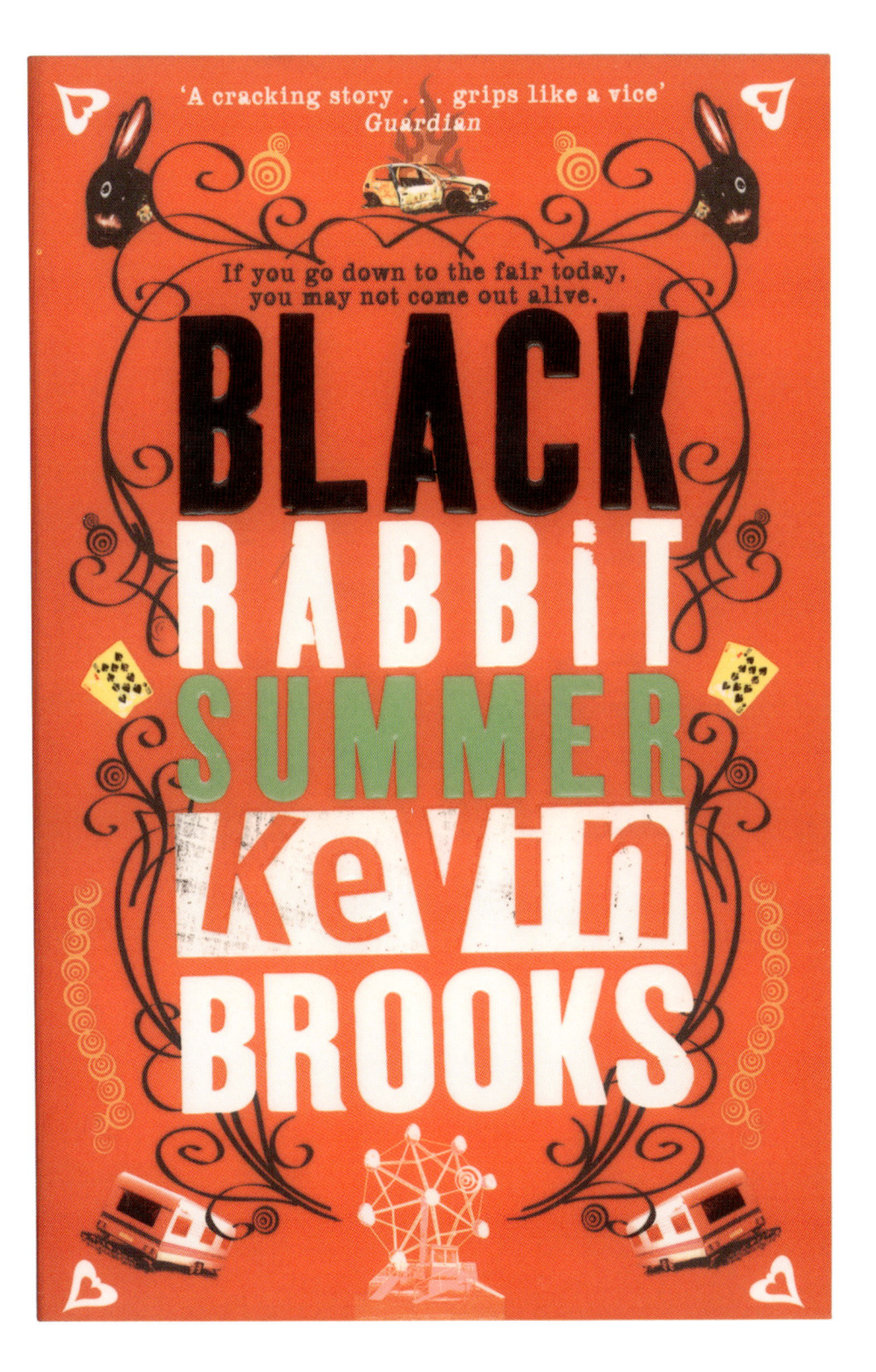

If you go down to the fair today,
you may not come out alive.

BLACK RABBIT SUMMER

Kevin Brooks

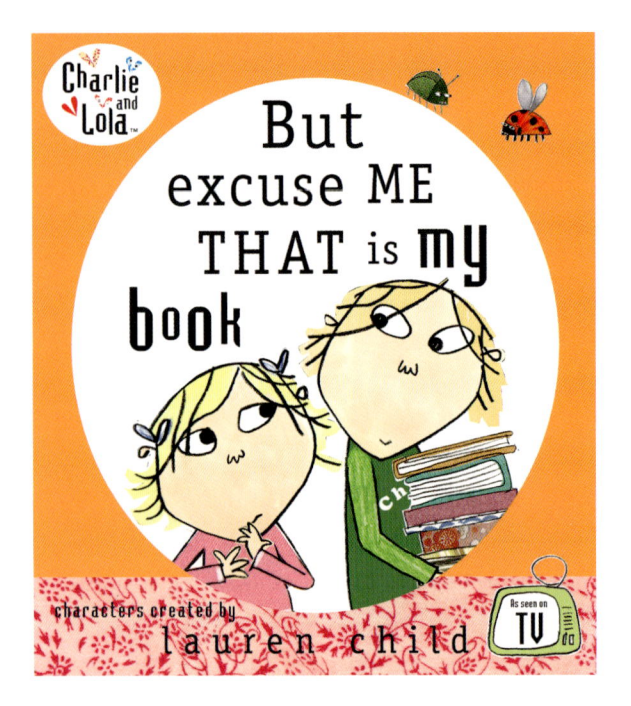

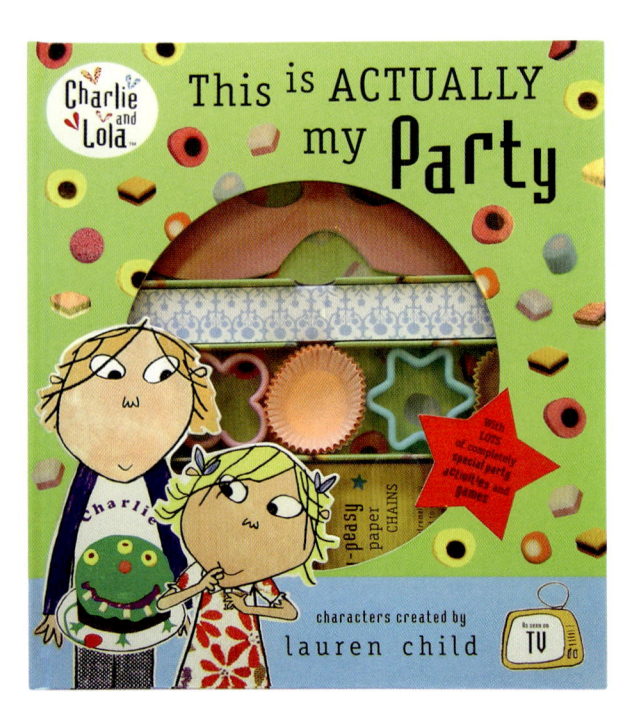

Picture books revitalized

Although no longer flagged as Picture Puffins, picture books are still very much at the heart of Puffin and, with many titles aimed at an early readership, introduce children to the joys of books.

The current list comprises both established and newly commissioned titles. Of those shown on the following pages, Jan Pieńkowski, Lynley Dodd and Katharine Holabird's books have been a part of Puffin for many years now, though Lauren Child and Ed Vere are relative newcomers. Taken together they show varied approaches to children's book illustration, from the more traditional illustrative style of Angelina illustrator Helen Craig, to the combination of old and new methods

Puffin by Design

employed by Pieńkowski, Child and Vere.

Pieńkowski's most recent titles make use of his silhouette technique (see pp. 114–5), although these latest books are presented as precious objects with paper-laminated hardback covers, the silhouette idea further explored through the use of intricate laser-cut pages.

Child has been phenomenally successful, particularly with the Charlie and Lola books and their collage of photography, painting and drawing. The original books were subsequently developed by Child and Tiger Aspect, and first shown on the BBC in 2005. The animated series had characters based closely on Child's original artwork and its success spawned further books based on scripts and animation from the series.

Angelina Ballerina is another character that has benefited from television exposure, and, like Lynley Dodd's Hairy Maclary, has been with Puffin for a number of years. As with other long-standing titles, both have their covers subtly 'freshened up' from time to time and continue to be popular.

Ed Vere's books have received critical acclaim. While at first glance they have some of the graphic simplicity of Pieńkowski's Meg and Mog books, the characters and narratives themselves are altogether edgier, reinforced by Vere's use of digital photo-montage backgrounds.

OPPOSITE: *But Excuse Me That Is My Book*, 2005. Illustrations by Lauren Child/Tiger Aspect Productions Ltd

Say Cheese!, 2007. Illustrations by Lauren Child/Tiger Aspect Productions Ltd

This is Actually My Party, 2007. Illustrations by Lauren Child/Tiger Aspect Productions Ltd

THIS PAGE: *Say Cheese!*, 2007. Illustrations by Lauren Child/Tiger Aspect Productions Ltd (inside spread shown)

V. Reinvention

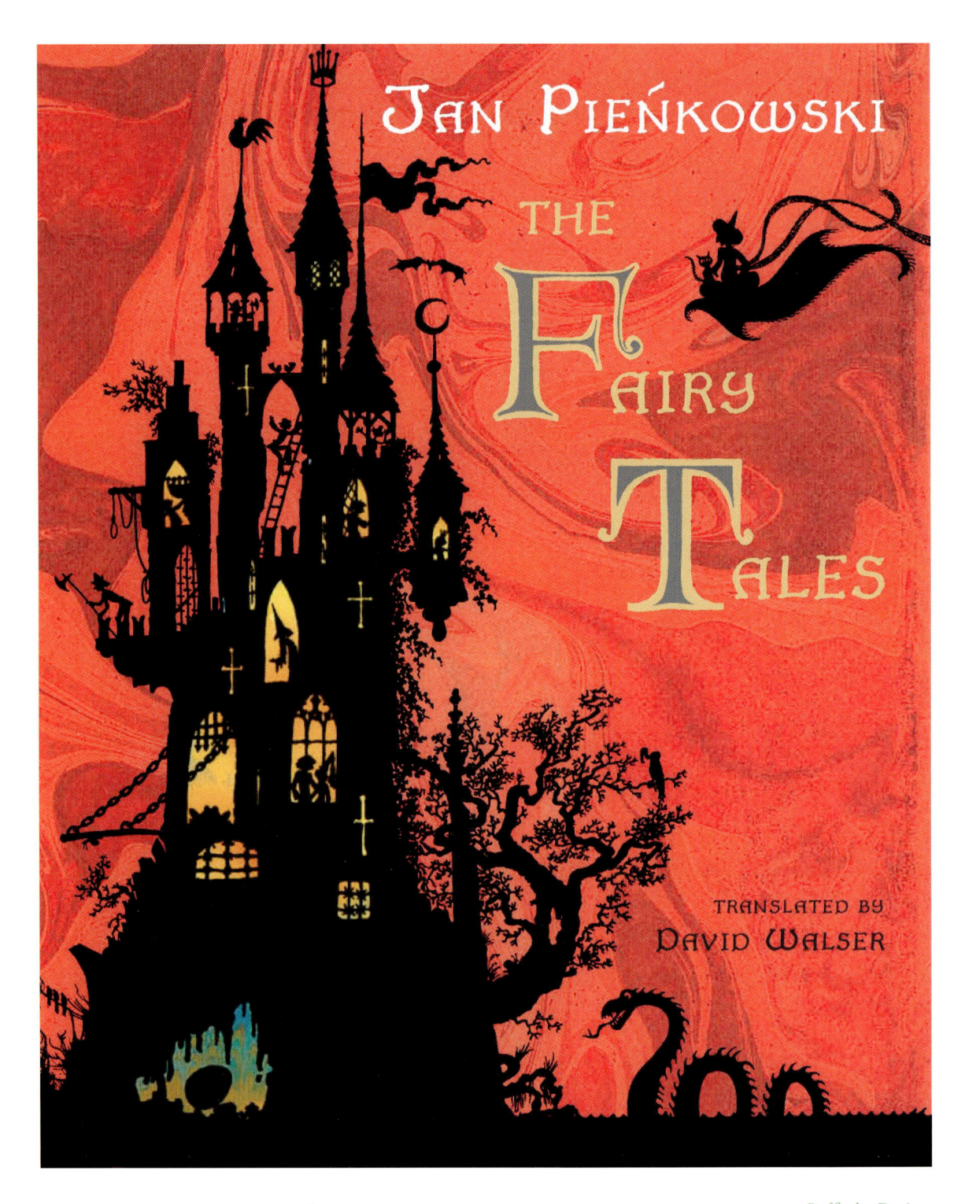

Jan Pieńkowski
The Fairy Tales

Translated by David Walser

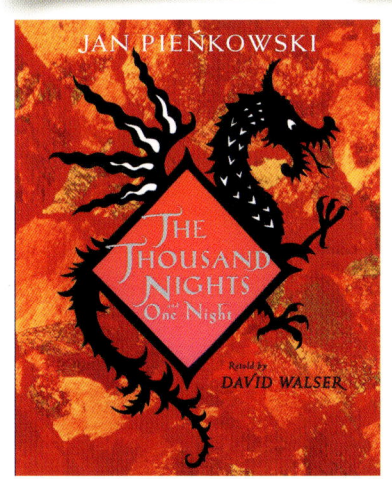

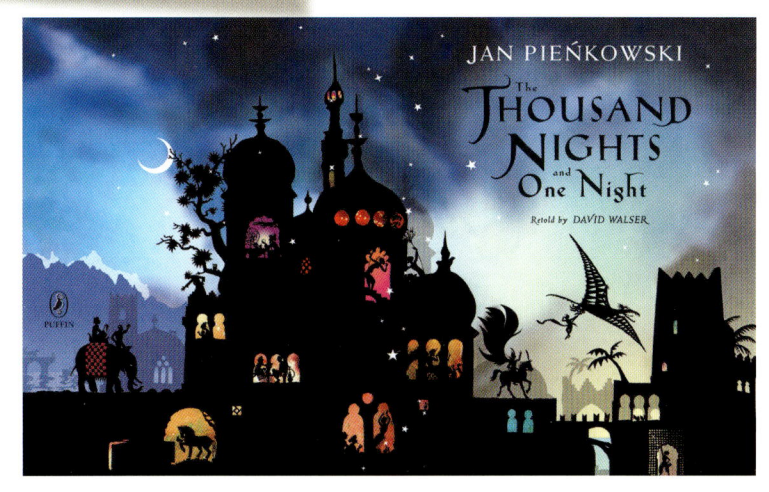

OPPOSITE: *The Fairy Tales*, 2005. Illustrated by Jan Pieńkowski

THIS PAGE: *Nut Cracker*, 2008. Illustrated by Jan Pieńkowski (cover and inside spread shown)

The Thousand Nights and One Night, 2007. Illustrated by Jan Pieńkowski (cover and inside spread shown)

THIS PAGE: *Angelina Ballerina*, 2007. Illustrated by Helen Craig

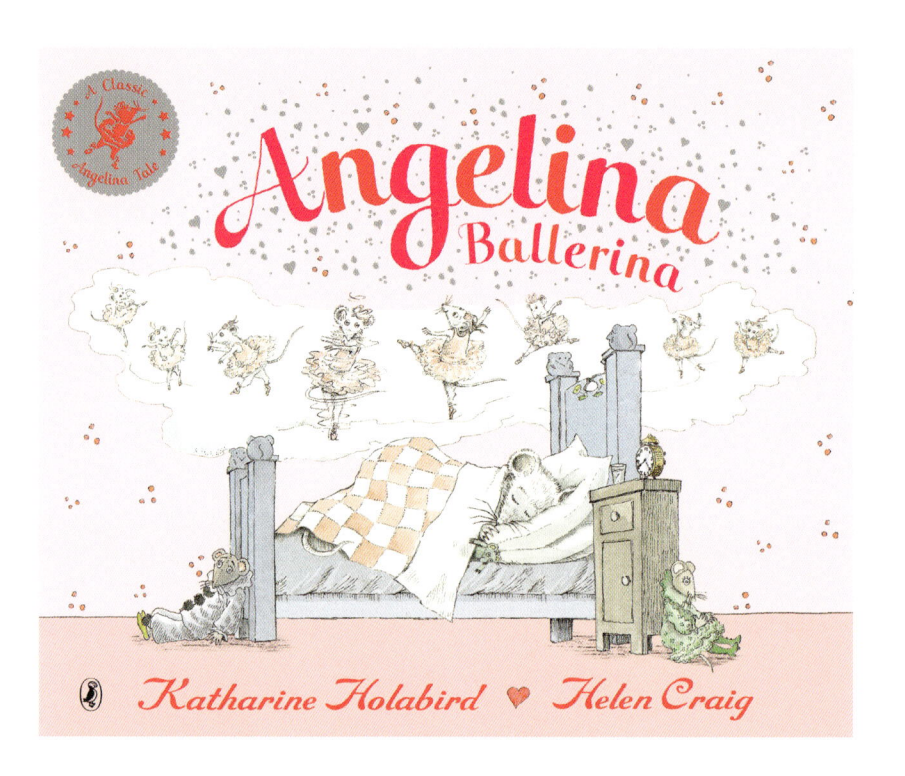

Hairy Maclary from Donaldson's Dairy, 2006. Illustrated by Lynley Dodd

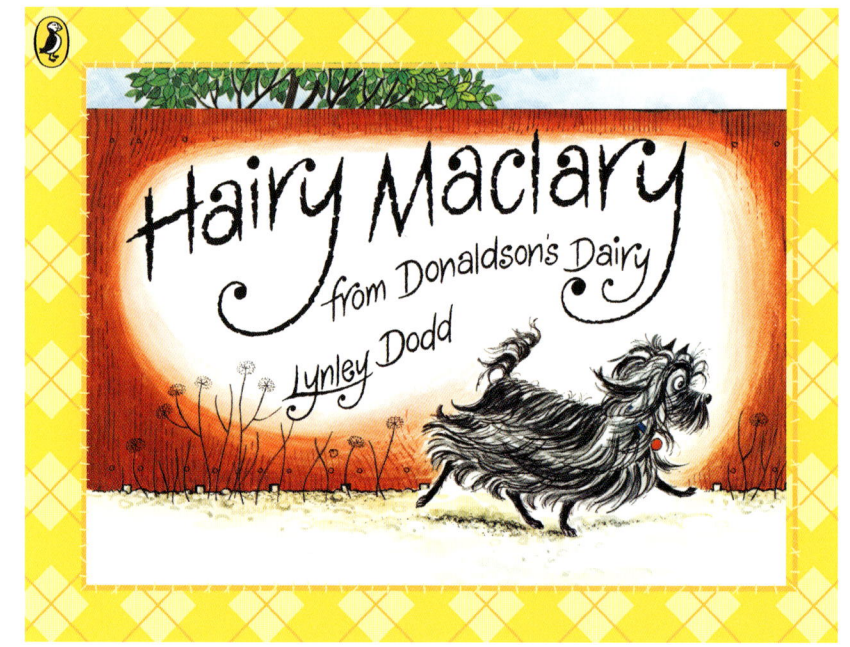

OPPOSITE: *Mr Big*, 2008. Illustrated by Ed Vere

The Getaway, 2007. Illustrated by Ed Vere

Chick, 2009. Illustrated by Ed Vere

Banana!, 2007. Illustrated by Ed Vere

V. Reinvention

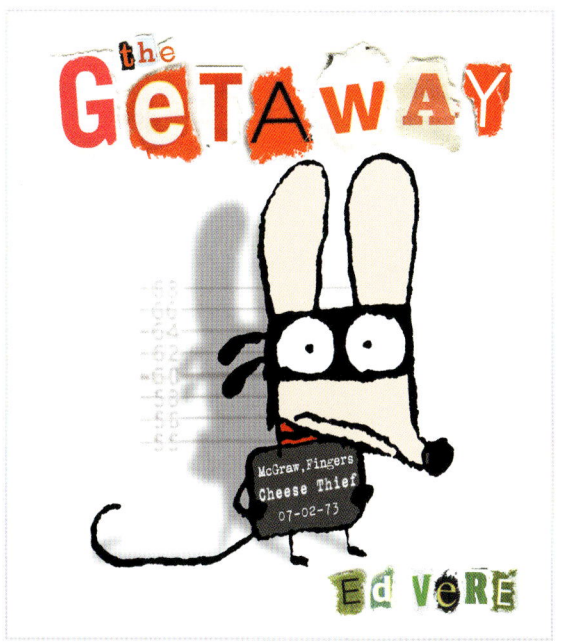

Goodnight Mister Tom, 2003.
Cover illustration by
Angelo Rinaldi

Puffin Modern Classics, 2003

The 2003 design for the Modern Classics is noticeable for its sophistication and confidence. The typographic treatment is more minimal than on any other Puffin books with letter-spaced OCR B capitals for series name and author, and a subtle flourish of a different font for the book title itself. All three elements are closely grouped and arranged top right with the Puffin logo, which allows for the maximum space to be given over to the image.

For some titles, for example *The Borrowers*, *Stig of the Dump* and *Charlotte's Web*, existing cover artwork already loved by generations of readers was re-used. Sometimes this was because that artwork had always been a condition of Puffin's original publishing agreement, sometimes because the art department and editors felt it continued to hold great appeal. A comparison with pages 101 and 111 will show how on *Charlotte's Web* and *Stig* the images have been tightly re-cropped for a more dramatic effect. On other covers the artwork is freshly commissioned.

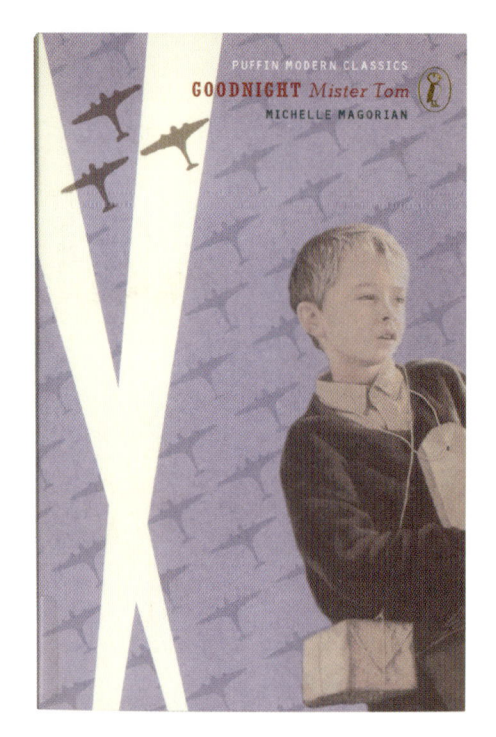

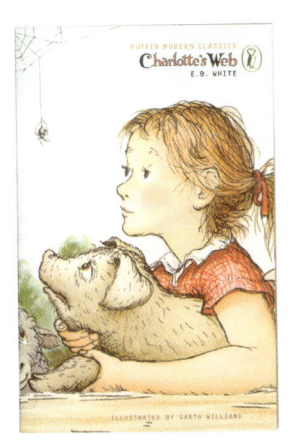

The Borrowers, 1993. Cover illustration by Diana Stanley

Stig of the Dump, 2003. Cover illustration by Edward Ardizzone

Charlotte's Web, 2003. Cover illustration by Garth Williams

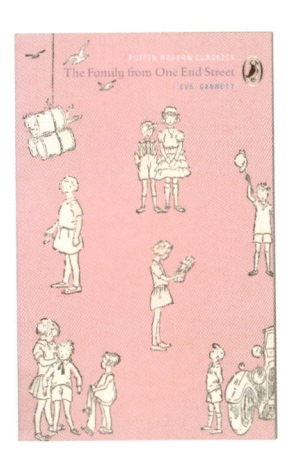

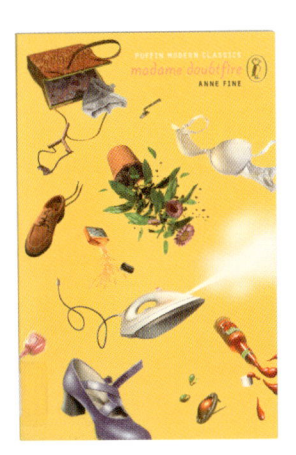

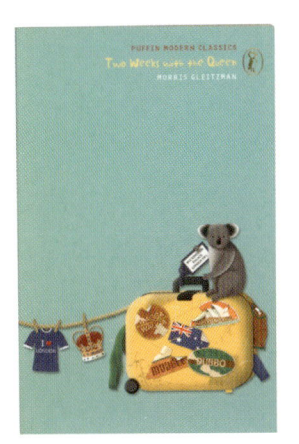

The Family from One End Street, 2004. Cover illustration by Eve Garnett

Madame Doubtfire, 2003. Cover illustration by Bob Lea

Two Weeks with the Queen, 2003. Cover illustration by Maura Millman

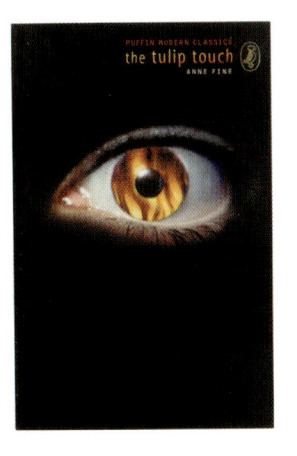

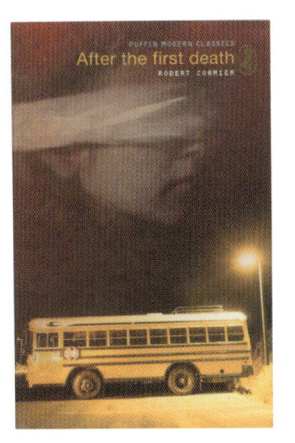

Smith, 2004. Cover illustration by David Frankland

The Tulip Touch, 2006. Cover illustration by Lee Gibbons

After the First Death, 2006. Cover photograph by Getty Images

V. Reinvention

Journey to the Centre of the Earth, 2008. Cover illustration by Chris Gall

The Call of the Wild, 2008. Cover illustration by Bill Sanderson

The Secret Garden, 2008. Cover illustration by Alice Stevenson

Alice's Adventures in Wonderland, 2008. Cover illustration by Chris Riddell

Little Women, 2008. Cover illustration by Kazuko Nome

White Fang, 2008. Cover illustration by Michael Halbert

The Wind in the Willows, 2008. Cover illustration by Adam Larkum

The Adventures of Tom Sawyer, 2008. Cover illustration by Bill Sanderson

Anne of Green Gables, 2008. Cover illustration by Lauren Child

Just So Stories, 2008. Cover illustration by Victoria Sawdon

Oliver Twist, 2008. Cover illustration by Steve Noble

Puffin Classics, 2008

As noted on pages 200–1, the 2003 Classics redesign was a gentle facelift that bought Puffin time with which to prepare a complete re-package. As with the re-launch of Penguin Classics in 2003 (see *Penguin by Design*: pp. 234–5) the brand-new cover look was created jointly with the Puffin US design team and was honed and finalized in close collaboration to suit both markets.

It has strong family similarities to its adult counterparts: the panel for author and title at the foot, the narrow white stripe for series name and logo, and a clearly defined, discreet area for the illustration. But there are significant differences too. Aside from the credit for the series name and introduction author's name, the typography of each title and author name is distinct to suit the subject matter, and while Penguin Classics still wear the black they first acquired in 1963, Puffins are colourful – again varied for each book – as befits children's literature.

The illustrations, which generally feature a distinctive character rather than tell part of the narrative, feature a strong black-and-white image with flat colours, and although many illustrators are used this restricted palette ensures a strong continuity. The reduced-size cropped illustration on the spine top, first introduced in 1993 and continued in 2003, ensures that the series remains recognizable on the bookshelf. The re-launch has been extremely successful in the US where the children's classic market is huge and highly competitive.

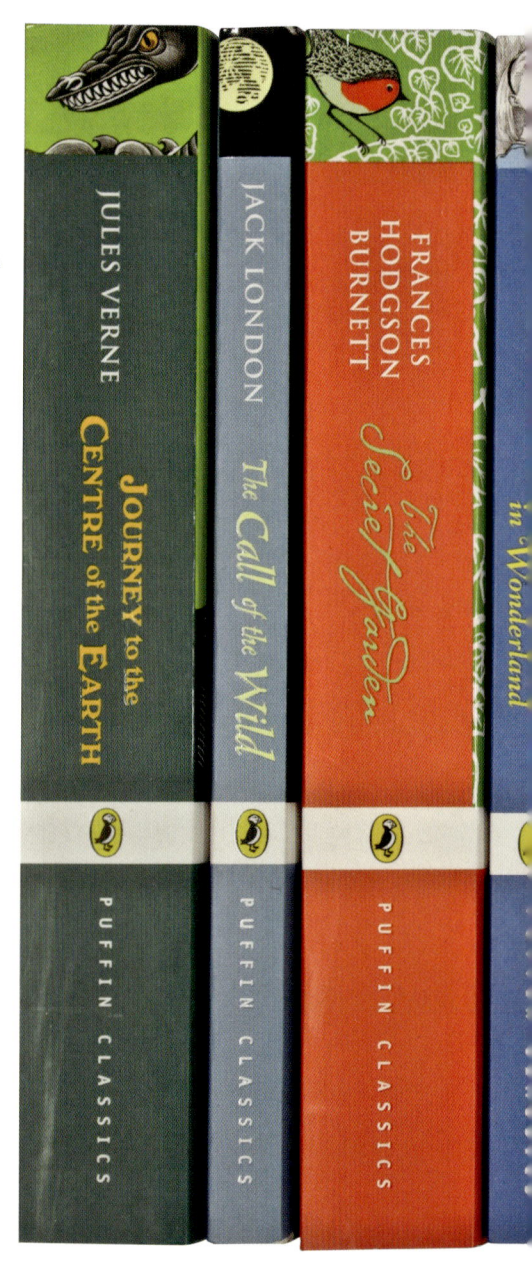

V. Reinvention

Kidnapped, 2009. Cover illustration by Ross Collins

Heidi, 2009. Cover illustration by Joe Berger

A Tale of Two Cities, 2009. Cover illustration by Bill Sanderson

The Happy Prince and Other Stories, 2009. Cover illustration by Ian Bilbey

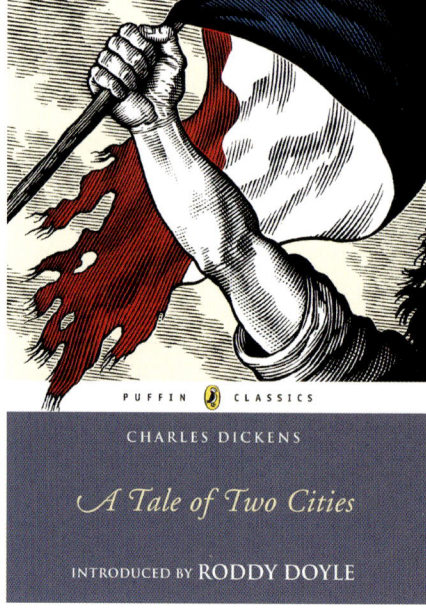

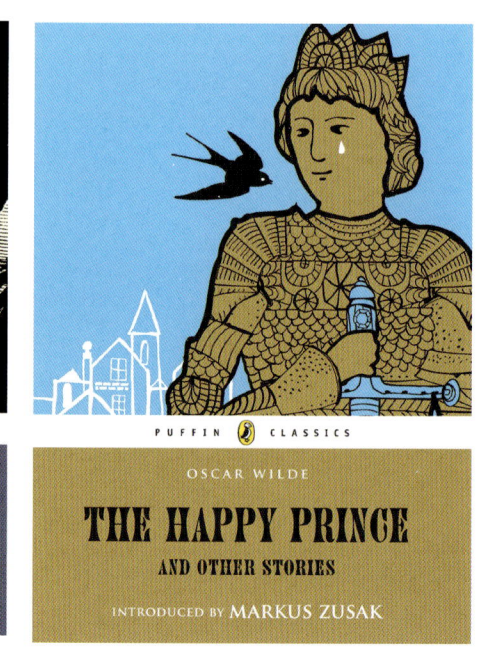

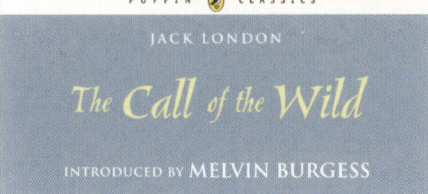

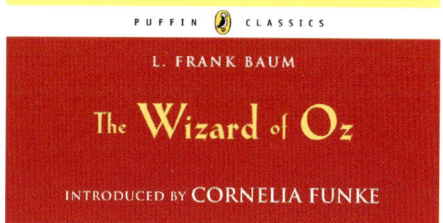

The Call of the Wild, 2008.
Cover illustration by Bill Sanderson

The Wizard of Oz, 2008.
Cover illustration by Tem Doran

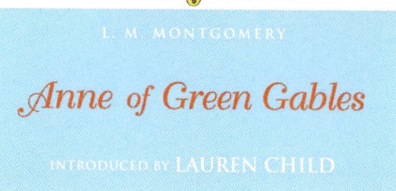

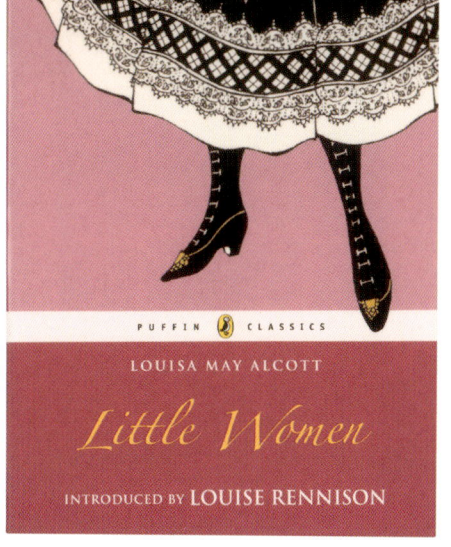

Anne of Green Gables, 2008.
Cover illustration by Lauren Child

Little Women, 2008.
Cover illustration by Kazuko Nome

V. Reinvention

Endymion Spring, 2006. Cover illustration by Bill Sanderson

OPPOSITE: *Once*, 2006. Cover design by Kate Clarke

The Gospel According to Larry, 2004. Cover design by Anna Billson

Then, 2009. Cover design by Katy Finch

Guantanamo Boy, 2009. Cover design by Tom Sanderson

Fiction today

Like contemporary Penguin fiction, Puffin fiction is characterized by a total freedom from the constraints of branding and logo, with each cover designed to reflect the contents and to appeal to the intended audience as directly as possible. While this approach took nearly thirty years to become acceptable for Penguin titles, it has been commonplace at Puffin from very early on in its history.

If there is a common theme to be seen in the selection of covers reproduced here it is in the central role of typography or lettering, with illustration being used to reinforce the mood or taking the form of a backdrop.

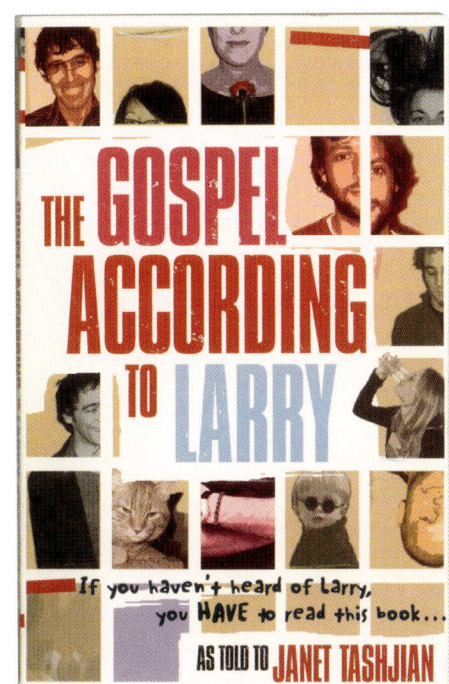

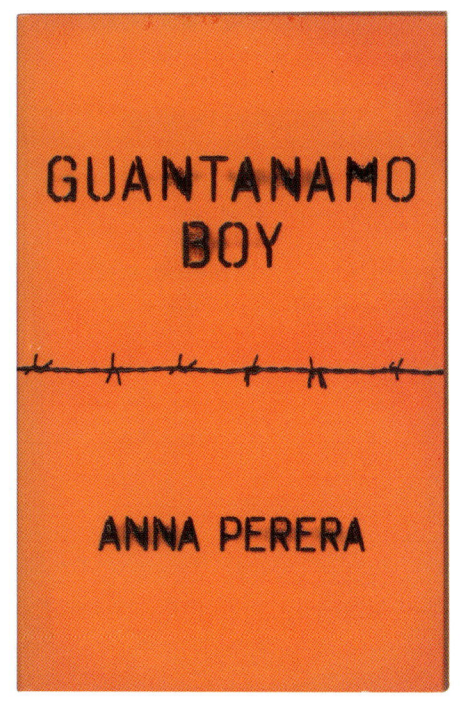

V. Reinvention 219

Bad Kitty, 2006. Cover illustration by Stanley Chow

The Glass Demon, 2010. Cover design by Tom Sanderson

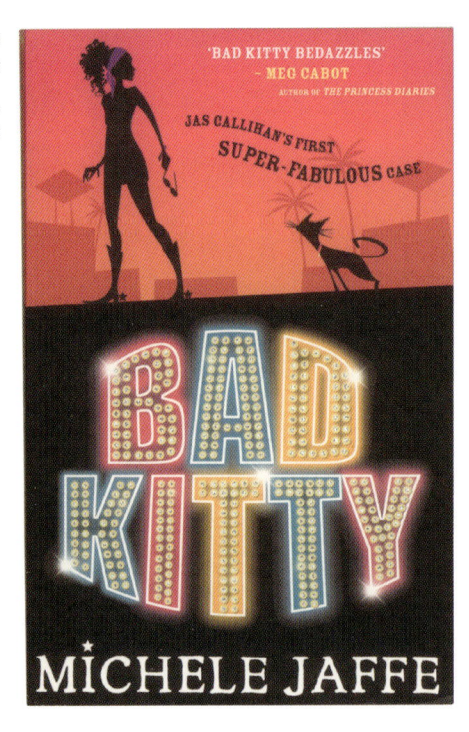

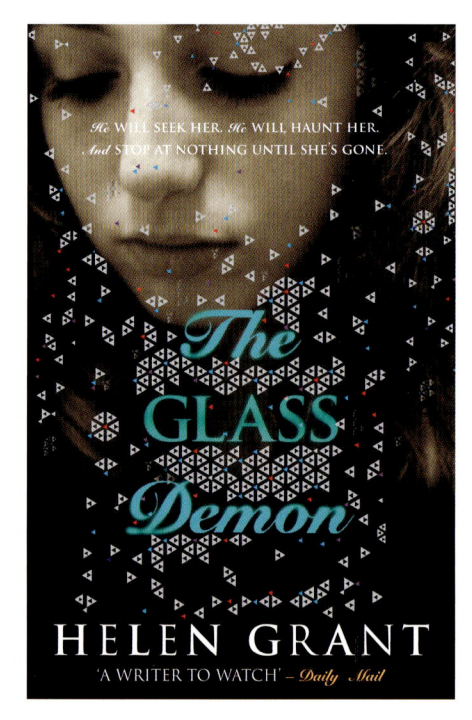

A Coyote's in the House, 2005. Cover illustration by Lauren Child

Ruby Red, 2007. Cover illustration by Alice Stevenson

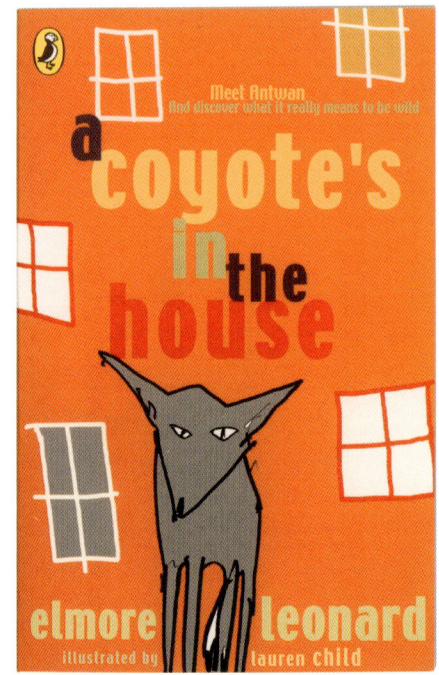

OPPOSITE: *The Luxe*, 2008. Cover design by Andrea C. Uva and Anna Billson

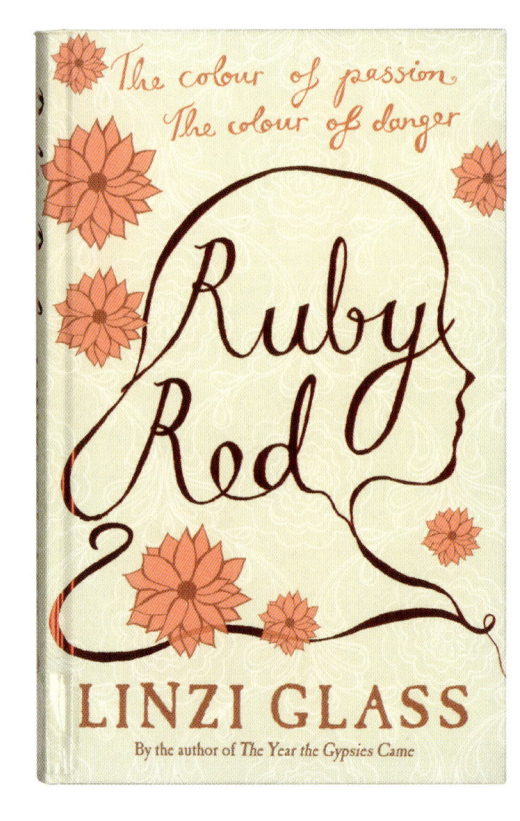

The Luxe

'All the glitz of *The O.C.* but with bigger frocks and more dashing boys' *Elle*

ANNA GODBERSEN

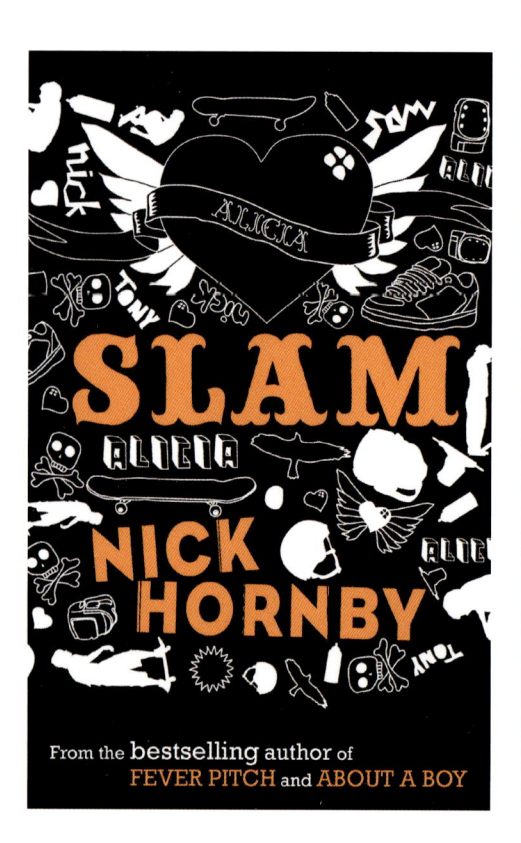

Slam, 2007.
Cover design by Studio Output
(full dust jacket shown to right)

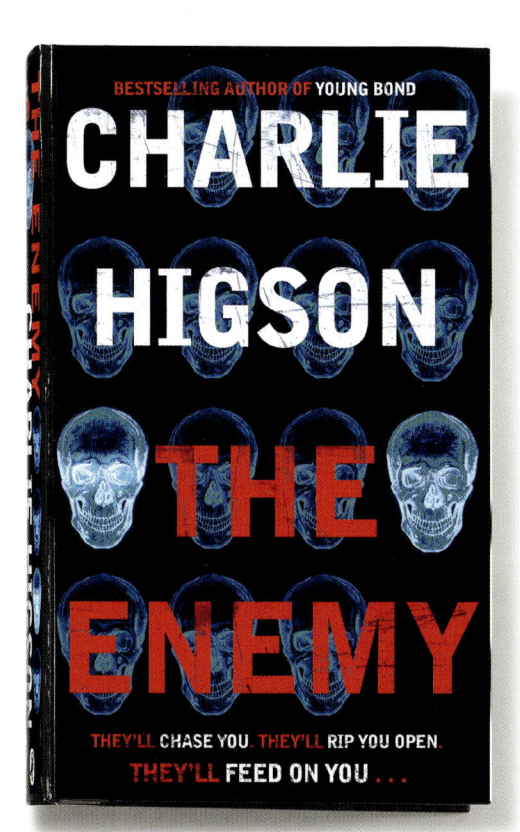

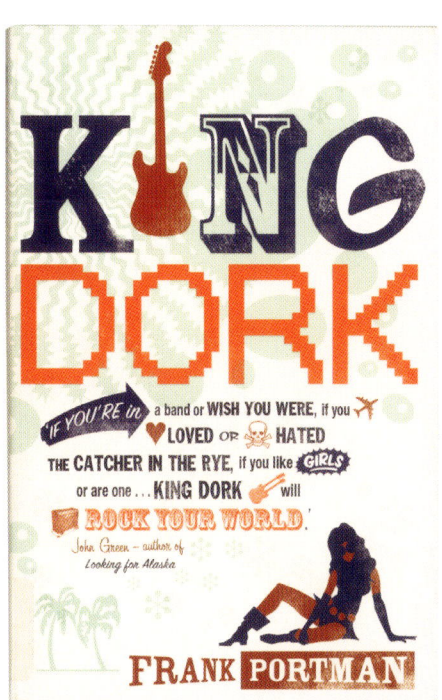

The Enemy, 2009.
Cover design by Tom Sanderson

King Dork, 2007.
Cover design by Tom Sanderson

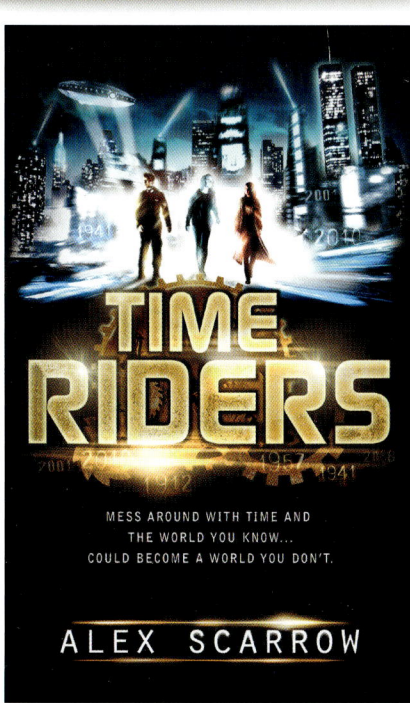

TimeRiders, 2010
Cover design by James Fraser; photography by Neil Spence

Spud, 2008.
Cover design by Tom Sanderson

Charlie and the Great Glass Elevator, 2001. Cover illustration by Quentin Blake

The author as brand I

The idea of packaging a single author's works, or a particular set of related titles, in a similar manner to encourage the collecting habit, is an old one and can be seen early on in the Puffin list with the visually connected Worzel Gummidge titles (see pp. 72–3) or the Narnia stories of C. S. Lewis (pp. 90–1), for example. Today, however, this has been honed to a fine art and is the result of close collaboration between the editorial, marketing and design departments.

While not the first illustrator of Roald Dahl's children's stories, Quentin Blake has been illustrating them since 1976, and to many the two seem inextricably linked. Blake began illustrating books in 1960 and formed strong partnerships with Joan Aiken, Russell Hoban, Michael Rosen and John Yeoman in addition to Dahl, as well as being an author in his own right. For the latest re-branding of Dahl titles Blake's existing illustrations have been re-used and reconfigured as necessary to work with the more prominent use of Dahl's name and the bellyband that contains the title. These are considerably better balanced visually than the previous design with its side bar and box, and make a very effective display en masse in bookshops.

Jeremy Strong's (b. 1949) first book for Puffin was *The Air-Raid Shelter* (1987). His books are humorous, the kind he wishes had been around when he was growing up, and this is reflected in the strong, colourful, economical illustrations by Nick Sharratt. The books on page 228 have a consistent look because of the uniform position of the author's name, but work visually because type is not used and, instead, the titles are all are drawn in the same style as the images.

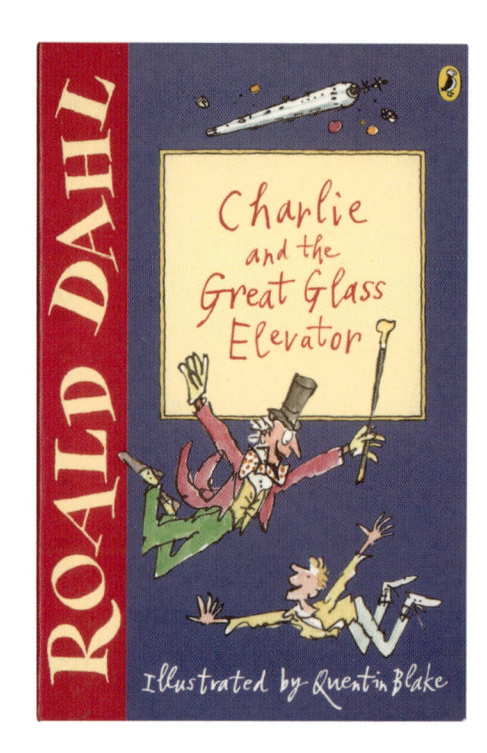

Other author brands are held together by the repeated use of a different kind of image style: soft-focus illustration and girly glittery letters for the Magic Kitten series and subsequent spin-offs, and the unmistakable face of Lara the spy dog bursting through prominent type for *Spy Dog* (see p. 229).

What makes the covers for Jeremy Strong's books work well also applies to those of Cathy Cassidy (b. 1962, see pp. 230–1), which have that same successful unity of drawn image and lettering.

OPPOSITE: *Charlie and the Great Glass Elevator*, 2007. Cover illustration by Quentin Blake

Roald Dahl

Charlie and the Great Glass Elevator

THE WORLD'S NO. 1 STORYTELLER

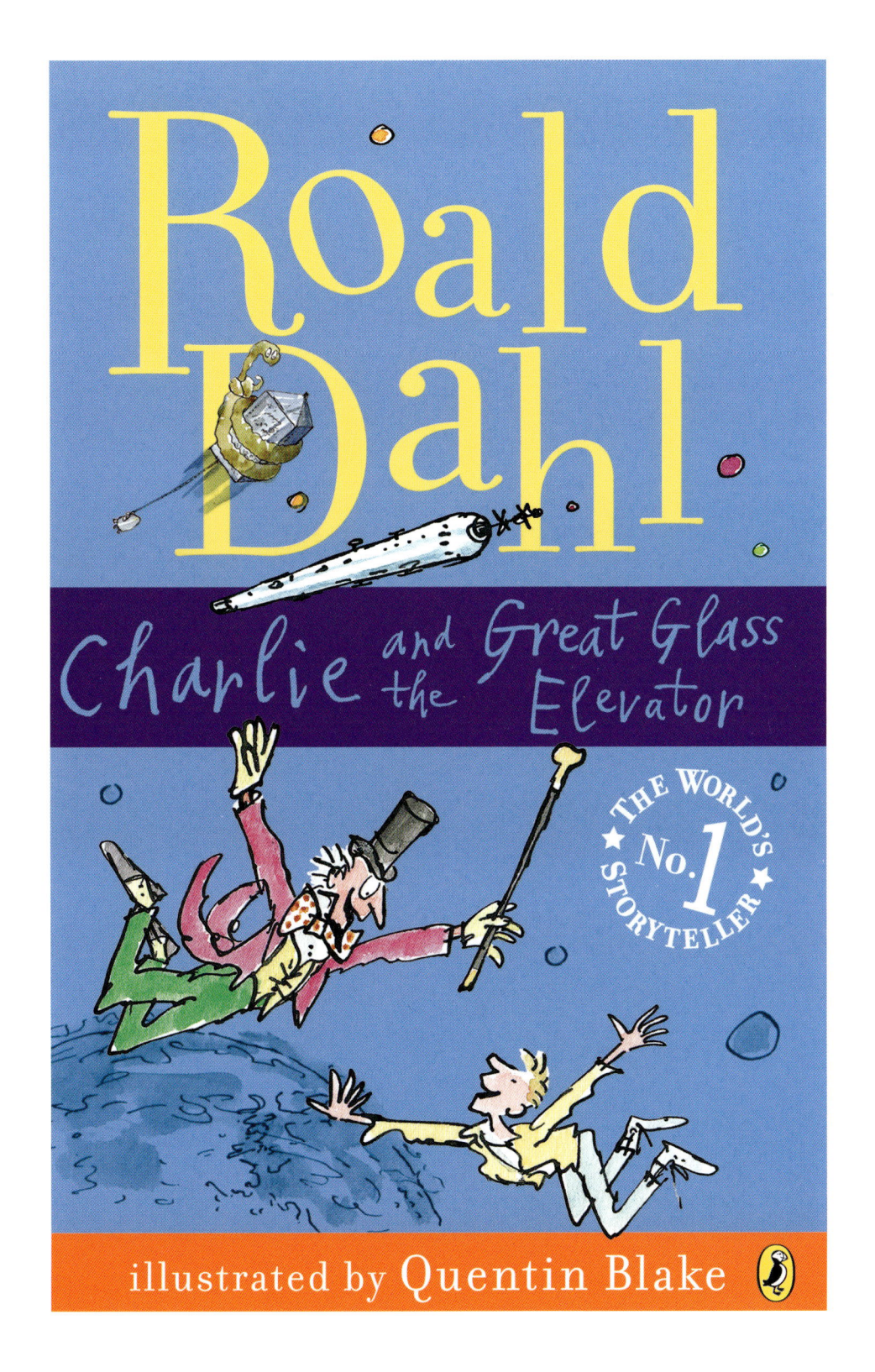

illustrated by Quentin Blake

Charlie and the Chocolate Factory, 2007. Cover illustration by Quentin Blake

The Witches, 2007. Cover illustration by Quentin Blake

The BFG, 2007. Cover illustration by Quentin Blake

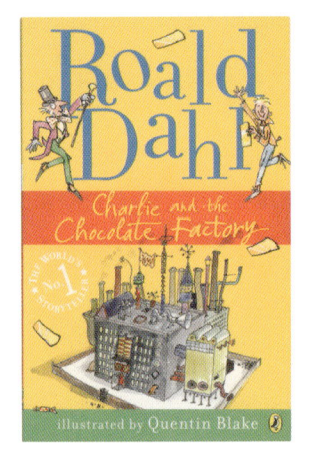

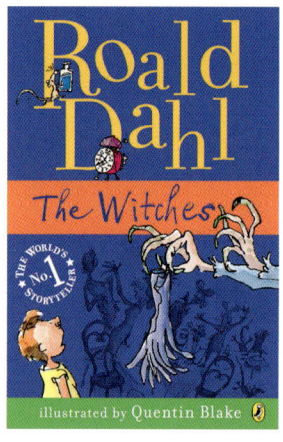

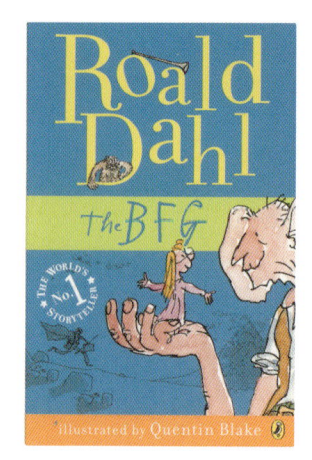

Fantastic Mr Fox, 2007. Cover illustration by Quentin Blake

Matilda, 2007. Cover illustration by Quentin Blake

George's Marvellous Medicine, 2007. Cover illustration by Quentin Blake

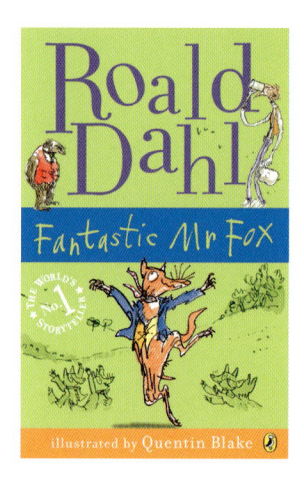

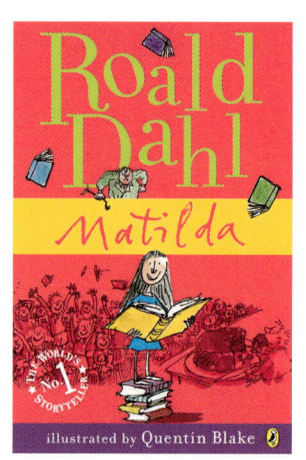

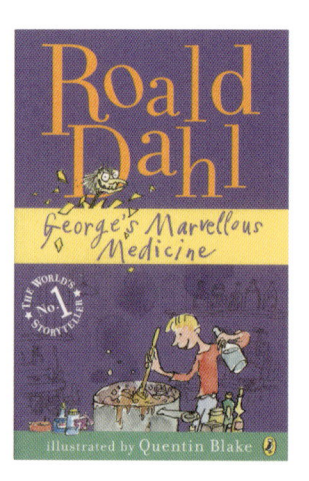

The Enormous Crocodile, 2007. Cover illustration by Quentin Blake

James and the Giant Peach, 2007. Cover illustration by Quentin Blake

Boy: Tales of Childhood, 2007. Cover illustration by Quentin Blake

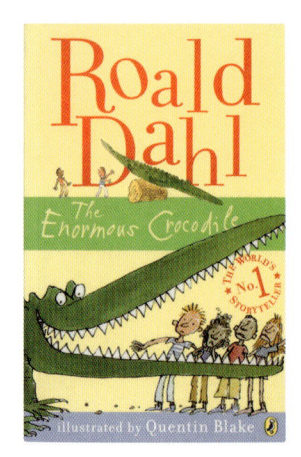

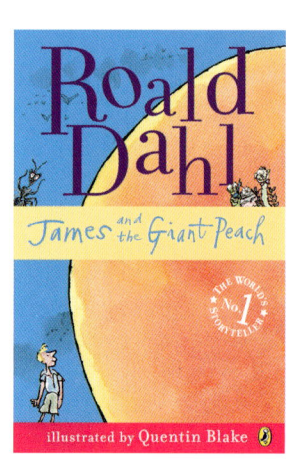

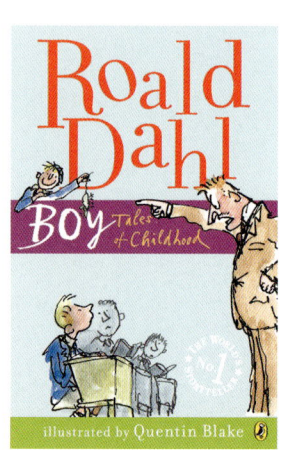

Charlie and the Chocolate Factory.
Inside illustration by Quentin Blake

The BFG. Inside illustration by Quentin Blake

V. Reinvention

The Hundred-Mile-an-Hour Dog, 2009. Cover illustration by Nick Sharratt

Krazy Kow Saves the World – Well, Almost, 2007. Cover illustration by Nick Sharratt

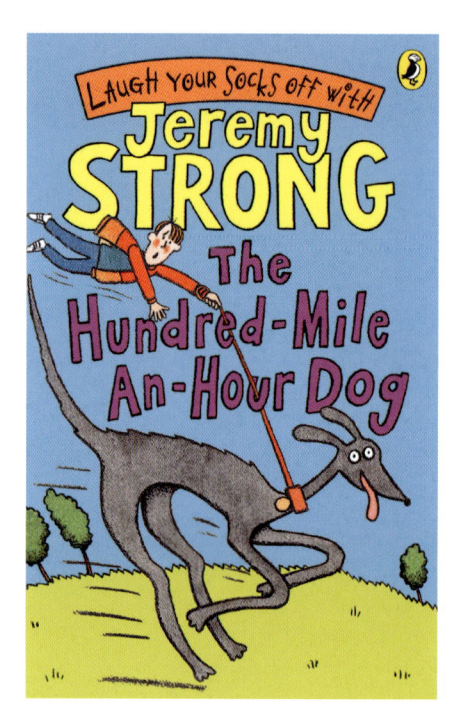

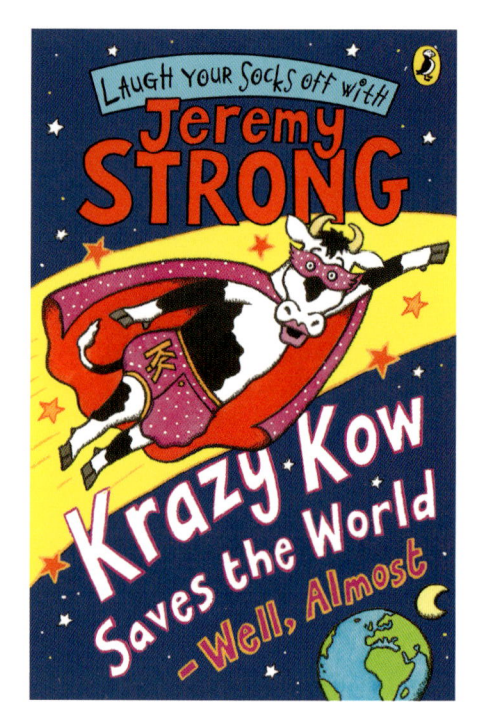

Beware! Killer Tomotoes, 2007. Cover illustration by Nick Sharratt

My Brother's Famous Bottom, 2007. Cover illustration by Nick Sharratt

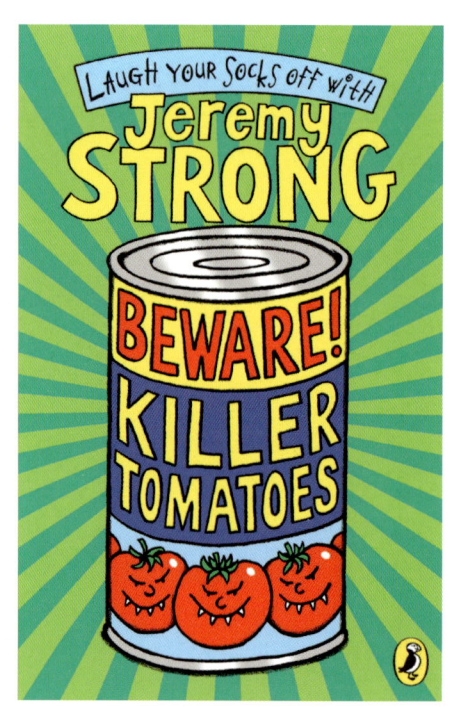

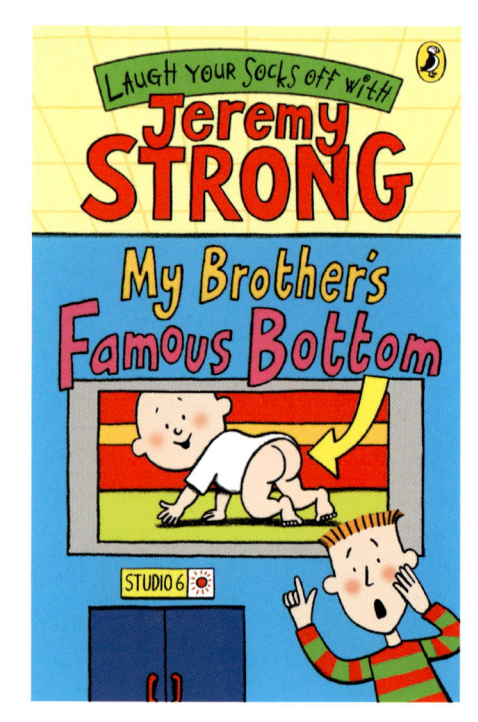

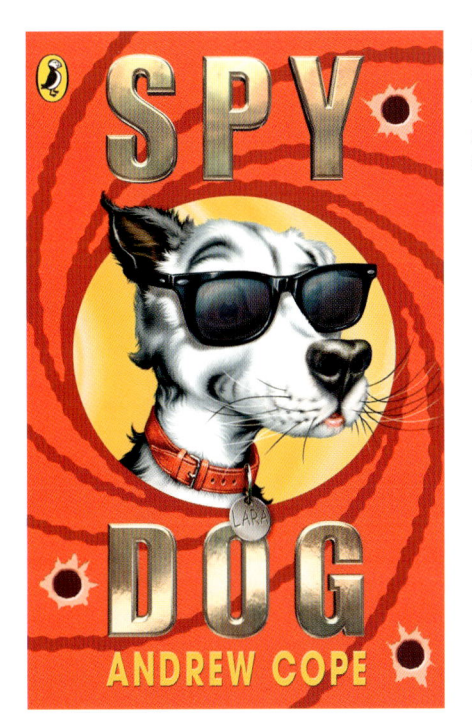

Magic Kitten: Seaside Mystery, 2007. Cover illustration by Andrew Farley

Spy Dog, 2005. Cover illustration by Andrew Farley

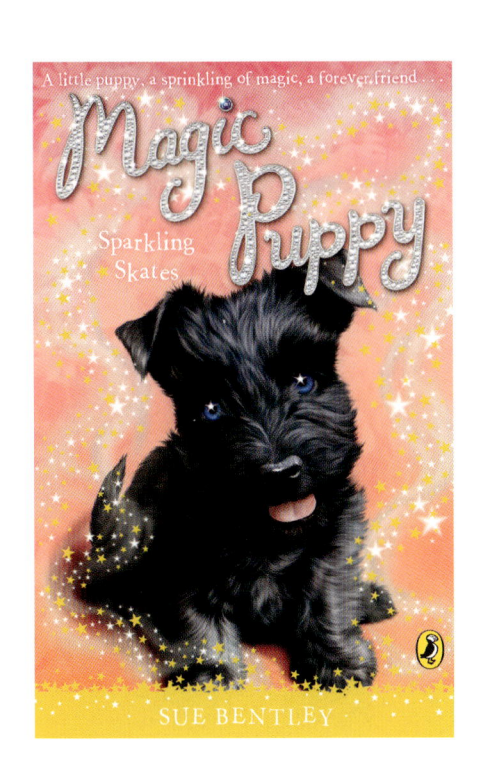

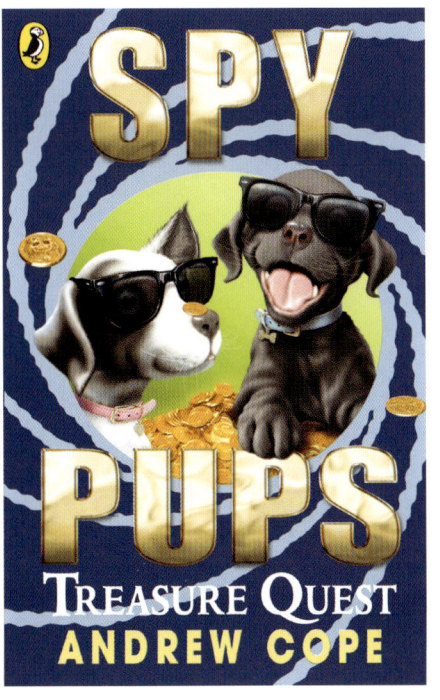

Magic Puppy: Sparkling Skates, 2009. Cover illustration by Andrew Farley

Spy Pups: Treasure Quest, 2009. Cover illustrations by Andrew Farley

GingerSnaps, 2008.
Cover design by Sara Flavell

Angel Cake, 2009.
Cover design by Sara Flavell

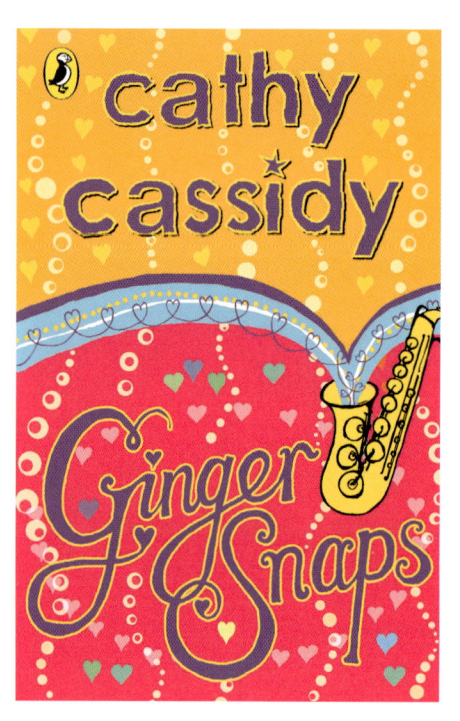

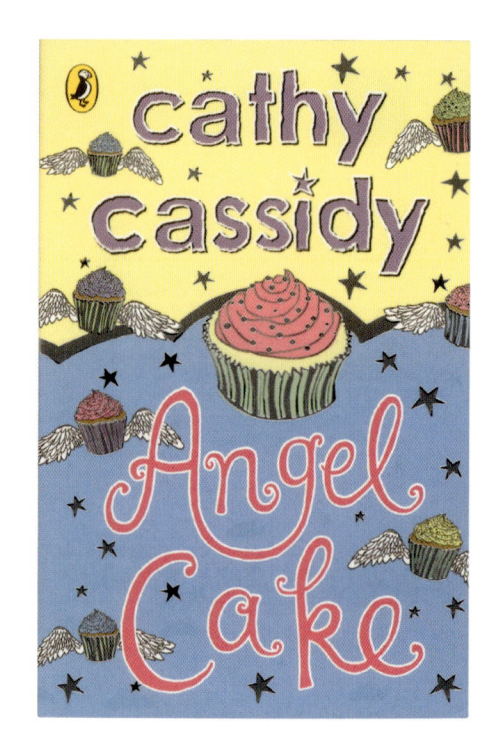

Driftwood, 2008.
Cover design by Sara Flavell

Lucky Star, 2008.
Cover design by Sara Flavell

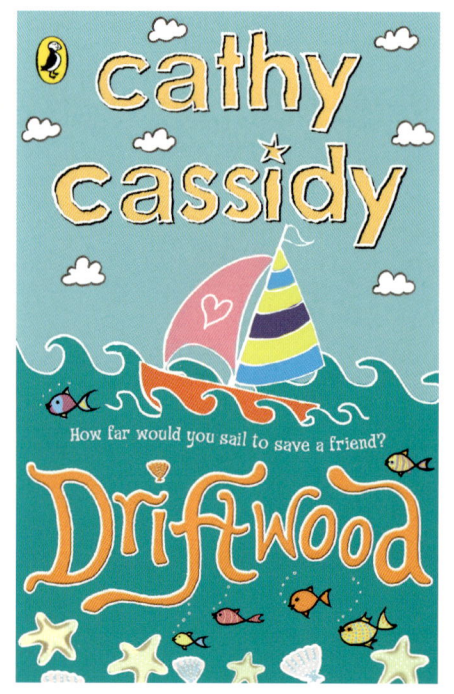

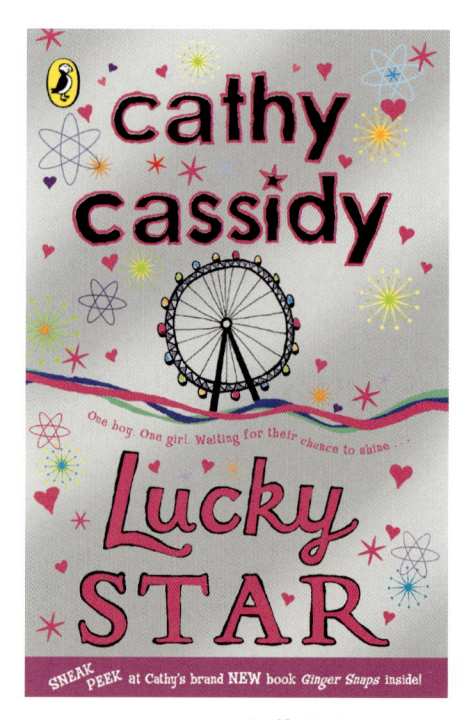

Dizzy, 2008

Indigo Blue, 2008

Scarlett, 2008

Sundae Girl, 2008

Lucky Star, 2008

GingerSnaps, 2009

Angel Cake, 2009

DIARY
of a
Wimpy Kid

a novel in cartoons

INTERNATIONAL BESTSELLER

Jeff Kinney

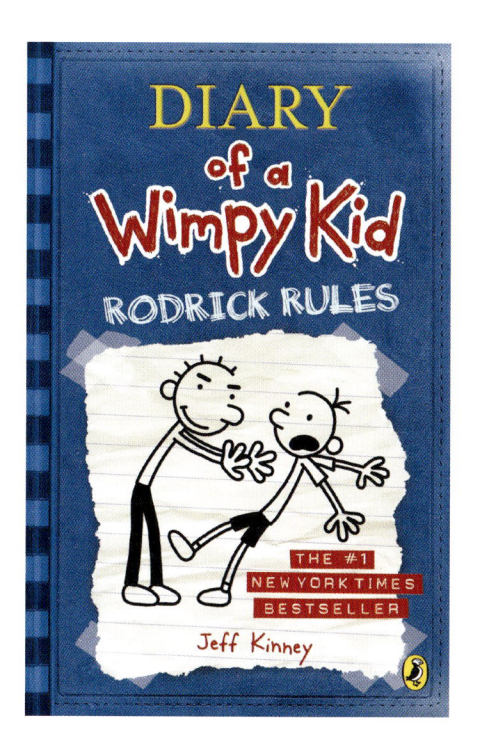

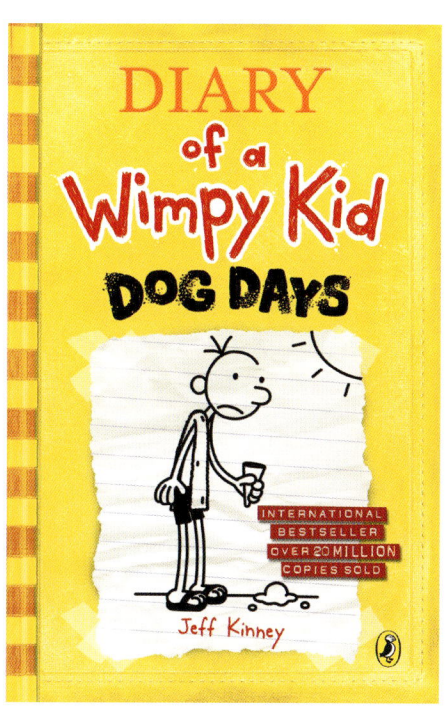

Diary of a Wimpy Kid: Rodrick Rules, 2009. Illustrated by Jeff Kinney

Diary of a Wimpy Kid: Dog Days, 2009. Illustrated by Jeff Kinney

Diary of a Wimpy Kid, 2008. Illustrated by Jeff Kinney (inside spread shown)

OPPOSITE: *Diary of a Wimpy Kid*, 2008. Illustrated by Jeff Kinney

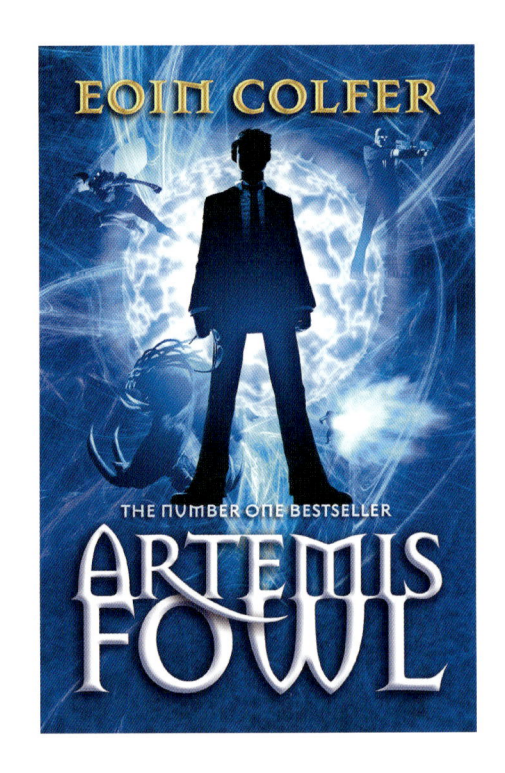

Artemis Fowl, 2006.
Cover illustration by Kev Walker

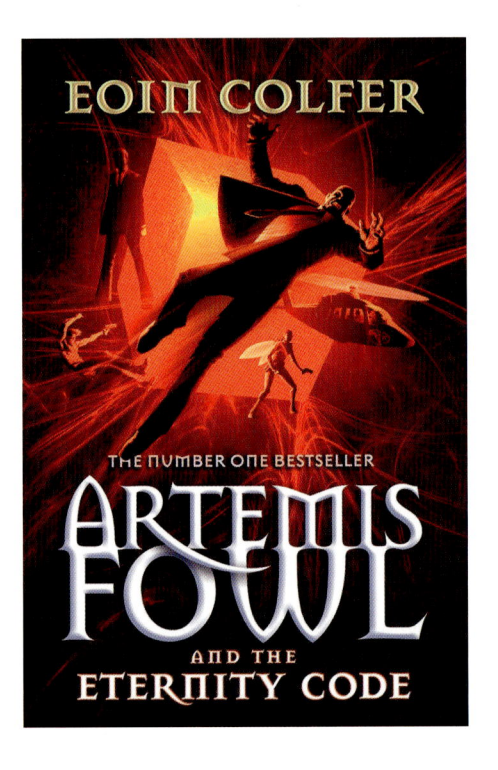

Artemis Fowl and the Eternity Code, 2006.
Cover illustration by Kev Walker

OPPOSITE: *Artemis Fowl*, 2002.
Cover illustration by Tony Fleetwood

The author as brand II

For Artemis Fowl by Eoin Colfer and the Percy Jackson series (see pp. 236–7) by Rick Riordan images are secondary to the name of each hero, which in each case becomes a typographic logotype. Artemis Fowl uses Jonathan Barnbrook's Mason typeface with a three-dimensional effect, while Percy Jackson is set in a distressed version of Cochin. For Charlie Higson's Young Bond series (see pp. 238–9) the similar idea of a logotype is used to create the signature look, though here it is the shape – making reference to the gunsight crosshairs of the Bond films but reminiscent to an older audience of the Thunderbirds' International Rescue – that carries the identity. Several of the Higson titles had an initial publication in hardback with distinctive, and very collectible, metallic laminated and de-bossed covers.

A softer approach to author identity is shown on the Meg Rosoff titles (see pp. 240–1), which feature an almost consistent use of Bembo. Here the author name font and decorative illustrations suggest mood rather than depict part of the narrative.

THE INTERNATIONAL BESTSELLER

ARTEMIS FOWL
Eoin Colfer

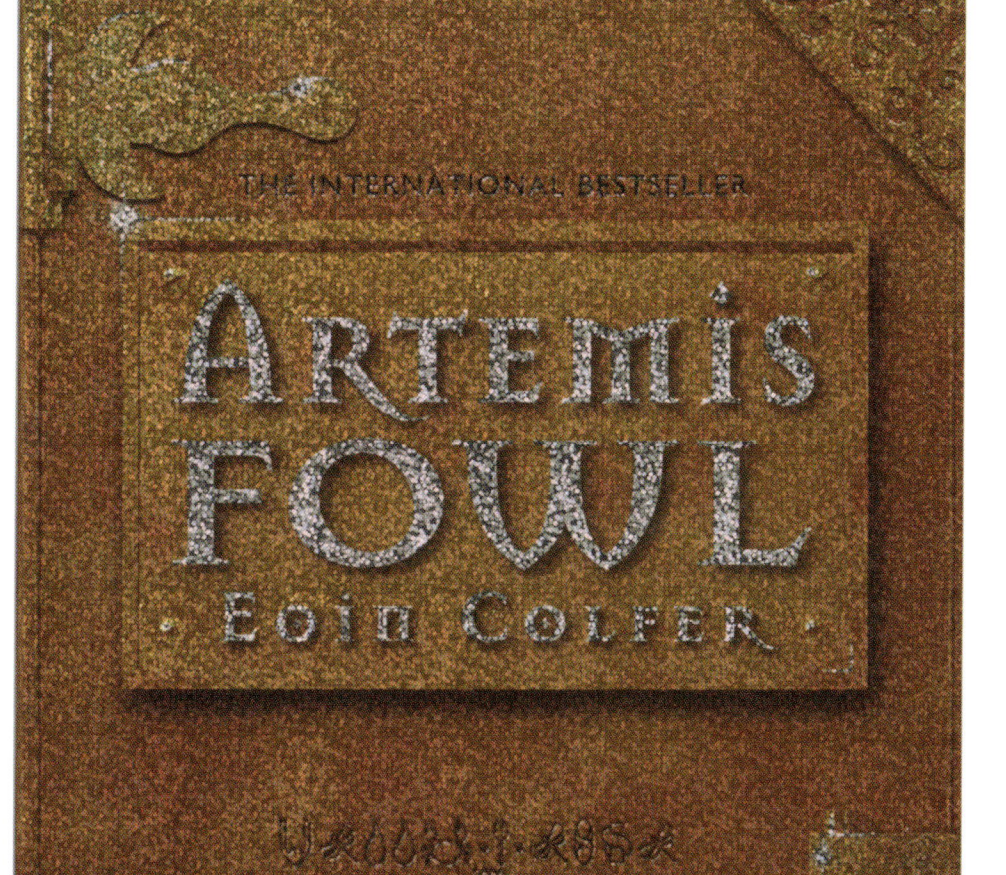

Percy Jackson and the Lightning Thief, 2008. Cover illustration by Christian McGrath

Percy Jackson and the Sea of Monsters, 2008. Cover illustration by Christian McGrath

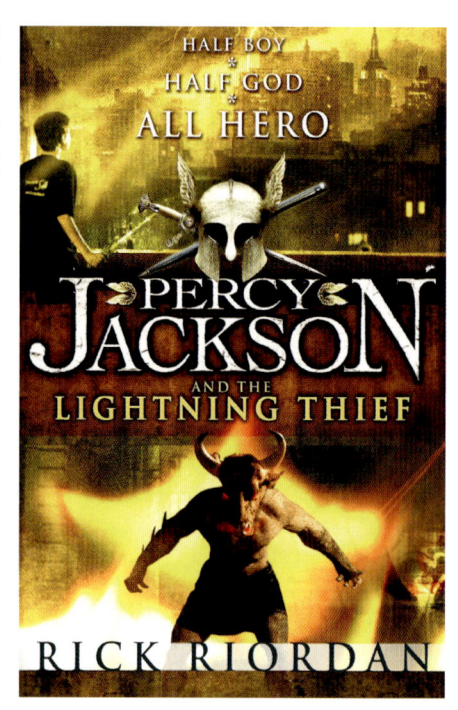

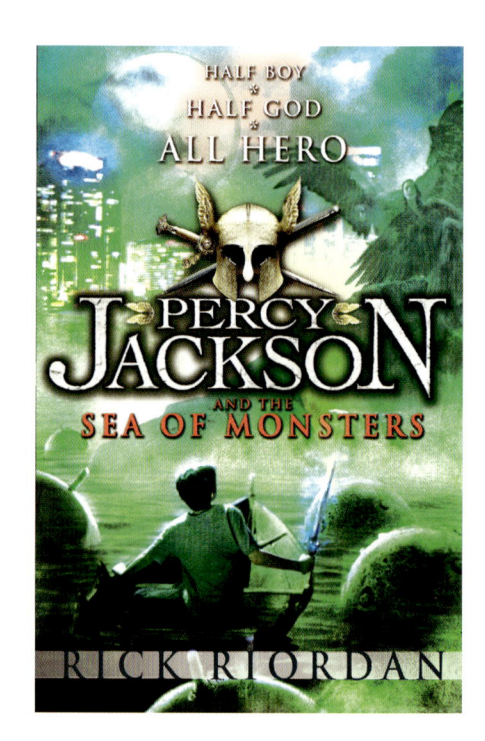

Percy Jackson and the Titan's Curse, 2008. Cover illustration by Christian McGrath

Percy Jackson and the Battle of the Labyrinth, 2008. Cover illustration by Christian McGrath

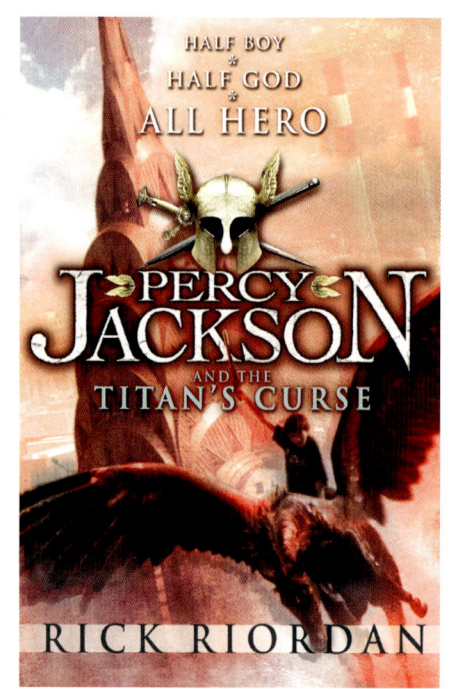

OPPOSITE: *Percy Jackson and the Last Olympian*, 2009. Cover illustration by Steve Stone

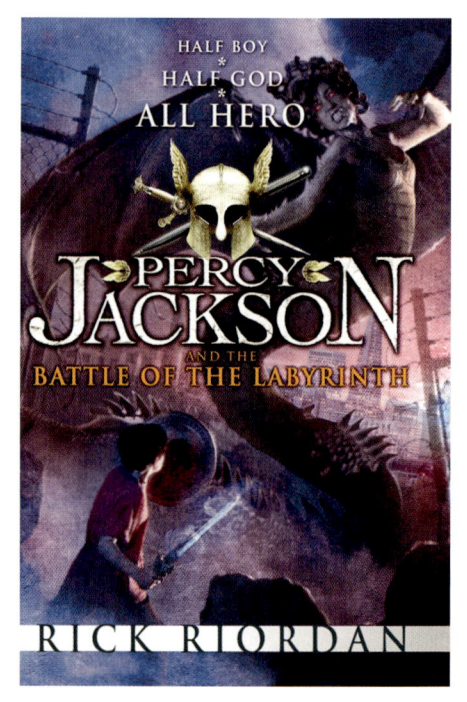

HALF BOY
*
HALF GOD
*
ALL HERO

PERCY JACKSON
AND THE
LAST OLYMPIAN

RICK RIORDAN

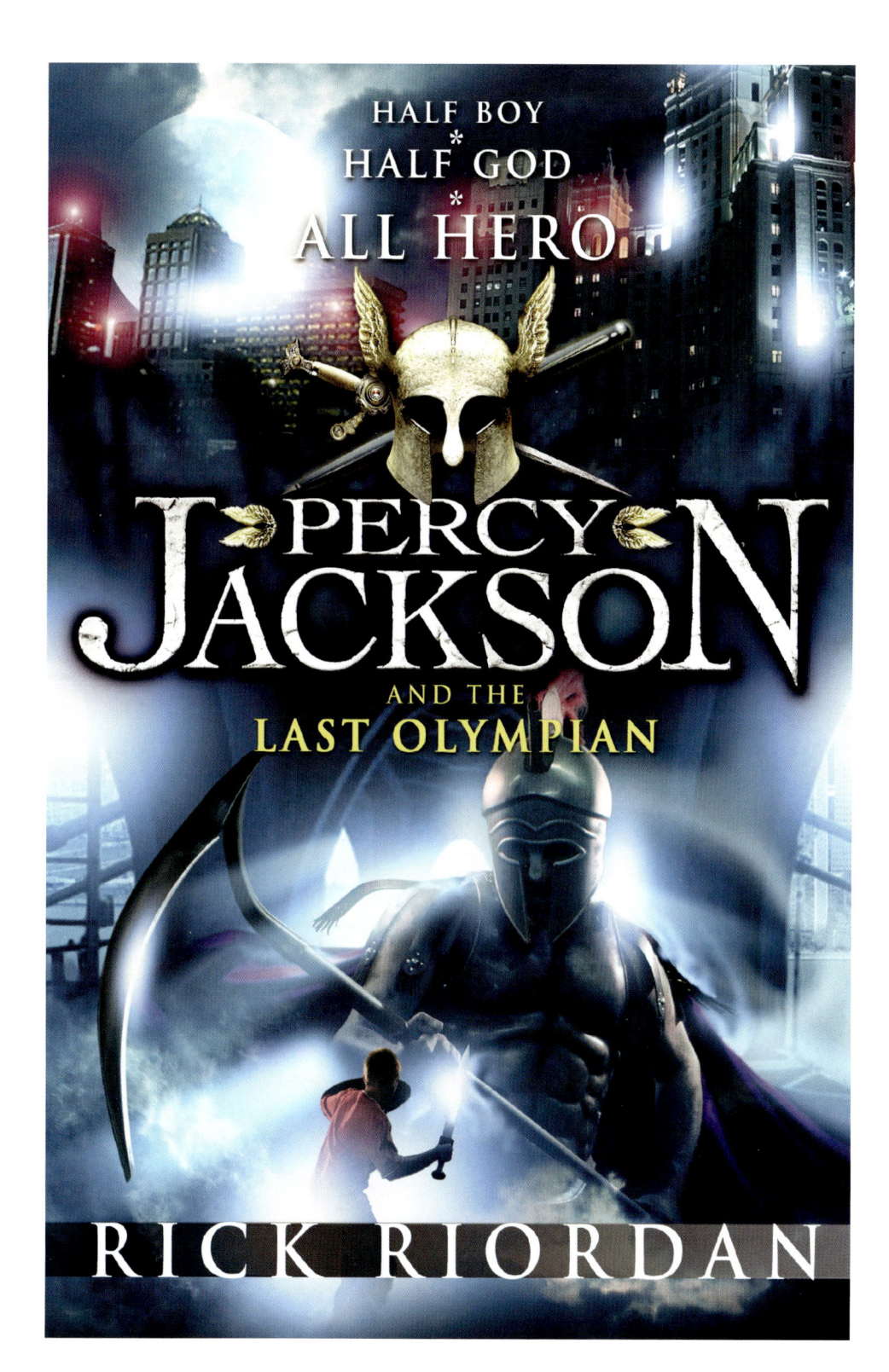

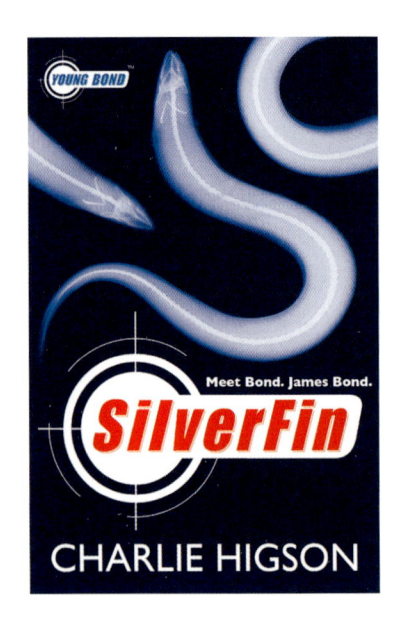

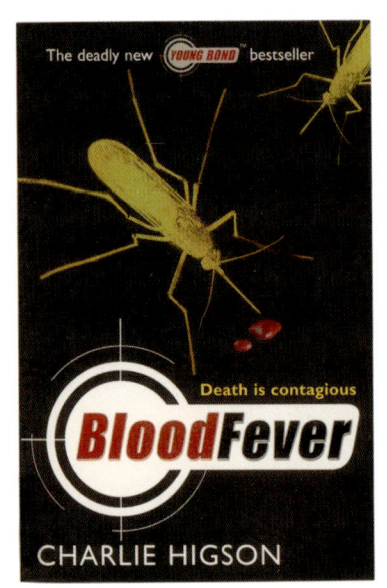

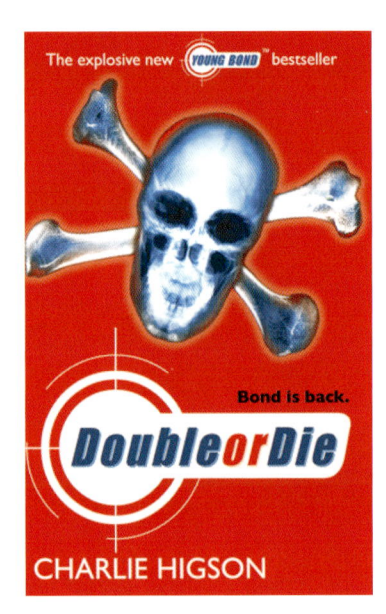

SilverFin, 2005.
Cover photography by Peter Dazely

Blood Fever, 2006.
Cover photograph by DK Images

Double or Die, 2007.
Cover photograph by Getty Images

By Royal Command, 2008.
Cover design by Tom Sanderson

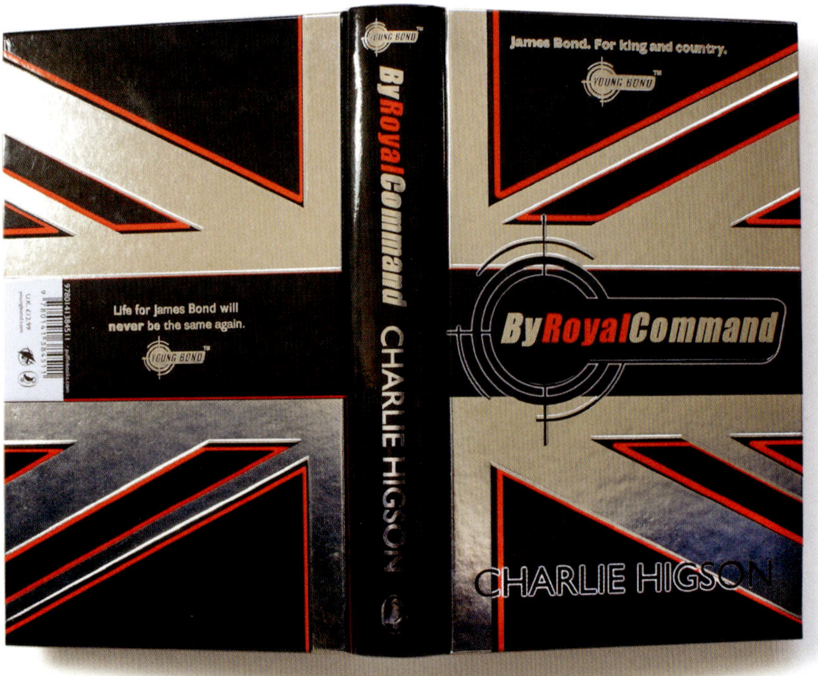

OPPOSITE: *Hurricane Gold*, 2007.
Cover design by Anna Billson
and Tom Sanderson

Puffin by Design

Young Bond

James Bond is staring death in the face.

Hurricane Gold

CHARLIE HIGSON

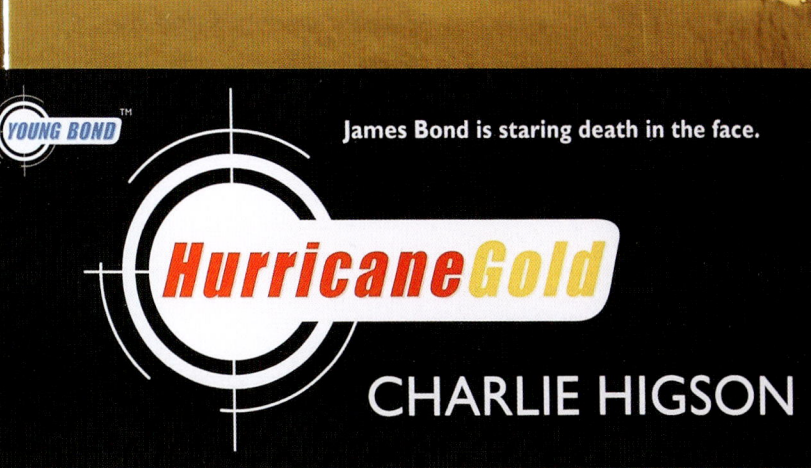

MEG ROSOFF

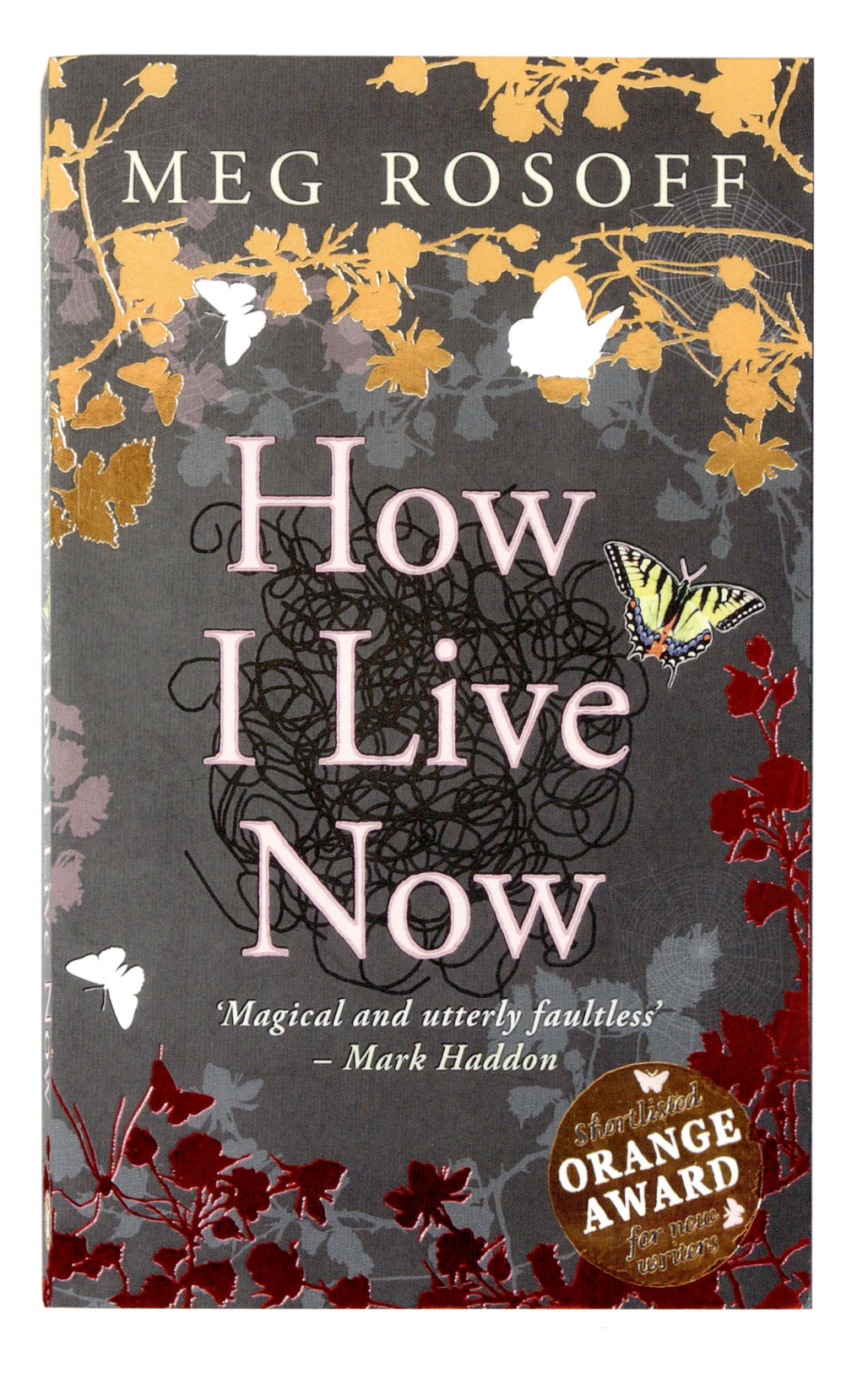

How I Live Now

'Magical and utterly faultless'
– Mark Haddon

Shortlisted ORANGE AWARD for new writers

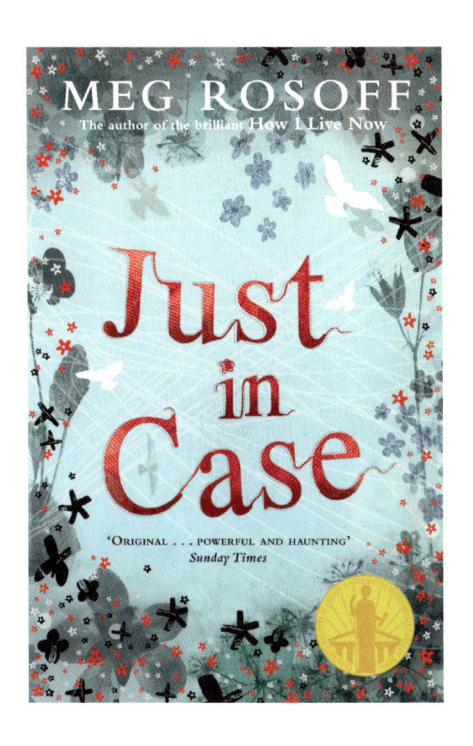

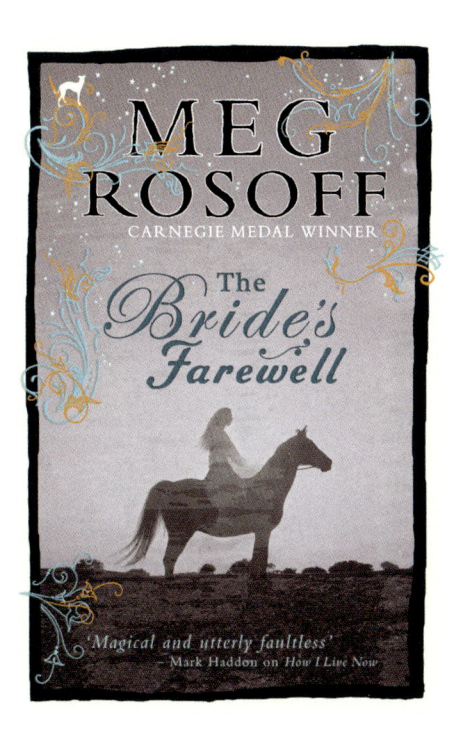

Just in Case, 2007.
Cover design by Katy Finch

The Bride's Farewell, 2009.
Cover design by Anna Billson

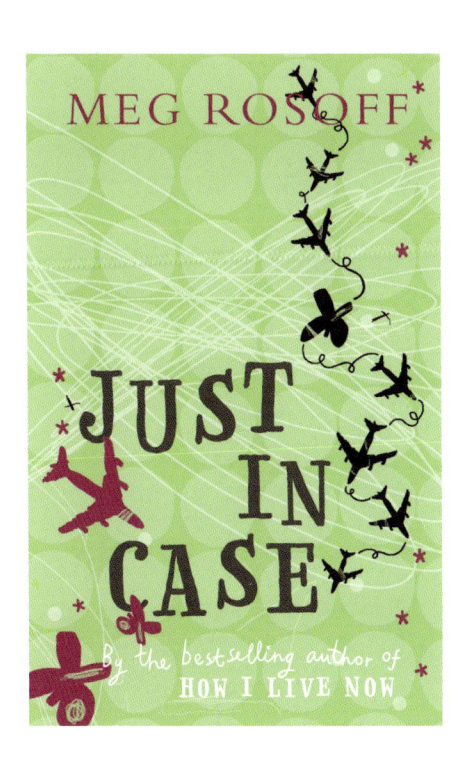

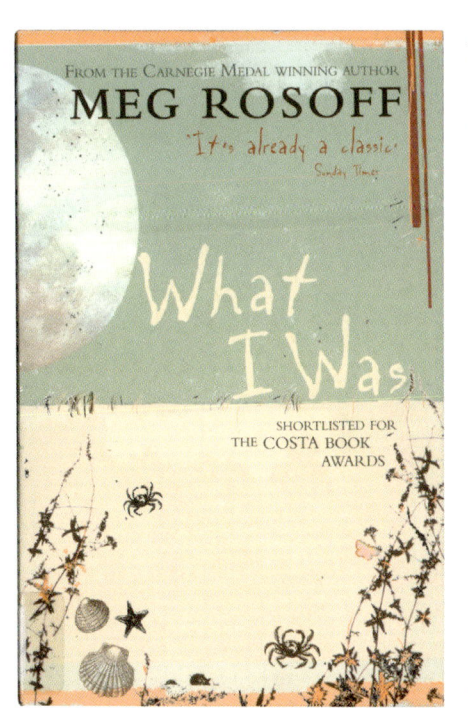

Just in Case, 2006.
Cover design by Anna Billson

What I Was, 2008.
Cover design by Anna Billson

OPPOSITE: *How I Live Now*, 2005.
Cover design by Tom Sanderson

That Summer

Sarah Dessen

Read her once and fall in love

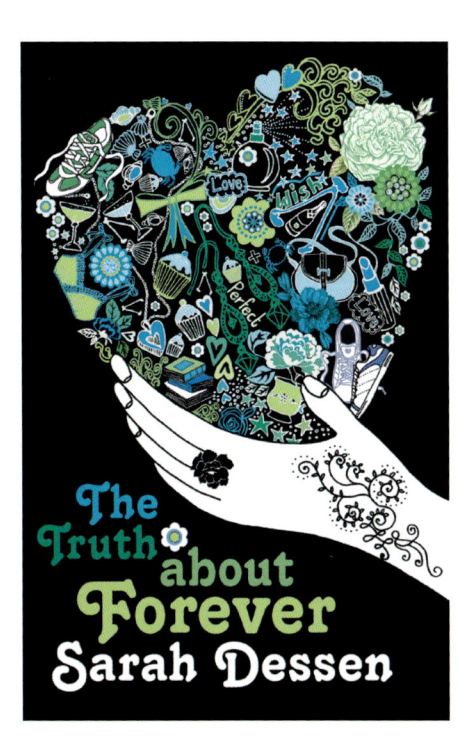

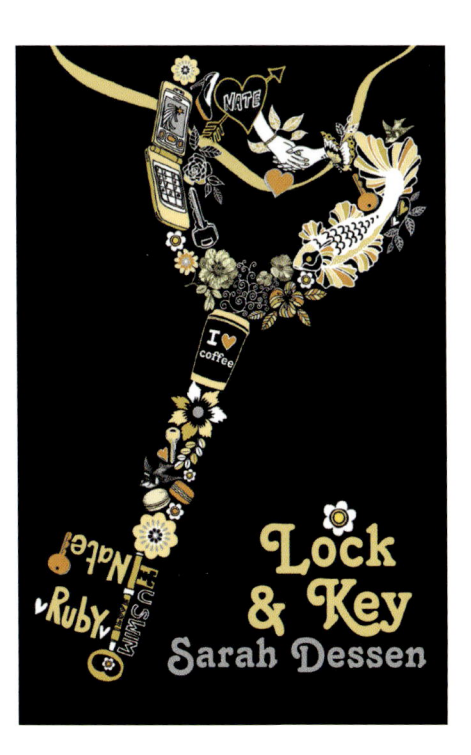

The author as brand III

Among very successful visual author brands are these recent covers for Sarah Dessen, in which the image plays a much more prominent role. Teenage and girly, but sophisticated with it – so striking and successful are they that the publisher of some of Dessen's other books has mimicked the design.

Long-established Puffin author Tove Jansson was also illustrator of her own books (see pp. 106–7), which gave her Moomin series of books a unity before author branding began to be fully exploited. Since her death in 2001, Puffin has continued to publish her longer story books, but in addition has bought the rights to develop the Moomin characters into a range of picture and novelty books for younger children. Puffin's in-house team have used Jansson's original line drawings from her comic-strip series drawn for the *London Evening News* in the 1950s, and reconfigured the artwork into colourful new illustrations, such as *Moomin and the Birthday Button*, for a pre-school readership. This new strand enables Puffin to publish related books and products in the way it already does for *The Very Hungry Caterpillar*, *Spot*, *Charlie and Lola*, and many others.

The Truth about Forever, 2007.
Cover illustration by Vici Leyhane

Lock and Key, 2009.
Cover illustration by Vici Leyhane

OPPOSITE: *That Summer*, 2009.
Cover illustration by Vici Leyhane

THIS PAGE: *Moominland Midwinter*, 2003. Cover illustration by Tove Jansson; design by John Fordham

The Exploits of Moominpappa, 2003. Cover illustration by Tove Jansson; design by John Fordham

BELOW: *Moomin's Little Book of Words*, 2010. Cover illustration by Tove Jansson; design by Goldberry Broad

Moomin's Little Book of Numbers, 2010. Cover illustration by Tove Jansson; design by Goldberry Broad

OPPOSITE: *Moomin and the Birthday Button*, 2010. Cover illustration by Tove Jansson; design by Goldberry Broad

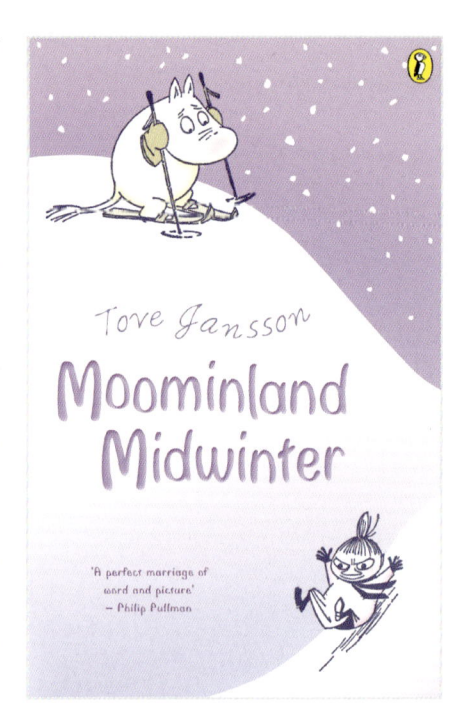

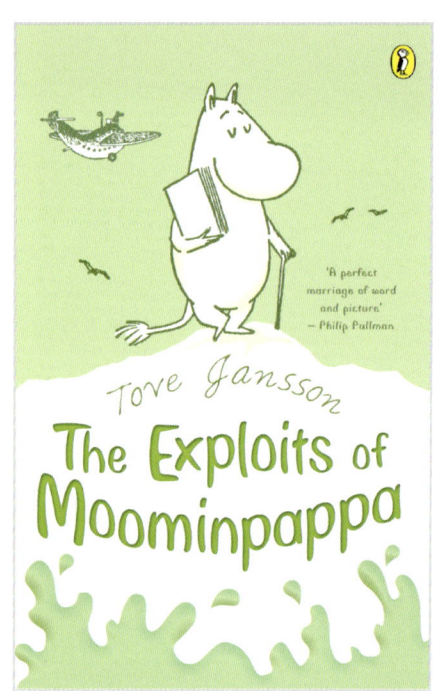

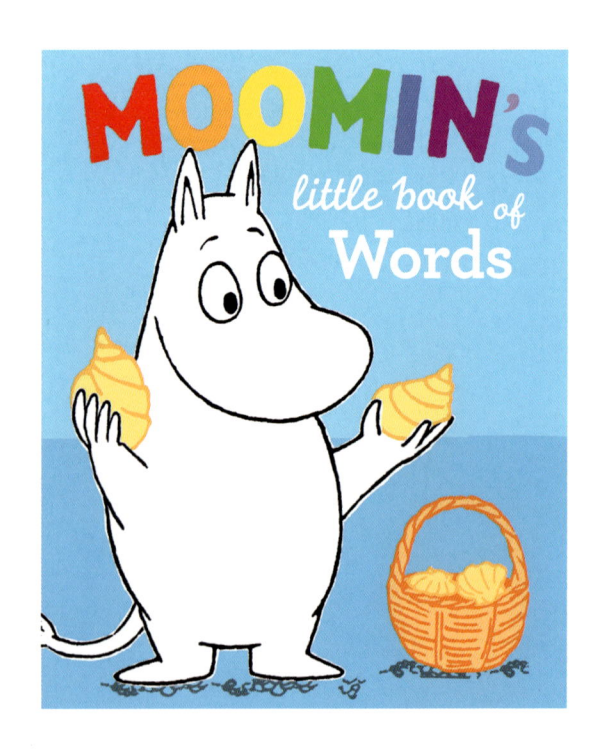

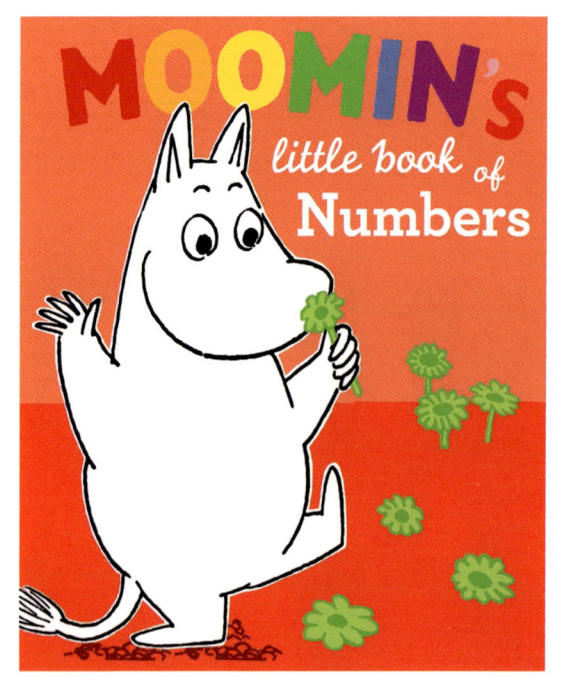

BASED ON THE ORIGINAL STORIES BY

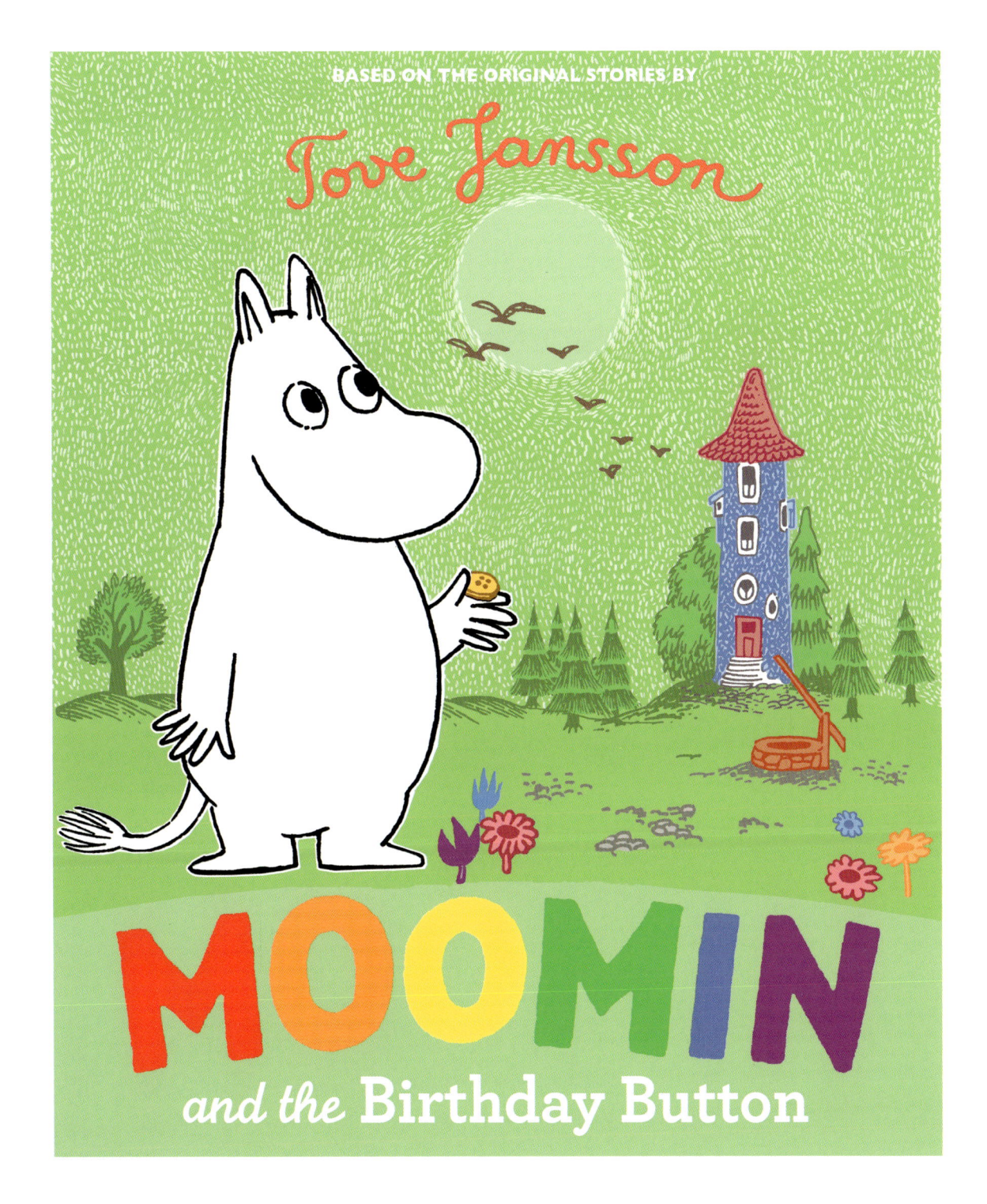

Tove Jansson

MOOMIN
and the Birthday Button

Is this the original drawing (? 1941) of
the Puffin symbol? Designer? [Bob Maynard]

2 prints
S/S
①

Return to
HPS

PS 1 (Dec. 1941) — first use
PS 15 (Dec. 1944) — last use
Designer?

PP 1 (Dec. 1940) — first use
Designer?

This differs in various details
from the drawing on facing page.

This is
printed
a bl...
on fa...
page

Logo Development, 1940–2010

1. Puffin, 1940
2. Puffin, 1941
3. Puffin, 1941
4. Puffin, 1948
5. Porpoise, 1948
6. Puffin, 1959
7. Peacock, 1963
8. Puffin, 1968
9. Practical Puffin, 1978
10. Puffin, 2003
11. Puffin birthday logo, 2010

OPPOSITE AND P. 6: Hans Schmoller's notebook showing logo history and development of all Penguin imprints

Puffin by Design cover shoot, 80 Strand, London, November 2009. Thanks to: Anna Billson, Penny Dann, Hannah Flynn, Eoghan Lynch, Alex Macilwaine and Daisy Mount. Jacket concept by Tom Sanderson

BY
DESIGN

BY
DESIGN

70 years of imagination

70 years of imagination
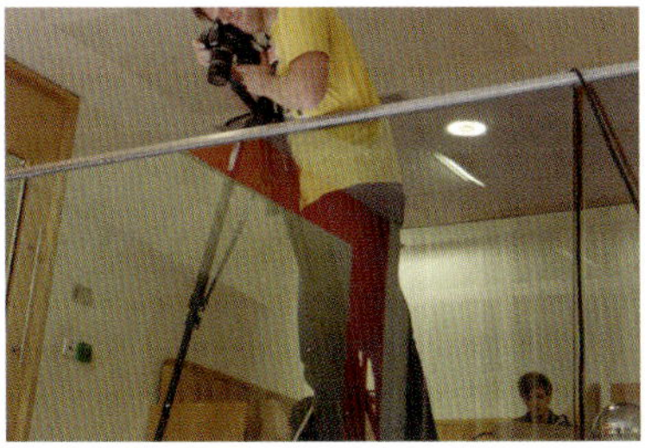

Bibliography and Sources

For the most comprehensive reading list on aspects of Penguin Books' history and development see:

Graham, T., *Penguin in Print: A Bibliography*, London: Penguin Collectors Society, 2003

Books and magazine articles

Although many issues of the Penguin Collectors Society *Newsletter* and *The Penguin Collector* have been consulted, only the most significant are listed below.

Artmonsky, R., *Art for Everyone: Contemporary Lithographs Ltd*, Artmonsky Arts, 2007

Backemeyer, S. (ed.), *Picture This: The Artist as Illustrator*, London: Central Saint Martins College of Art & Design in association with Herbert Press, 2005

Carrington, N., 'A Century of Puffins', *Penrose Annual*, Volume 51, 1957, pp. 62–5

—, 'The Birth of Puffin Picture Books', Penguin Collectors Society *Newsletter*, 13, 1979, pp. 62–4

—, in Bawden, E., *Life in an English Village*, Harmondsworth: King Penguin, 1949

Edwards, R., *A Penguin Collector's Companion*, London: Penguin Collectors Society (revised edition), 1997 (revised as Yates, M., *A Penguin Companion*, London: Penguin Collectors Society, 2006)

— (ed.), *Happy Birthday Puffin*, London: Penguin Collectors Society (Miscellany 6), 1991

Gritten, S., *The Story of Puffin Books*, Harmondsworth: Puffin, 1991

Hare, S., *Allen Lane and the Penguin Editors*, Harmondsworth: Penguin, 1995

—, 'The History of the Drowning Porpoises', *The Penguin Collector* 64, June 2005, pp. 36–40

—, 'The Life History of Life Histories', in Chadwick, P., *Life Histories* (Puffin Picture Book 116), London: Penguin Collectors Society, 1995

— (ed.), *Penguin by Illustrators*, London: Penguin Collectors Society, 2009

Holman, V., *Print for Victory: Book Publishing in England 1939–45*, London: British Library Publishing, 2008

Horne, A., *The Dictionary of 20th Century British Book Illustrators*, Woodbridge: Antique Collectors' Club, 1994.

Hunt, P. (ed.), *Children's Literature: An Illustrated History*, Oxford: Oxford University Press, 1995

Lewis, J., *Penguin Special: The Life and Times of Allen Lane*, Harmondsworth: Penguin Viking, 2005

McPhee, H., *Other People's Words: The Rise and Fall of an Accidental Publisher*, Sydney: Picador, 1973

Powers, A., *Children's Book Covers: Great Book Jacket and Cover Design*, London: Mitchell Beazley, 2003

Reynolds, K., & Tucker, N. (eds.), *Children's Book Publishing in Britain since 1945*, Aldershot: Ashgate, 1998

Rogerson, I., *Noel Carrington and his Puffin Picture Books* (exhibition catalogue), Manchester: Manchester Polytechnic Library, 1992

Smith, G., 'Autolithographic Progress and Plastic Film', *Penrose Annual*, Volume 43, 1949, pp. 71–3

Smith, G., *Colour and Autolithography in the 20th Century* (exhibition catalogue), Manchester: Manchester Metropolitan University (Special Collections), 2006

Somper, J., *The Story of Puffin*, Harmondsworth: Puffin, 2001

Williams, R. (ed.), *Puffin Picture Books and Others*, British Paperback Checklist, Volume 19, Scunthorpe: Dragonby Press, 1996

Websites

www.puffinbooks.com
   The company's own website with information about all titles, background information, author interviews and more.

www.puffinclubarchive.blogspot.com
   A fansite about the original Puffin Club, which was founded in 1967.

www.puffinpost.co.uk
   The online successor of the printed magazine that was the most visible aspect of the original club. Launched on 2009 by The Book People.

www.penguin.co.uk
   Penguin Books' main website, which focuses on the adult titles but with links to the other divisions.

www.pearson.com
   Website of the parent company that owns Pearson Education, the Financial Times Group and the Penguin Group.

www.sevenstories.org.uk
   Based in Newcastle upon Tyne, Seven Stories: the Centre for Children's Books contains, among other treasures, Kaye Webb's archive and book collection.

www.penguincollectorssociety.org
   Founded in 1974 and now with more than 500 members, the society, an educational charity, aims to help to preserve and conserve Penguin books, and material relating to Penguin, and ensure the ready availability of that material for present and future research.

Archives

www.bristol.ac.uk/is/library/collections/specialcollections/archives/penguin
   The Penguin Archive contains the archives of Penguin Books Ltd from its foundation in 1935 to the 1980s, with continuing deposits up to the present day. A four-year AHRC-funded project to create an online catalogue began in 2008.

Index

To avoid excessive length, books are indexed only if they are referred to in the text or appear in more than one cover design; titles are indexed under their authors. Italic entries refer to illustrations.

Achilleos, Christos 178
Adams, Richard 99, 118
   Watership Down 99, 118, *119*
Ahlberg, Allan 150–1, 191
   Peepo! 150, *156–7*
Ahlberg, Janet 150–1, *156–7*, 191
Ahlberg, Jessica 198
Aiken, Joan 113
   The Kingdom Under the Sea 114, *115*
   A Necklace of Raindrops 114
   The Wolves of Willoughby Chase 114
Aitchison, Janet
   The Pirate's Tale 123
Alcott, Louisa M.
   Little Women *78*, *79*, 217
Alldridge, Elizabeth 77
Allen & Unwin 12
Ambrus, Victor 139
Ardizzone, Edward 58, 59, 98, 110, 165, 195, 213
   The Little Girl and the Tiny Doll (with Aingelda Ardizzone) *164*, 165
   Paul the Hero of the Fire 58, 98
Arnold, James 86
Attenborough, Liz 147, 148, 190
autolithography/lithography 12–13, 14, 46, 52, 56

Badmin, S. R. 46
   Trees in Britain 14, 46, *47*
   Village and Town 46
Bailey, Peter 198
Bantam Picture Books 17
Bareham, James 179, 183
Baron (photographer) 87
Barrett, Peter 102, 109, 128

Bassett-Lowke, W. J. 33
   A Book of Trains (with F. E. Courtney) 52, *130*
   Marvellous Models and Models to Make (with Paul B. Mann) 53
   Waterways of the World 33
Battley Brothers 60
Bawden, Edward 38
Bawden, Paul 141
Baxter, David 133
Baynes, Pauline 90, 91, 100, 101, 118, 119, 166
Bell, Bill 195
Bennett, Jill 112
Bergen, David 183
Berger, Joe 216
Berry, Erick 68
Best, Herbert
   Garram the Hunter 65, 68
Bibby, Cyril
   The Human Body (with Ian T. Morison) 53
Bilbey, Ian 216
Billson, Anna 191, 219, 221, 239, 241
Binder, Pearl 12, 24, 25
   Misha Learns English 24
Birch, Caroline 194
Biro, Val 132
Blake, Quentin 113, 114, 124, 127, 184, 195, 224, 225, 226, 227
Bledsoe, Judith 102
Bloomfield, Diane 93
Blyton, Enid 79
Bond, Michael 105
   A Bear Called Paddington 105
   Paddington at Large *104*, 105
   Paddington at Work 105
   Paddington Helps Out 105
Book People, The 192
Borland, Polly 192

Bossert, Patrick 175
   You Can Do the Cube 147, *174*, 175
Briggs, Raymond 150, 158–9, 191
   Father Christmas 151, *159*
   Fungus the Bogeyman 151, *158*
   The Snowman 151, *158*, 191
Broad, Goldberry 244
Brough, Jack 42
   Printing (with Harold Curwen) 14, 42
Burkert, Nancy Ekholm 113
Burns, Jim 178
Burton, Virginia Lee 59

Caldecott, Oliver 66
Calvocoressi, Peter 98–9
Campbell, Bruce
   Bird Watching for Beginners 86
Campbell, Rod
   Dear Zoo 146
Carle, Eric
   The Very Hungry Caterpillar 150, *154–5*, 191
Carrington, Noel 12–13, 14, 17, 19, 24, 26, 29, 33, 58, 60, 98
Carroll, Lewis 80
   Alice's Adventures in Wonderland *81*, 182
Cassidy, Cathy 191, 224
Chadwick, Lee 17
Chadwick, Paxton 21, 60
   Life Histories 17, 60
   Pond Life 60
   Wild Animals in Britain 60
   Wild Flowers 60
Chadwick, Peter 168
Chapman, Dorothy 56
Child, Lauren 191, 192, 206, 207, 217, 220
Chow, Stanley 220
Clark, Margaret 96
Clarke, Kate 219
Cleary, Beverly
   Fifteen 168, *169*
Clifford, Rowan 165
Coghlan, Eileen 77
Colfer, Eoin 190, 234
Collins, Ross 216
Cooke, Geraldine 176

Cope, Andrew
   Spy Dog 224, 229
Corder, Zizou
   Lionboy *194*, 197
Country Life 12, 13, 24, 26
Courtney, F. E. 52
   A Book of Trains (with W. J. Bassett-Lowke) 52
Cowell's (printer) 13, 14, 26
Cox, Steve 162
Cracknell, Alan 182
Craig, Helen 206, 210
Crews, Donald 160
   Freight Train 160, *161*
   School Bus 160
   Truck 160
Curwen, Harold 38, 42
   Printing (with Jack Brough) 14, 42

D'Achille, Gino 201
Dahl, Roald 113, 124, 191, 224
   The BFG 113, 184, 226, *227*
   Charlie and the Chocolate Factory 99, 113, 226, 227
   Charlie and the Great Glass Elevator 224, *225*
   Fantastic Mr Fox 112, 113, 196, 226
   James and the Giant Peach 113, 226
   The Twits 113
   The Witches 113
Davies, Roland 18
   Great Deeds of the War 14, 17, *18*
Davis, Julia
   No Other White Men 73, 76
Denton, John
   On the Railway 130, *133*
   On the Road 130, *131*
Dessen, Sarah 243
Dixon, Norman and Margaret
   The Puffin Quiz Book 82, *126*
Dodd, Lynley 191, 206, 210
Dolley, Christopher 98
Doran, Tem 217
Dorrell, Sheila 17
Dovey, L. A.
   Cotswold Village 49
   Half-Timbered Village 49

Dow, Francesca 191, 192
Drummond, Violet 58, 59
   The Flying Postman 58
Dumayne, John 30
Dunn, Gavin 201
Dunn, Laurence 33, 52
   A Book of Ships 52
Dunn, Richard 170
Dyson, Sylvia 71, 76

Ede, Janina 109
Edwards, Gunvor 106
Edwards, Lionel 20
Edwards, Peter 137
Emett, Rowland 40
   The Emett Festival Railway 41
Emmanuel (illustrator) 177
Evers, Alice 88

Faber & Faber 97
Facetti, Germano 66, 97, 136
Farley, Andrew 229
Feiffer, Jules 102
Festival of Britain 41, 26
Fighting Fantasy 147, 149, 176–8
Finch, Katy 219, 241
Fine, Anne
   Madame Doubtfire 186, 213
Fitch Perkins, Lucy 89
Flavell, Sara 230
Flax, Zena 102
Fleetwood, Tony 235
Forbes Watson, Anthony 190
Fordham, John 244
Fortnum, Peggy 89, 104, 105
Frankland, David 213
Fraser, Helen 191
Fraser, James 223
Frederick Warne 147, 150
Frost, Eunice 65, 68

Gabler, Grace 42, 68, 71, 74
Gall, Chris 214
Gardner, James 14
   On the Farm 14
   War in the Air 14, 19
Garnett, David
   The Battle of Britain 14, 18, 19

Garnett, Eve 71, 213
Gernat, Mary 92
Gibbings, Robert 70
   Coconut Island 68, 70
Gibbons, Lee 213
Gibson, Robert 132
Gladstone, W. E. 68
   The Puffin Puzzle Book 82
   The Second Puffin Puzzle Book 82, 83
Glover, Trevor 148
Godwin, Tony 66, 96, 97
Goodfellow, Peter 142, 143
Gordon, Margaret 164
Gorey, Edward 167
Gourdie, Tom
   The Puffin Book of Lettering 42
Graham, Eleanor 64–5, 66, 79, 85, 93, 101
   The Children Who Lived in a Barn 66, 92, 93
   The Puffin Book of Verse 93
   A Puffin Quartet of Poets 93
   The Story of Jesus 66, 93
Grahame-Johnstone, Janet and Anne 102
Green, Roger Lancelyn 66, 85
   King Arthur and His Knights of the Round Table 84, 85
   The Tale of Troy 85
   Tales of the Greek Heroes 85
Greenland, Peter 170
Gregory, Bill 197
Gregory, Peter 130, 133
Gribble, Diana 135
Grimmond, William 68, 69, 88
   Jungle John 68
Guppy, Coral 180

Hagerty, Leonard 30
Halbert, Michael 214
Hale, Kathleen 12, 13, 14, 24, 26
   Orlando's Evening Out 26, 26–7
   Orlando's Home Life 26
Hale, Philip 141
Hall, A. H. 70, 74, 78
Hamilton, Patricia 139
Harding, Robert 202

Hardy, A. C.
   A Book of Ships (with Laurence Dunn and M. J. Hardy or Winston Megoran) 52–3
Hardy, Patrick 146
Hare, Steve 17
Harlequin 17
Hart, Dick 102
Hart, Tony 40, 41
   Puppets 41
Hartrick, A. S. 50
Harwood, John 56, 57, 58, 59, 70, 72, 73, 76
   Aladdin and His Wonderful Lamp 58, 59
   The Old Woman and Her Pig 56, 57
Heath Robinson, W. 71
Heaton, Peter 56
Helweg, Hans 167
Higson, Charlie 191, 234
Hill, Eric 150
   Where's Spot? 146, 150, *151*
Hodges, C. Walter 77
   Columbus Sails 73, 77, 85
Hogarth, Grace 58
Holabird, Katharine 206
Holland, James 14, 18
   War at Sea 14, 18
   War on Land 14, 19
Holmes, Sally 167
Hood, Alun 172, 180
Hooker, John 135
Horse, Harry 198
Hosking, Eric 86
Hough, Charlotte 79
Houghton Mifflin 58, 59
Howes, Geoff 174, 175
Hughes, Shirley 124, 162, 163
Humphreys, Sally 172
Hutchings, Tony 173
Hutton, Clarke 28, 29, 50, 51
   The Tale of Noah and the Flood 50

Illingworth, Leslie 138
Isotype Institute 44
Ivey, Richard 195

Jackson, Carolin 38

Jackson, Steve 176
   The Warlock of Firetop Mountain (with Ian Livingstone) 147, *149*, 176
James, Will
   Smoky 65
Jansson, Tove 107, 108, 243, 244–5
   Comet in Moominland 106, *108*
Jaques, Faith 113
Jarrett, Dudley 59
Jezard, Alison
   Albert 164
John, Simon 141
Johnston, Arnrid 18, 20
Jones, Laurien 136
Jones, Peter 149
Jones, Peter Andrew 176
Jones, Richard 172
Jones, Steve 179

Kearney, David 187
Keeping, Charles 140
Kennedy, Richard 136
Ker Wilson, Barbara
   Last Year's Broken Toys 136
Kestrel 146, 147
Kettle, Stuart 164
King, Clive
   Stig of the Dump 97, 110, *111*, 187, 212, 213
King-Smith, Dick
   The Sheep-Pig 184, 194, 199
Kinney, Jeff 191, 232–3
Kitchen, Bert 170
Knights, John 173
Kurth, Heinz 130, 132, 133
   Build a House 130, *133*

Lacey, Tony 146–7, 150, 169, 175
Ladybird Books 150
Ladyman, Phyllis
   About a Motor Car 54
Lake, Anthony 75, 78
Lancashire, David 134, 135
Lane, Allen 7, 12, 13, 14, 19, 64, 66, 96, 98
Lane, John 7
Lane, Richard 7

Index   253

Larkum, Adam 214
Le Guin, Ursula 99
Le Vasseur, Peter 138
Lea, Bob 213
Leacroft, Helen and Richard 38, 44
  The Building of Ancient Egypt 38
  Building a House 44, 130
Leslie, Cecil 78
Lewis, C. S. 91, 99
  The Lion, the Witch and the Wardrobe 90, 91
Leyhane, Vici 242, 243
Lilly, Charles 194
lithography *see* autolithography
Livingstone, Ian 176
  The Warlock of Firetop Mountain (with Steve Jackson) 147, 149, 176
Lloyd, Margery
  Fell Farm Holiday 65–6, 80, 88
Lobban, John 132
Lynch, Patricia
  Strangers at the Fair 73, 77
Lyne, Michael 30

McAllister, David 173
McCaig, Ian 177, 180
McCulloch, Derek
  Cornish Adventure 65, 68
McDonald, Jill 96, 97, 122–3, 124, 126
McGinn, Peter 132
McGrath, Christian 236
McGregor, R. J.
  The Secret of Dead Man's Cove 80
  The Young Detectives 80
McGrogan, Patricia 116
McKee, David 181
McPhee, Hilary 135
Maitland, Antony 101
Makinson, John 191
Manham, Allan 141
Mann, Paul B. 53
  Marvellous Models (with W. J. Bassett-Lowke) 53
'Marber grid' 136

Marriott, Pat 108, 114
Marsh, James 182
Marshal, K.
  David Goes to Zululand 73, 75
Martin Jr., Bill 150
Marx, Enid 28, 29
Masefield, John
  The Box of Delights 101, 103
Matthews, Derek 165
Mayer, Peter 99, 146, 148
Maynard, Bill 68
Megoran, Winston 52
Middleton-Sandford, Betty 85
Miles, John 40, 41, 60
  Noah's Ark 41
Millar, H. R. 89
Millar, Ian 178
Millard, P. F. 20
Millman, Maura 213
Milnes-Smith, Philippa 190, 191
Molesworth, Mrs
  The Cuckoo Clock 65
Morison, Ian T.
  The Human Body (with Cyril Bibby) 53

Nathan 14
Newnham, Jack 134
Nickless, Will
  The Ugly Duckling 58, 59
Nicoll, Helen 114, 150
Nicolle, Patrick 22
Noble, Steve 214
Nome, Kazuko 214, 217
Norton, Mary
  The Borrowers 187, 212, 213

Oxford University Press 50, 58, 97

Pallant Sidaway, G. E. 22
Parker, Brynhild 20
Parker, Richard
  A Moor of Spain 85
Parks, Peter 21
Pask, Helen 169
Pau, Johnny 181
Peacock Books 97, 136–43, 146, 147, 162, 168, 203

Pearce, Philippa
  A Dog So Small 101
Penguin Australia 98, 135, 148
Penguin Books 7–8, 64, 88, 98–9, 136, 176, 190–1
  Classics 66, 147, 182
  King Penguins 65
  Peregrine Books 136
  Specials 65, 86
  Viking 147
Penguin Collectors Society 17, 60
Père Castor 12
Pevsner, Dieter 66
Phillips, W. Francis 137
photolithography 14, 52
Pieńkowski, Jan 114, 115, 150, 152–3, 191, 206, 207, 209
Platt, Gillian 132
Porpoise Books 14, 29, 58–9, 98
Potter, Beatrix 147
Potter, Margaret and Alexander
  The Buildings of London 49
  A History of the Countryside 48–9
Preston, Mark 185
Primrose, Jean 106
Puffin Books 8
  and Australia 98, 135, 147
  audio books 147
  film and TV tie-ins 120–1
  foreign-language editions 14, 135
  logos 38, 68, 105, 106, 136, 150, 203, 246–7
  and USA 58, 147–8, 160, 214
  SERIES
  Baby Puffins 14, 56–7
  Classics 8, 147, 180–3, 191, 200–1, 214–17
  Cut-out Books 14, 40–1, 49
  Fantail 147
  Modern Classics 8, 184–7, 191, 194, 212–13
  New Puffin Picture Books 98, 130–3
  Peacock Books 97, 136–43, 146, 147, 162, 168, 203
  Picture Books 12–14, 17, 18–55, 66
  Picture Puffins 98, 146, 150–61, 206
  Pied Piper (US) 148
  Pocket Puffins 147

  Porpoise Books 14, 29, 58–9, 98
  Practical Puffins 98, 134–5
  Puffin Plus 147, 168–73
  Read Alone 147
  Read Aloud 147
  Story Books 14, 64–6, 68–85, 88–93, 194
  Young Puffins 105, 147, 162, 164–7
Puffin Club 97–8, 148, 192
  Puffin Post 97, 99, 122–3, 192
Puffin School Book Club 148

Ransome, Arthur 116–17
  Peter Duck 116
  Swallows and Amazons 116, 117
Ravilious, Eric 12, 13
Redlich, Monica
  Jam Tomorrow 68, 71
Reiniger, Lotte 84, 85
Renny, Juliet 102, 103
Rey, H. E. 28, 29, 59
  Mary Had a Little Lamb 29, 59
Riddell, Chris 199, 214
Rinaldi, Angelo 201, 212
Riordan, Rick 191, 234
Roberts, John 133
Roberts, Lunt 30
Rodgers, Frank 187
Rojankovsky, Feodor 12
Rose, Jim 98
Rosoff, Meg 191, 234
Ross, Victor 37
  English Fashions 37

Sancha, José 24, 25
Sanderson, Bill 214, 216, 217, 218
Sanderson, Tom 203, 204, 205, 219, 220, 223, 238, 239, 240
Sandy, Laurence 30
Sawdon, Victoria 214
Schmoller, Hans 41, 247
Searle, Ronald 96
Serjeant, R. B.
  The Arabs 38

Sewell, Anna
   Black Beauty 79
Sewell, John 136
Sharratt, Nick 224, 228
Sikes, Mary 30
Skibulits, Anne
   A Tea-Time Story 50, 51
'S.J.' (illustrator) 70
Smith, Arthur 21
Smith, Duncan 176
Smith, Geoffrey 13
Stanley, Diana 213
Stearn, Nick 203
Stebbing, Hilary 28, 29
   Extinct Animals 29
   Pantomime Stories 28, 29
Stevenson, Alice 214, 220
Stevenson, Robert Louis
   Dr Jekyll and Mr Hyde 180, 181, 183
   The Suicide Club 136, 137
   Treasure Island 78, 79
Stone, Steve 237
Stower, Adam 199
Strong, Jeremy 224
   The Air-Raid Shelter 224
Stroud, John 34
   Airliners 34, 34–5, 130
Studio Output 222

Talbot Kelly, R. B. 20, 40, 41
   Paper Birds 41
Taylor, Geoff 180
Taylor, Richard 23
Taylor, Sally 200
Tenniel, John 80, 81
Terry, Mike 184
Thomson, George L. 42
   Better Handwriting 42
Todd, Barbara Euphan 65
   The Television Adventures of Worzel Gummidge 120
   Worzel Gummidge 56, 65, 67, 72, 73
   Worzel Gummidge Again 72, 73
Tolkien, J. R. R. 79, 91, 96, 101
   The Hobbit 96, *100*, 101
Townsend, Jack 37
   The Clothes We Wear 37
Transatlanic Arts 17
Travers, P. L.

Mary Poppins 97
Trier, Walter 24, 25
Trix (illustrator) 40
Tschichold, Jan 52
Tuckley, Nigel 83
Tunnicliffe, C. F. 21
Turner, Sidney, R. 30
Turngren, Annette
   Flaxen Braids 73, 74
Tyler, Gill 198

Uva, Andrea C. 221

Van Deelan, Fred 196
Van der Maat, Dick 187
Veale, Sidney E.
   How Planes Fly 34
Venables, Bernard 20
Vere, Ed 191, 206, 207, 210
Verne, Jules
   Around the World in Eighty Days 180, 181
Viney, Mark 181
Vriesendorp, Madelon 140

Walford, Astrid 78, 79
Walker, James 173
Walker, Kev 234
Webb, Kaye 17, 60, 91, 96–9, 101, 118, 122, 124, 135, 136, 146, 150, 192
White, E. B.
   Charlotte's Web 101, *187*, 212, 213
   Stuart Little *108*, 199
White, Gwen 75
Whybrow, Ian 191
Wildsmith, Brian 93, 102, 108
William Collins 97
Williams, Garth 101, 108, 187, 199, 213
Williams, Stuart 186
Williams, Ursula Moray
   Adventures of the Little Wooden Horse 164, 166
Williamson, Thames
   North After Seals 73
Willis, Jeanne 191
Woodcock, John 82
   Binding Your Own Books 82

Wren, E. A. 34
Wright, Lyndie 165

Yee, Chiang 14, 24, 25
   The Silent Traveller 24, 25
Young, Edward 68

Acknowledgements

When I left Puffin out of *Penguin by Design* I wasn't intentionally creating future work, there simply wasn't room, so my first thanks must go to Francesca Dow, Managing Director of Puffin, and Anna Billson, Puffin Art Director, for inviting me to complete the story.

The book's development owes much to a number of people. The designer, Tom Sanderson, whose appreciative eye greatly aided book selection and who came up with a class evocation of a 1950s Puffin Story Book for the cover. My editor, Helen Levene, and copy-editor, Jennie Morris, who patiently steered the project, asked the right questions and seemed to understand when to leave me alone. Also at 80 Strand, Tony Lacey was generous with his recollections, Eoghan Lynch assisted Tom in picture research and scanning, and Richard Duguid provided clarification towards the end of the writing process. At Penguin's own library in Rugby, Sue Osborne and Rob Pitchford always made me welcome and answered questions with good humour; at University of Bristol Library Special Collections, Rachel Hassall, Hannah Lowery and Michael Richardson did likewise.

Anyone who writes about any aspect of the Penguin story owes a massive debt of thanks to the Penguin Collectors Society and its members, and I am no different. Their publications and the friendly advice of members has been invaluable, with Steve Hare in particular, selflessly providing clues, somewhere to stay en route to Bristol and covers of books that Penguin no longer have.

Others helped in more general ways: Catherine Dixon, Andrew Hall and David Pearson gave encouragement when needed; Muss and Dave Cope provided somewhere to stay during visits to Rugby; and Kate Lyons, Micheline Mannion and Shoko Sata took over various design jobs in my studio.

My final thanks are to my family, Jackie, Beth and Felicity, for their continuing patience and support.

Picture credits

All books have been scanned from originals in the Penguin Archive in Rugby by MDP Ltd, except pp. 10–11, 56–7 (photo: Phil Baines), pp. 6, 246 (photo: David Pearson), courtesy University of Bristol Library Special Collections; pp. 14, 58–9, 62–3 courtesy Steve Hare (photo: Phil Baines); pp. 94–5, 144–5, 188–9 reproduced directly from artwork, courtesy Puffin Books. Images featured on pp. 2, 3, 5, 9 from various Puffin and Penguin publicity materials. Photo portraits are from University of Bristol Library Special Collections, except p. 146 courtesy Tony Lacey; p. 190 courtesy Francesca Dow (photo: Justine Stoddart); p. 191 courtesy Anna Billson (photo: Justine Stoddart). Back cover-flap illustrations from *A Child's Alphabet* [1945] by Grace Gabler. Cover concept and photography Tom Sanderson.